THE
INNER RADIANCE

TEACHINGS OF
THE ORDER OF CHRISTIAN MYSTICS

THE INNER RADIANCE

TEACHINGS OF THE ORDER OF CHRISTIAN MYSTICS
THE "CURTISS BOOKS" FREELY AVAILABLE AT
WWW.ORDEROFCHRISTIANMYSTICS.CO.ZA

THE
INNER RADIANCE

Transcribed by
HARRIETTE AUGUSTA CURTISS
and
F. HOMER CURTISS, B.S., M.D.
Founders of
THE ORDER OF CHRISTIAN MYSTICS
and
AUTHORS OF THE "CURTISS BOOKS"

2012 EDITION

REPUBLISHED FOR THE ORDER BY
MOUNT LINDEN PUBLISHING
JOHANNESBURG, SOUTH AFRICA
ISBN: 978-1-920483-04-3

Dedication

This edition is lovingly dedicated to the Memory

of the Founders of

The Order of Christian Mystics

Pyrahmos and Rahmea

and to

The Teacher of the Order

who on earth was called

Helena Petrovna Blavatsky

"Ministers of Christ and Stewards of the Mysteries of God."
1 Corinthians 4 vs. 1

TABLE OF CONTENTS

PREFACE

The material for this volume has been available for several years, but the long illness of Mrs. Curtiss, and the subsequent great growth of *The Order of Christian Mystics* as a result of our extensive lecture tours and our exhibit at *A Century of Progress* exposition in Chicago during 1933 and 1934, together with the tremendously increased activities which followed, have further delayed its preparation for publication.

But this delay has not been wholly unfortunate, as it has enabled us to include several chapters dealing with present-day conditions in the world which have been in great demand and which we are glad to make available to all in permanent form.

We trust that this new material will enable our readers and students to understand more intelligently the revolutionary conditions through which humanity is now passing, while the more general philosophical and spiritual material will give them both philosophical and scientific, as well as spiritual, reasons for a greater realization of their *vital* and *personal* relation to both the lower and the invisible kingdoms of lives which surround them in Nature, their relation to their fellow-men, and to that great Cosmic Source of all light, life and consciousness, that Eternal Being, whom men call God.

—The Authors.

CHAPTER I

THE INNER RADIANCE

"And the light shineth in the darkness; and the darkness comprehended it not" *St. John*, I, 5.

"For God, who commanded the light to shine out of the darkness, hath shined into our hearts, to give the light of the knowledge of the glory of God in the face of Jesus Christ." *II Corinthians*, IV, 6.

Back of all evolution there is an inner power, a manifestation of life, an Inner Radiance which pushes the unfoldment of all forms of life—from atoms to planets—on to their destined perfected manifestation. The essence of this Inner Radiance is the out-breathing of the Supreme Being, the Divine Breath, which manifested as the sacred Word which brought all things into expression, and which in man becomes embodied in flesh as the Divine Dweller.

Science has proved that every form of life expresses some aspect of radiant energy or Inner Radiance; in fact, each form is fashioned by and exists for the express purpose of permitting its particular aspect of that Inner Radiance to manifest on Earth, much as the hard shell of the wholesome nut exists for the purpose of enabling the soft, tender meat to survive and manifest in conditions which without the outer shell would crush and destroy it and prevent its expression here on Earth.

Every physical form is but an aggregation of material and other substances held together by, and through which, a particular aspect, current or vibration of the divine One Life finds expression. And only by the steady pressure from within outward of the gyrations of the Inner Radiance, this mysterious life-force, can the inner and unseen

pattern unfold, materialize in matter and evolve into the full
expression of perfection it is intended to manifest. For, like the
nut, the inner pattern[1] which was breathed out by the Creator
through the Divine Mind, must have a protecting covering of
physical substance ere it can fulfill its destiny, which destiny
was imprinted upon it ere it was sent forth into manifestation.
And it is through the evolution of these outer forms[2] which are
continually modified to accommodate the progressive unfolding
of the inner pattern, that the Inner Radiance moulds all physical
matter ultimately to embody God's will for that form.

These outer forms are not created in an instantaneous flash; for
after God spake the Word and the inner patterns or ideals were
projected into manifestation, it required untold ages for their Inner
Radiance to overcome the inertia of matter and mould that dense
and resistant substance into the meshes of the delicate, ethereal
inner patterns so as to permit their progressive unfoldment and
correct materialization in the physical world.

It requires tremendous constructive power to unfold and
evolve these outer forms; to gather the materials and transform
and synthesize them into living tissue; to collect the tons of earth
which compose a giant tree, for example, and to absorb and lift
hundreds of feet into the air the countless barrels of water which
are daily required by such a tree. All the outer forms which
protect and more or less crudely outpicture their inner patterns
are therefore sustained and evolved by the dynamic cohesive
power of their Inner Radiance, the downpouring and inflowing
of the life-aspect of the Godhead; that ever-renewing Inner
Radiance of the Divine which constantly pushes all forms on
to perfection; that Eternal Urge upward and onward from the
primitive to the perfected through the progressive new presentation
and new revealing of the inner pattern or Ideal of all things.

---

[1] For details see *The Truth About Evolution and the Bible*, Curtiss, Chapter III.
[2] *Ibid*.

This is equally true of suns and cosmic systems as it is of the lowliest forms. All are but manifestations in matter of the Divine One Life.

This law applies to man as well as to all other expressions of the cosmic currents of the One Life. To accept the statement that "God formed man of the dust of the ground," and to ignore the previous statement that "God created man in His own image and likeness" is to accept the letter which killeth all true understanding of the subject—the mere shell of the nut—and ignore the Spirit or Inner Radiance which maketh alive. For just as in the nut there is its kernel, which is destined to unfold into the tree, and which is wrapped in the hard outer shell, so in man there is an inner kernel—called the Christ Child—whose Inner Radiance, although wrapped in the swaddling clothes of the outer shell or personality and therefore little realized and understood, is ultimately destined to accomplish its mission, namely, to spiritualize the flesh and unfold the inner pattern of the Divine Real Self. But only as we remove the restrictions of the swaddling clothes, by allowing the Christ Child to manifest through us, can we enable Him to grow up and become the Carpenter who can utilize all the experiences of life as tools and all the conditions of life as materials with which to make our body a temple of the Living God, leaving behind as chips the superficial things of the outer life.

Once man realizes that his Real Self is truly a Ray of God, made in His image, and allows that Image of God[3] to manifest, the whole world will be changed. Man is therefore far more than the physical form—which was not created but *formed* or evolved[4] out of the dust of the ground—through which his Inner Radiance manifests. Man is a microcosm or an epitome of the universe. The same Eternal

---

[3] See "The Image of God" in *The Truth About Evolution and the Bible*, Curtiss, Chapters XIX, III.

[4] For details see *The Truth About Evolution and the Bible*, Curtiss, Chapter III.

Being from whose Divine Mind the inner pattern of all lower forms were projected also projected the Inner Man,[5] created in His image and likeness and destined to be the Lord of Creation and His highest manifestation on this planet.

The Inner Man or first Adam of the first chapter of *Genesis* was the Real Self or Spiritual Man, while the second Adam of the second chapter of *Genesis* was but the outer, physical form or animal body into which the Spiritual Man was to incarnate. But only when the Earth and its lower forms had evolved to the requisite point did this human-animal form appear. And only when this human form had evolved to a point where it contained the necessary organs and centers could the Spiritual Man be breathed into that human form. And it was only after the incarnation of the Spiritual Man into the body of flesh that man "became a living Soul" and the unfoldment (evolution) of man as we know him began.

If this fundamental distinction between the outer form or body of man and his Inner Radiance is understood, the so-called conflict between religion and science[6] disappears, for both are true in their own realms; one is talking about spiritual man and the other about his physical body. Only as we allow the Inner Radiance of the Spiritual Man to shine forth in our hearts and manifest in and through the body of flesh can we express our Real Self, the Image of God, which shall illumine, guide and ultimately redeem from ignorance and sin—transgression of the Law—the man of flesh.

Because of the effect of the Inner Radiance on the evolution of the outer form, one of the chief characteristics of all living things (forms) is change. This is due to an ever-progressive unfolding of the inner pattern, a new manifestation or ideal for each form. That which is incapable

---

[5] See *"The Origin of Man"* in *The Voice of Isis*, Curtiss, 288.
[6] For details see *The Truth About Evolution and the Bible*, Curtiss, Chapter III.

of change has ceased to grow and will soon cease to live. Then the lower forms of life of which that higher form was made up, or connected with—atoms, cells, bacteria, etc.,—will have a brief form of separate existence until the old body of which they were a part is entirely disintegrated. Then the Inner Radiance which formerly inhabited the now disintegrated form is freed to manifest in the higher worlds, and in its next incarnation must build up and inhabit a new form which will be less limiting to its unfoldment and manifestation.

This Law of Change is a Law of Life and applies to peoples, civilizations, customs, ideas and religions as well as to physical forms. When the Inner Radiance, or the Spirit which quickeneth, no longer finds free expression through a previous form of manifestation—no matter how vital and radiant with life and power that form may once have been— that form, be it civilization, custom, idea or religion, becomes but an empty shell; for its Inner Radiance has withdrawn to seek a new avenue or form of manifestation.

Applying this Law of Change to religion, we will readily understand that every form of religion must unfold and change its mode of expression in accord with the advances in man's conception of the universe and its laws, if that religion's Inner Radiance is to continue to shine forth anew and reveal its inner pattern more perfectly.

Like the rose whose petals, at first folded tightly over its inner golden center, gradually unfold and open its heart to the Sun and permit its perfumed breath to pour forth upon the air, so must religion follow the same Law of Change (growth). The "air" of mankind which religion must perfume is composed of the principles and ideals which it inbreathes and which vitally affect the spiritual, moral and social health of the nations. Air, when illumined and vitalized by the rays of the Sun, becomes to the physical universe the very breath of God, whose Voice pronounced the Word that was made flesh. Sunshine and air have been essential factors in the formation of all flesh since the beginning, but air, too, must change or it becomes "dead air" and often poisonous.

The inner mystical truths upon which the outer forms—creeds and ceremonies—of all religions are built remain unchanged throughout the ages, for they are spiritual verities eternal in the heavens. But the outer forms which veil and only partially express them must evolve, and should grow ever more transparent that the Inner Radiance of Divine Truth may shine through more brightly to illumine the minds of men and reveal all the Divine Truth that it is possible for man's spiritual unfoldment in each age to grasp.

If, instead of evolving and more clearly revealing its Inner Radiance, a religion becomes materialized through adherence to the letter of its man-made dogmas and creeds, then it ultimately disintegrates and disappears, after having served its purpose for a cycle, as though blown away by the winds of heaven. But if it is willing to modify its former conceptions, its Inner Radiance will illumine the heart and mind of someone, or of many, to break through the crust of misconception and materialization which has gathered around it, that new conceptions of its vital truths may shine forth in forms suited to the New Age.

Thus do all religions have their reformers and regenerators. And the old forms of expression drop away as the petals of a rose which has spent its life-force fall to the ground, although its Inner Radiance still persists, either as a seed of a new rose or is indrawn into the bush that it may manifest greater beauty and fragrance in another, or perhaps several more blossoms on the same bush. Therefore, the crying need of religion today is to put forth new blossoms from the same Eternal Roots of Divine Truth. For no longer can the man-made interpretations of the medieval ages satisfy either the intellect or the heart-hunger of enlightened minds of the present twentieth century, the beginning of this new Aquarian Age. Hence, if our present-day religions are to remain a vital factor in the lives of modern men and women, there must be a new and vital interpretation of the world-old spiritual principles concerning the manifestation of the Divine to man and within man, such as *The Order of Christian Mystics* is endeavoring to set forth.

In former ages the heat and light of the Sun were about the only forces recognized by the mass of mankind as coming from it, but today we know that the visible rays constitute only a small part of the Sun's vital forces. Important as the visible rays are to the life of man and the planet, it is the downpouring of the invisible rays (ultra-violet, etc.) of the Inner Radiance of the Sun which penetrates to the center of the planet and there forms the four inner realms of radio-active ethers which, together with the upward-streaming rays from the various radio-active substances in the Earth itself, are the most potent and which have the most important effects upon health, vitality and growth, whether of planets, animals or men.

Just so it is with the Spiritual Sun. For although the spiritual Inner Radiance, which has manifested visibly in the various world religions and teachers, has been of great importance in the outer spiritual life of mankind, yet it is only the inner, invisible and mystical rays of the Christ-light—which has always manifested under various names, even though unrecognized and unknown by the mass of mankind—which has been the most potent force in the inner spiritual life of humanity.

And just as we have now reached an Age in which we have begun to recognize the invisible rays of the Sun and begun to understand something of how to use them for health, healing, growth and vitality, so we have reached an Age when we must recognize and learn to use through actual practice—through prayer, meditation, aspiration and radiation in speech and conduct—the invisible rays of the Spiritual Sun, the Christ-light, for our spiritual health, healing, growth and vitality. For it is this, at present little known, mystical Inner Radiance of the Christ-light which *must be recognized and used* to bring humanity a truer understanding and fuller appreciation of the laws of Its manifestation as set forth in the *Gospel* story. "That Light was the true Light, which lighteth every man that cometh into the world." But the Light shone in the darkness of man's incomprehension and he recognized it not, just as the invisible rays of the Sun and of radium have shone forth in the physical world for countless ages until the expansion of man's consciousness enabled him to recognize and use — although as yet only partially — their powers.

To obtain the healing, revitalizing and regenerating effect of the Sun's invisible rays, we must deliberately expose ourselves to the direct light of the Sun, for the healing rays are cut off if the light passes through ordinary window glass. Likewise, to obtain the regenerating, redeeming and illuminating effects of our Inner Radiance from the mighty I Am Presence within, we must have certain definite periods daily when we *deliberately expose ourselves* to, or bathe in, the inner mystical Christ-light or the Inner Radiance of an individualized Ray of that Eternal Being which is sent to Earth to draw all things unto Him that all may have life, and life more abundantly. Hence the vital necessity for a specific time each day for meditation, prayer and worship.

Every advance in science which results in the alleviation of the hardships, discomforts, sorrows and suffering of humanity comes, firstly, because enlightened minds have deliberately turned their attention to the unknown forces and laws of Nature and meditated upon them until they have conceived something of their possibilities and uses. Then comes the recognition of those forces and their deliberate application to the problems of humanity. In a similar way, if we wish to quicken our spiritual growth and unfoldment, we too must *deliberately turn our attention* to the unknown forces and laws of the spiritual life and meditate upon them.[7] In other words, just as we have solar and radium solariums in our sanitariums, so we must establish a spiritual solarium, as it were, in which we consciously bathe in the Inner Radiance of the Christ-light of the I Am Presence within.

To help us gain this realization and apply its power to our personal lives, we should visualize our Real Self, not as a finite mortal, but as a great and glorious *immortal spiritual being*, the mighty I Am Presence, overshadowing us and endeavoring to find ever greater and greater expression through us, according to our recognition of and response to His divine guidance. We should picture Him so radiant with the spiritual emanations of His divinity that He is bathed in a dazzling white light which pours down over us, fills our aura and thus surrounds us with its snowy whiteness, much as though we were encased in a giant bottle of snowy white glass. Every time we visualize this ideal of our Real Self and reach up in aspiration to and correlate with its divine reality, we enlarge the channel through which that Inner Radiance can descend into our human personality. There its presence will help us to overcome our limitations, redeem our mistakes, illumine our minds and fill our lives with its radio-active emanations, so that we will unconsciously be a blessing to all we contact, just as the perfume of the rose unconsciously delights all who contact it.

As we make a practice of this we will gradually begin to recognize and respond to many invisible rays of spiritual light, life and truth which formerly were unknown and unsuspected by us. Once we recognize them we will be able to apply these forces as health, happiness, spiritual uplift and unfoldment in our lives and radiate them to others, thus helping to counteract, and ultimately entirely banish, the seemingly inevitable ills of mankind. Thus will we manifest

---

[7] Using our *Prayer for Light*, the *Prayer to the Divine Indweller*, etc. See *Prayers of the O.C.M.*, Curtiss, 1-6

not only physical health and intellectual growth, but spiritual health and intellectual illumination which will make our lives spiritually radio-active. And thus will the Inner Radiance shine forth in blessing upon all mankind because we have removed the swaddling clothes that obscured the Christ-light within; because we are unfolding new petals on the Rose of Life, and we have begun to bring the Inner Radiance into visible manifestation in joy, health, power and happiness in our outer lives.

CHAPTER II

THE GOD MAN

"We know that whosoever is born of God sinneth not; but he that is begotten of God keepeth himself, and that wicked one toucheth him not. And we know that we are of God, and the whole world lieth in wickedness." *I John* V, 18-19.

"God is in us of a truth." *I Corinthians*, XIV, 25.

"Thus every mortal has his immortal counterpart, or rather his Archetype, in heaven. This means that the former is indissolubly united to the latter, in each of his incarnations, and for the duration of the cycle of births." *The Key to Theosophy*, Blavatsky, 59.

The object of physical existence is still one of the greatest mysteries for most of humanity, even in these days of great scientific advance and enlightenment. But it is still a mystery only because the attention of the most progressive minds of the world has been focused on material things, problems and aims in the world outside of the Self, instead of being focused within to find out what the Self really is and its object in manifesting in the physical world.

In these days of turmoil, of uncertainty and of wavering faith, of growing antagonism and even atheism, the understanding of this mystery is of far more importance to our Soul-growth and even to our worldly welfare than any amount of information on psychic or occult topics, however informative and intellectually interesting they may be.

The fundamental concept for us all to realize and firmly establish in our minds is that *we are essentially Spiritual Beings* here and now, as much so as we will ever be; that we have nothing to do with Earth conditions except when we come down from our heavenly home to manifest for a few short years in this world of matter. But when we are

once incarnated in these bodies of flesh, we so lose the memory of
our heavenly home and *who we really are* that we often manifest
so little of our Real or Divine Self or I Am Presence that we seem
to be but mortals instead of Immortals, and seem to be limited to
the functions of the bodily organism in which we find ourselves.

This feeling arises because of our lack of proper training and
teaching as to the difference between the human personality and
the Real Self which is striving to find expression through it. Most
persons have, therefore, never really conceived of the fact that
the Real Self of us is an individualized Ray of the Divine, and
therefore necessarily is made in the image and after the likeness
of God or the sevenfold Elohim; *an actual emanation* from or
particle of the Godhead that has been consciously projected from
Himself for the purpose of manifesting Himself in individuality in
the worlds of matter and form. Since we are His direct emanations
we naturally contain all the potencies and powers of the Godhead,
such as the God-consciousness to grasp and understand the truth
which shall make us free from the bonds of ignorance and illusion,
the Divine Will to manifest that Truth, the Divine Love to cherish
and bring it forth, and the Divine Life to vitalize and establish it
as a living power in our lives.

We must therefore never for a moment entertain the old
medieval conception that we are worms of the dust, poor
miserable sinners, weak human creatures, mere human animals.
For we are far more than animals, more even than human beings.
Instead of piteously praying for God to come down and save us
from the results of our own ignorance, mistakes and selfishness,
we must realize that God is right here all the time now, within
us as the God Man, made in His image and after His likeness.
Hence God does not need to come down. He merely needs to
be *recognised* within and *be allowed to manifest* without. As
our text says: We know that whosoever is born of God sinneth

not; but he that is begotten of God keepeth himself, and the wicked one toucheth him not."

We are indeed Sons and Daughters of God, children of the Most High, who are seeking to manifest our Divine Selfhood here on Earth through bodies of flesh. "And if children, then heirs; heirs of God, and joint heirs with Christ."[1] Even if the God Man within is as yet only in the babe stage of His unfoldment and manifestation, He nevertheless is filled with the love, the power and the glory of the Divine. And the more we meditate upon Him and *strive to express* His divine qualities, the more He grows in His power to manifest them through us and guide our personality. There is therefore nothing that cannot be accomplished in His name if we realize in all its intensity, in the depths of our hearts, that we, the Real Self, are Divine here and now; that *we are Gods in the process of manifestation* in matter. Hence the ancient axiom: "Men are mortal gods and gods are immortal men."

However, some may ask: Where does the animal part of us come in? Here we must realize clearly that the animal part *is not us*, is not the Real Self, the God Man. We possess an animal body not because we are the highest type of animal, but because it is a highly evolved physical instrument which is absolutely necessary for the God Man to manifest through in this world of form and matter.[2] It is given to us so that when we reach the stage of unfolding consciousness wherein we recognize our Divinity, when we realize that we are more than mere animals, *more than mere mortals*; that we are truly Sons and Daughters of God; when we realize our power to reach up in consciousness to the throne of our Father, to become one with Him, to feel His love and His power and His blessing filling us, then we will have a perfected and trained instrument through which to manifest our Sonship and Daughtership here on Earth,

---

[1] *Romans*, VIII, 17.
[2] For details see *The Truth about Evolution and the Bible*, Curtiss.

even as it is done in heaven. Thus shall our life on Earth become
a mirror of our celestial life.

But how are we to perfect our human instrument so that the
God Man can manifest through it? First, we must recognize that
the animal nature, with all its passions, appetites and desires, has
been fashioned and given to us by the Father for our use.[2] It is
therefore not to be despised or ill-treated. For there is nothing that
He has made, from the lowest one-celled microscopic organism
up to man, or from the sands of the seashore up to galaxies of
blazing suns, that has not a manifestation of His divinity within
it, whether seen or unseen, whether understood or not understood
by us. Hence, we should think of everything we contact on Earth
as being a partial manifestation of God. By so doing we can gain
a greater understanding of God and a greater power to help us
manifest the God Man within.

For there is nothing manifested that is not made by God,
except the inharmonious, impure and abominable things *which
are created by man* through the *perversion* of his creative powers
of mind and body because of his ignorance, his disobedience to
the inner guidance, and his selfishness and perverse wickedness.
Every thought we think and every word we utter creates after its
kind in some realm.[3] It either adds to the inharmony and misery
of the world or it helps humanity onward and upward, and it also
sinks down into the lower kingdoms and blesses and lifts them
up. Hence there must be no refusal to face anything, no denial of
obvious facts or of the existence *to us* of the things that our senses
report, but a willingness to *see and recognize each manifestation
for what it is* and either use it, learn a lesson from it or pass it by
as the God Man within may direct.

Realizing our real, Divine Nature and our power to
transcend and control our animal self, we must strive in every
way to train and perfect and uplift it by radiating and ex-

---

[3] For details see *Realms of the Living Dead*, Curtiss.

pressing in our daily lives the powers and forces that come from the God Man within: our highest aspirations, our intuitions, our highest thoughts and ideals, so that their radioactive power will refine and make the animal nature and the whole human personality more and more responsive to the God Man within. Thus will the lower nature and all its faculties be purified, uplifted and glorified to their highest uses in the service of the God Man for His manifestation on Earth.

But the manifestation must be from the Divine within, radiating and expressing outwardly. No amount of assumed or outward show of religion or pretence or claim of spiritual advance, no hypocrisy or self-delusion, can long cover up or conceal the real character or stage of unfoldment of the God Man within. Each person unconsciously but inevitably reveals his stage of unfoldment in his outer conduct. Daily, hourly, in every act of life and in all our contacts with others we evidence and prove the degree of our realization and manifestation of the God Man within.

It is comparatively easy to demonstrate our God-consciousness and our God-powers in the higher, finer realms whose substance is so immediately responsive to our every thought. But we can only complete the full cycle of expression of the God Man by demonstrating His characteristics and powers in the dense and relatively unresponsive conditions of Earth-life, and thereby gain the rudiments of self-knowledge through the physical senses. It is therefore both *our duty and our privilege* to learn to utilize our divine powers of will, wisdom and love here in the physical world. And since we are Sons and Daughters of God we must learn to live like Gods; must practice thinking and speaking and acting as near as we can imagine Gods would do here and now.

We must strive to manifest that absolute poise which results from an inner quietude. Manifest serenity under all conditions because of our realization of our high destiny: manifest self-control because the Real Self controls: patience and no need for hurry because we realize the timelessness of Eternity in which we live; purity because of mastery of the flesh: radiant health without because of Life Divine within: cheerfulness and happiness because of our inner joy: kindliness of speech and act because of our great love: a melodious voice because it has lost its power to wound:[4] a quizzical humour because of our understanding of man's foolishness: tolerance because of man's ignorance: courage because of a realization of our immortality: a soft answer that turneth away wrath because we do not respond to inharmony and realize man's spiritual childishness: words and deeds of helpfulness and comfort because of our great compassion and our desire to help others: unselfishness and charity because of our inner store of riches. The necessity for demonstrating the degree of our unfoldment in our daily conduct was clearly recognized by that illumined leader and founder of Quakerism, George Fox. He and his followers believed that the visible "signs" of the inward grace must be manifested outwardly. In every act of life they kept in mind the necessity of evidencing the real, positive proof of their realization of the God Man within, which they gained by meditation upon Him in regular periods of silence and communion with Him. It was not alone the manifestation of His power from within which carried them through persecution and martyrdom, that so puzzled and baffled their persecutors. It was their unfailing kindness, their gentleness in word and act, their courtesy, their tender care of the weak and ailing, their uncompromising stand against all inharmony and sin, even the mildest forms of wrongdoing, which demonstrated the power of the God Man within to guide them in the practical affairs of daily life. Theirs was the strength of gentle non-resistance, yet none could be so staunch and unyielding when faced with a question of principle or faith. No personal sac-

---

[4] "Before the voice can speak in the presence of the Masters, it must have lost its power to wound." *Light on the Path*, Collins.

rifice was too great, no suffering was too much, no imprisonment or persecution half so terrible in their eyes as to *lack courage* and *fail to live up to* the Divine Guidance of the God Man within as revealed to them through prayer and meditation. And we can do no better today than to emulate that attitude of mind and that daily practice of the presence of God in our lives.

To the extent that we recognize and correlate with the God Man within, the more we feel the warmth of His burning love, the more we feel His sympathy for all mankind, the more we realize His Christ-consciousness, the more do we respond to and radiate His qualities and forces to the upliftment and blessing of all we contact. For the more we are blessed by a realization of His God-powers within, the more we are able to bless, help, comfort and enlighten others. As we respond to the harmony and joy of His presence within, so will we be gloriously happy, kind, poised and serene under all conditions. We will thus be a shining example of what humanity, as manifestations of the God Man, should be: not by seeking to dominate others or to compel them to be or do what we think is right, but by inspiring them to manifest their own God Man within.

We must remember that this physical world is the realm in which we must learn to demonstrate our divine characteristics, just as a violin factory, wherein the material instrument is manufactured, is necessary before the musician can demonstrate the Soul-rapture of his musical genius. Our short visit to this Earth-plane should therefore be regarded as a great privilege, *another opportunity to manifest* as much of the God Man within as we have been able to unfold during all our previous incarnations.

But the God Man within cannot force us to follow His guidance nor can He manifest within us against our will. He therefore must have, first, *our recognition of His presence within*, and then our glad and *willing obedience* and help, so that He may find expression in and through our daily lives. For even God and His Archangels cannot manifest in the human kingdom except through us as Their instruments of expression. They are our Archetypes and we Their counterparts, Their mystic shrines, temples of the Living God. If we make mistakes, if we give way to temptation or to impure or destructive thoughts or words, nevertheless the God Man is still within us, but crucified by and suffering from all the inharmonies of our creation. He does not condemn or scold us, but speaks to us in the Still Small Voice.

As we recognize our mistakes and strive to correct and redeem them. He holds out His hands in love and says: "Come unto Me and I will give you rest and peace. I will give you My power to overcome. Only ask for it. Only take it and use it to master the personality and make it your servant. For the uplifting of humanity and all the lower kingdoms is a mighty task and I need your help. *Come and help Me* to uplift and bless all manifested things. Thus will you become My Chosen Ones. Thus will you learn to manifest Me, your Real Self, the God Man within."[5] Then will we be able to demonstrate that; "The gods are come down to us in the likeness of men," as the people of Lycaonia said of Paul and Barnabas.[6]

---

[5] See lesson *His Chosen Ones*, Curtiss.
[6] *Acts*, XIV, 11.

CHAPTER III

AS IN THE DAYS OF NOAH

"As it was in the days of Noah, so shall it be also in the days of the Son of man . . . . until the day that Noah entered into the ark, and the flood came, and destroyed them all. . . . Likewise also was it in the days of Lot; . . . . the same day that Lot went out of Sodom it rained fire and brimstone from heaven, and destroyed them all. Even thus shall it be in the day when the Son of man is revealed." *St. Luke*, XVII, 26-30.

Everything in the universe finds expression in rhythmic waves of cyclic expression: periods of outgoing into manifestation and indrawal into obscuration and rest. History therefore ever tends to repeat itself in greater or lesser cycles. Nations, peoples and races tend to pass through similar conditions, especially toward the close of their greater and lesser cycles. And just as at the close of the cycle of the year all Nature passes through the disagreeable conditions of rain, mud, frost and snow, as a result of the storms of the closing cycles of the year, so do nations and humanity as a whole have to pass through similar conditions of stress and strain at the close of their respective seasons or cycles. This is due both to planetary and to national causes. Through their cyclic revolutions the planets periodically tend to return to their former relations to each other and therefore tend to subject this Earth and its humanity to conditions similar to those which obtained in previous ages when the planets formed the same combinations and relationships with each other and with the Earth.

Astrologers tell us that as the Sun (in 1931) was in adverse aspect to Saturn, Uranus and Jupiter, and especially as Saturn was afflicting Uranus, it tended to retard all progress. Such combinations have a very adverse influence both upon finance and labor as well as upon agriculture. Hence we are now experiencing planetary influences which tend to bring about "hard times," unemployment, financial depression and panics, as well as unusual storms, droughts, floods, crop failures and famines. These generally adverse influences did not cease until Saturn passed out of the thrifty but earthbound sign of Capricorn into the airy but erratic sign Aquarius on November 20th, 1932, although they were modified for the better by the benign rays of Jupiter, the planet of finance, when it passed out of Leo into Virgo on August 11, 1932. But since astrology teaches that we should "rule our stars," instead of passively and helplessly giving way to their influences as if they were fate, the results are greatly intensified by man's personal reaction to the planetary influences, that is, whether he gives way to them or utilizes them for his learning and his ongoing.

The most important factor, therefore, in such unusually upset conditions of humanity as we find at present is the individual and collective Karma which man himself has created in the past and has not entirely redeemed. This unredeemed Karma naturally accumulates toward the end of the greater and lesser cycles, at which time it must be faced and redeemed or it will overwhelm all those whose personal advance has not enabled them to learn their lessons and thus escape participating in any but the general or racial Karma. As the combinations of planetary aspects and influences are now similar to those which existed at the close of the former great cycles in the days of Noah and of Lot, humanity is facing a similar crisis.

Again today we see "that the wickedness of man was great in the Earth, and that every imagination of the thoughts of his heart was only evil continually. . . . The Earth also was corrupt before God, and the Earth was filled with violence . . . . for all flesh has corrupted his way upon the

Earth."[1] And since the great mass of mankind today will not listen to the prophets of this age any more than they did to Noah and to the angels who came to Lot, similar cataclysms[2] must take place to cleanse the Earth and prepare for the new and spiritually advanced conditions of the incoming Aquarian age of Altruism. "Even thus shall it be in the day when the Son of man is revealed." For only so can humanity be cleansed, awakened and prepared for the greatest event in the two-thousand-year cycle of the Aquarian Age, namely, the descent and manifestation of the Christ as the coming Avatar.[3]

Noah symbolizes those illumined ones or prophets of the Lord who are able to hear His voice and give out His loving counsel and helpful warnings to mankind. Those "of the household of Noah" are all those who are willing to listen *and heed* the words of the many modern prophets of the Lord in all races and languages and religions who are warning their respective peoples to prepare for great changes in the Earth and all outer conditions, as well as for the near advent of the Son of Man, whether as the reappearance of the Asiatic Rigden Jyepo in Shambhala or of the phenomenal manifestation of the Christ in America. Therefore it is most important to broadcast the Cosmic Philosophy which explains the conditions which humanity is facing, and also the how, why and when of His coming, so that this knowledge shall be the leven that shall leven all humanity and give all who will, the understanding and the help which will enable them to pass through the coming conditions in safety and help them to prepare for His coming.

It should be understood that it matters not what the Soul has done in the past or is doing today: it is still divine and is beloved of the Christ. The Great Law, therefore, metes out to every Soul not the Karma of punishment, not of ar-

---

[1] *Genesis*, VII, 5, 11, 12.
[2] Such as recently raised the coast of New Zealand 70 feet. See our 1931 *Annual News Letter* for further examples, also *Coming World Changes*, Curtiss.
[3] See "The Doctrine of Avatara," *Voice of Isis, Curtiss*, Chapter X.

bitrary tests merely to wring their hearts and overwhelm them with suffering, but our Karma is apportioned by the Lords of Karma[4] to each of us so that it will act as the law of adjustment which brings to each one at just the right time that which shall ultimately awaken him to a realization of the Christ within and to his divine heritage. Or, if necessary, it may remove us from incarnation to prevent us from generating further adverse Karma until we have learned our lessons and have attained greater growth and unfoldment.

The planets come back into their same relative positions at the appointed time, not to punish mankind, but again to touch the hearts of men with their vibrations of purification and redemption and to pour out the forces needed by man to cleanse himself and his environment and creations. Only that which is not cleansed and cannot respond to the octave of vibration of the new cycle needs to be swept away and allow this little planet to pass safely through its "days of tribulation" and again prepare for the coming of the Son of Man; for planets, like nations and individuals, must be tested and proved or disintegrate and be withdrawn from manifestation.

While all planets are His temples, yet at this particular cycle this Earth has been chosen as His sanctuary in the midst of them all, because it is here that He has chosen to manifest again to teach us to recognize Him and the help He can give us to awaken us to a fuller realization that we are His children and therefore Divine, and to bring to us the memory of our heavenly home and the great mission for which we are incarnated here in the flesh. Only a God of Divine Love would create man in His image and watch over his evolution and unfoldment through the long ages of ignorance and lack of realization and mistakes until he awakened to the realization of the I Am Presence of the Christ within

---

[4] See Chapter XV herein.

and learned to listen to His guidance and serve Him on Earth even as it is done in heaven.

Our Karma comes, therefore, not merely as a mechanical reaping of that which we have sown in the past, but because those past experiences have left certain tendencies, vibrations or grooves in our lives, in our characters, in our dispositions, which we must either fill up or perfect into constructive channels of expression and realization. To bring this about, some need one thing, some another. Some need "hard times," poverty, sickness, surprising experiences, perhaps disappointment and disillusion because of the dark shadows of their past lives. But that which comes is just that which is needed to wake us up and bring to us a realization of our Real Selves and our mission on Earth.

Think you that the Lord of Love sends these things as mere punishment? As mere tests? Not so. All these things come in the greatest love. For like humanity in general, and also the planet, even His awakened ones must be cleansed and readjusted and strengthened and fitted to do their part in preparing for His coming. Although we can always contact the Christ within when we turn to Him in prayer and aspiration, ere we are worthy to greet the Coming One face to face, we must prove that we have worked out or transmuted the old Karma which so often clings to us like a vampire, sapping our spiritual and psychic life and making us far from that which we should be manifesting.

We cannot trust and rely upon Him utterly, however, until we have conquered our fears. We cannot truly believe until we have faced and conquered our doubts. We cannot have perfect health until we have been cleansed from all impurities and live in harmony with Nature's laws. But since we know that all that comes to us is but part of our training for His service, we can pass through it willingly and understandingly. And with His help we can triumph over all our experiences, and so, from our own experience and realization, be able to help, enlighten and comfort those who are in distress and spiritual darkness around us.

The book of *Revelation* in the *Bible* is an allegorical presentation of the conditions which the world must pass through at the close of the cycle of the Fifth Great Race. And as we are now passing through the closing days of the fifth sub-race we must naturally expect to pass through similar conditions, but in a lesser degree. Many persons fear to read *Revelation*, both because they cannot understand its symbology and because of the many dire disasters and terrible sufferings which it outpictures as the result of the cleansing process. They therefore often fail to read the last chapter, in which there is depicted the conditions which will prevail during the Sixth and Seventh Great Races after the cleansing has been completed.

To a less perfect degree similar conditions should prevail as we enter the sixth sub-race after the cleansing of the fifth sub-race which precedes His coming. For after His coming, if the humanity that survives the cleansing will live according to the Divine Law of love, harmony, purity, brotherhood and co-operation *under His guidance*, then indeed "there shall be no more curse." The results of the former curse of inharmony and impurity will have been adjusted and wiped out and humanity, having learned its lessons, will no longer generate the antagonism and inharmonies with which mankind cursed the Earth and himself during the previous cycle. Also then "there shall be no more night there; and they need no candle, neither light of the Sun; for the Lord God giveth them light."

In other words, when we realize the light of the Christ within we will no longer struggle blindly in the darkness of spiritual ignorance, nor will we turn to the "candle" of our human intellect, nor to the authorities of the outer world which correspond to the physical Sun, for guidance; for the light of the Christ within will thenceforth light our path through life and illumine all our problems and give us the peace and happiness which should be his here and now.

But to help humanity to pass through the troublous times of the necessary cleansing which must come, and be able to enter into the new conditions of peace, love, harmony and co-operation, all those who are "of the household of Noah" must set to work seriously, now while there is yet time, to build an Ark of the Lord wherein all who will may enter and be saved. Not only are all the spiritually awakened ones needed in this great work, but also all the enlightened minds of the race; those who are leaders in science, literature, religion and art, as well as in the fields of economics, industry, politics, etc. All should be brought to realize the significance of present-day conditions and use all their talents to further the constructive working out of the revolutionary planetary changes and the results which these changes will have upon mankind. All should be made to understand that it is a great cosmic event that is being prepared for and not merely the adjustment of man's Karma; for this is the cycle "when the Son of man shall be revealed."

Spiritually, this Ark of safety for humanity is the spiritual aura of the Coming One, which is so vast as to include all mankind to the extent that they "tune in" to the vibratory rate of His life, love and power. Yet into His aura there is drawn the essence of all the aspirations, the loving thoughts, kind words and helpful deeds of all those who are seeking, even if ever so blindly and ignorantly, to do His will or more understandingly to prepare for His coming; in fact, the constructive forces of all who are united in the one idea of preparing both themselves and humanity for His advent

Since all our spiritual vibrations are thus united in Him, to that extent *we become a part of Him and He of us*. Then literally "in Him we live and move and have our being." Through such an aura of the united spiritual forces of God and man the Master can more directly reach into the hearts of mankind and help to awaken their consciousness of the Christ within and thus help to save great masses of humanity from the suffering they would otherwise undergo during these "days of tribulation." Those who thus respond to His presence constitute the Elect, because they have elected to follow His guidance. And it is for the Elect's sake or because of their activities among their fellow men that we are promised that *the days of tribulation shall be shortened*, else there should be no flesh left alive.

In the physical world *The Order of Christian Mystics* can be made into a corresponding Ark—one among many such that are needed—in which *all who will listen to its message* will find not only a warm welcome, fellowship and encouragement, but also that comfort, peace and sense of security which comes from an understanding of the Law and the Divine Plan which is working out through the present stormy trials in their lives and the turbulent conditions in the world.

The planks of this Ark of the Order are the universal spiritual principles which its Teachings present, all indissolubly bound together with the indestructible bonds of love. Hence they embrace all kingdoms and creatures, as well as mankind. And those who will enter into this Ark and *rely upon its planks and follow the guidance* of its Captain will surely pass through the deep waters of these changing conditions in safety and learn the lessons of such events. Even though they may be storm-tossed and wave-bound at times, they will surely land upon the mountain top of the higher consciousness when the storm is over. Then will the dove of peace bring them the olive branch of true understanding and realization.

With this understanding we need not be dismayed if in the next few years we see even more extraordinary changes and revolutions, both in the Earth itself and *in all conditions of life*, than in the past few years; if we witness revolutions, new wars and what appears to be the world gone mad, turned upside down. For we will know that all this is only the process of cleansing and purifying; the painful breaking out of the diseases which have been hidden in the body of humanity during the past cycle that they may now be recognized and cured.

Since we have the planks of this Ark of Safety already sawed, planed and fashioned and ready for our use in the clear, scientific and inspiring explanations of life and the ultimate destiny of mankind and the planet, as set forth in the Teachings of this Order, *it is our duty to help to spread this understanding* of life to all who will listen.

Our responsibility is therefore great, almost beyond our present comprehension. Realization of this duty and responsibility and a faithful and self-sacrificing acceptance of it "in His service" will be the measure of our love for Him. Therefore, let us all make haste to spread abroad the call of the prophets. Let us use the planks of spiritual truths to build an Ark of Safety for ourselves, for our neighbours and for all mankind. Then shall the flash of lightning that shines from the East unto the West at the time of His coming be the flash of spiritual intuition that shall reveal to us the truth of His coming and how we may serve Him in helping to succour and save all who will listen.

CHAPTER IV

SPIRITUAL CO-OPERATION

"In that place I beheld a fountain of righteousness which never failed, encircled by many springs of wisdom. Of these all the thirsty drank, and were filled with wisdom, having their habitation with the righteous, the elect and the holy." *The Book of Enoch*, XLVIII, 1.

"But whosoever drinketh of the water that I shall give him shall never thirst; but the water that I shall give him shall be in him a well of water springing up into everlasting life." *St. John*, IV, 14.

At this period of manifestation, or the New Aquarian Age into which humanity is now entering, the most important question confronting all classes and all nations, in one way or another, is that of co-operation. In a vague way this is spoken of as the one thing most essential to bring peace out of discord and to harmonize the many divergent views of life and the seemingly conflicting interests of classes and nations. Yet without unselfishness and spiritual enlightenment each tends to hold tenaciously to his own idea of what co-operation means. Each is assured in his own mind that if all the rest of mankind would co-operate with his pet theory all would be well, hence the difficulty of securing practical co-operation even among those who are striving for it.

The majority of advanced thinkers admit that only true co-operation in its highest and best sense can at this time bring about a solution of the world's problems, and such international events as the acceptance of the Dawes' plan, the Locarno Treaty, the London Conference on the reduction of naval armaments, the Kellogg-Briand Treaty, etc., indicate a decided advance toward the practical working out of this ideal. Yet the great mass of mankind must also understand what true co-operation means; hence the need to spread a knowledge of its principles.

Because co-operation is a fundamental principle underlying the whole manifested universe, when its principles are widely understood and practiced, it will manifest peace, harmony, prosperity and plenty in its predestined and God-ordained manner among men, just as it does among the planets of the solar system, among the organs of the body and among the parts of the growing tree or plant. Let us realize then that the present individualistic and disorganized expression of thought and interaction among men and nations is abnormal, and is but a passing phase of adjustment preparatory to ushering in the New Era, just as storms and disagreeable conditions mark the transition from winter to spring.

This New Era will mark the next step in the increased unfoldment of the minds and hearts of all mankind; for by passing through the stress and strain of coming world conditions and learning their lessons, we may the more quickly develop the innate possibilities which, in the majority of mankind, are now like seeds deeply buried in the soil of the earthly or physical consciousness. Although with the great majority this development may require considerable time, just as a deeply buried seed must be left alone for a long time ere it can unfold according to the inner pattern of that which it is destined to become, yet this New Era will see an ever-increasing overshadowing of all devoted hearts and enlightened minds by the Divine Wisdom received through the spiritual faculties!

Divine Wisdom is always a God-given gift, not an intellectual attainment; for while knowledge is man's intellectual understanding of a fact or a truth, wisdom is the inner knowing and realization of that which the intellect conceives. Hence, it is often possessed by those who have little intellectual development. On the other hand, the intellect may be highly developed—through training, study,

etc.,—yet if the unfoldment of the *spiritual* consciousness be
lacking, the intellect alone can never receive or grasp Divine
Wisdom. For "The natural man receiveth not the things of the
spirit of God; for they are foolishness unto him: neither can he
know them, because they are spiritually discerned."[1]

During this new springtime of humanity we are told that
the time is very near when that which may be likened to an
examination as to the fitness of each and all to go into the New
Era will be upon us. All who can pass such a testing will be
given new and greater powers and have greater responsibilities
for promoting the advancement of humanity and the globe, while
all who fail will have to step aside or, to continue the simile, will
be dismissed from this day at school for a time until they have
had an opportunity for further study elsewhere (in the higher
realms) that they may come back at some future cycle when they
will be better prepared to pass the examination. But with these
latter we have little to do in this lesson; for we desire to give all
the explanation and help possible to those earnest ones who are
determined to pass their examinations and tests, and advance and
help the world here and now in its time of greatest need.

As this new spiritual consciousness springs into manifestation
the great Gardener of Souls must carefully train, prune and divest
this spiritual growth of the many opposing parasitic forces which,
like plant pests and diseases, may attack it or which may have
been acquired during its gestation. Some of these adverse forces
and conditions have been brought over by the individuals from
past lives, perhaps even while the spiritual seed was preparing
for its enfoldment, while some may have been acquired from
the Earth conditions in which the seed is germinating, just
as the seed of a plant may be contaminated by disease in the

---

[1] *I Corinthians*, II, 14.

soil or in the very manure which has been supplied to help on its growth.

But while the above conditions are karmic, both racial and personal, there is still another karmic condition not usually known or understood which accounts for a great deal of the evil in the world and for much of the definite opposition to all things good. This is the force of evil created by the so-called "fallen" angels[2] who became the terrible sorcerers and black magicians whose monstrous iniquities caused the sinking of the continent of Atlantis. Many of these evil beings are still living in and teaching and exercising their powers from the astral world, and it is the sum-total of their evil machinations which is called the force of the Antichrist which is now having such a widespread manifestation in its effort to blot out all forms of worship and religion in Russia. It is this concentrated force of evil, which draws to itself all mankind who can be influenced by it, and forms the invisible army which consciously opposes every effort for the good, the enlightenment and the uplift of mankind put forth by the army of the Christ. And it is this army of evil forces which is today fighting the terrible Battle of Armageddon in the astral world and which is beginning to be precipitated upon the physical plane.

As we have explained elsewhere,[2] the giants which were created by the unlawful and unholy relations of the fallen angels with the daughters of men—also referred to in *Genesis* vi—were giants not alone in stature, but also in intellect and in their control over the forces of Nature. Possessing superhuman powers, they were able to bring into manifestation on Earth many forces of tremendous power, which were withheld from the knowledge of that infant humanity, and use them to dominate, enslave or destroy mankind. And it is some of these same forces which are being rediscovered today—such as poison gas, the so-called

---

[2] See lesson *The Ministry of Angels*, Part 1, Curtiss.

"death ray," etc.,—and their physical aspect only too often being used to destroy instead of uplift mankind.

It is still the influence of these diabolical Atlantean sorcerers which directs the forces of evil which are forever fighting against the forces of good, and which has been responsible—working through those who have opened themselves to their influence—for much of the degradation of the human race ever since. Not only have these evil forces opposed every effort and every movement for the enlightenment and advancement of humanity, but their sorcery and black magic have created a great vortex of evil which draws into it many an unwary Soul, and whose influence spreads out over mankind as an astral cloud of temptation and evil suggestion, influencing to evil rather than good all who open the door of their minds to selfish or evil thoughts. Hence, only as we determine to shut out evil and inharmonious thoughts and fill our minds with thoughts of the Inner Radiance of the Christ-light will our minds be impervious to the astral influence of this cloud, for then there will be no room or opening for its entrance. But thank God that we are now fighting in the last days of this terrible warfare, for "Iniquity passes away like a shadow, and possesses not a fixed station"; hence the good must ultimately prevail.

All followers of the Christ should consciously enrol under His banner, not only that they may pass safely through the awful cataclysms and possible carnage which are so soon to manifest, but that they may help to neutralize and counteract the evil and prevent the suffering such disasters will bring. These changes in Earth conditions are destined to come, for they are a part of the regeneration and evolution of the planet, but they can come gradually and gently if the prayers of mankind are sent out with such power as to counteract the destructive vibrations of the evil generated in the past

The first definite work that each can do, and it is by no means an insignificant one or over-easy to perform, is at each period of meditation and devotion and every time the thought occurs during the day, invoke the aid of the higher spiritual powers and thus give them an avenue of manifestation on Earth through true and unselfish prayer[3] for the salvation of humanity and the speedy success of the predestined victory of good over evil. This can be done without regard to race, religion or creed, and will constitute true spiritual co-operation; for prayer has a mighty and magical radio-active spiritual power which holds at bay and dissipates the forces of evil. To the enemy it forms a barrier of living Light, something like a screen of fire-mist, through which they cannot penetrate, while to all who are striving to follow the Christ, it is like a benediction of blessing, comfort and protection.

Let us remember then that as members of God's enlightened host we each have a pressing duty and an inescapable responsibility to perform and a definite part to play in the salvation of mankind and the mitigation of the coming disasters.[4] For the evil created by the fallen angels and their followers all down the ages has about run its cycle and must now be conquered once for all, that the surviving humanity may enter the New Era un-handicapped by the terrible burden of its past evil Karma. Let us therefore co-operate with the Divine in its effort to manifest through us in peace, love and harmony. For only by the increased development and broadcasting of peace, love and harmony can the accumulated evil of the past and the opposition to all good in the present be overcome without cataclysms of disaster and suffering, and allow mankind to co-operate unselfishly for the best good of all.

Another most important phase of spiritual co-operation is a united, wise and determined effort to prepare ourselves and the minds of our fellowmen for the advent of the Lord

---

[3] Such as the Prayer for World Harmony in *Coming World Changes*, Curtiss, 114, and *Prayers of the O. C. M.*, Curtiss, 14.

[4] *For* details see *Coming World Changes*, Curtiss.

of Life who is so soon to manifest on Earth to give mankind the teachings for the New Age. We should let no one discourage us by statements that, because He may not appear *publicly* before 1975, He will not make Himself known to His faithful followers long ere that time. In fact, He is even now being seen and felt and heard by those who can correlate with Him or "meet Him in the air," and is giving all sincere and aspiring hearts His personal help, comfort and loving counsel.

Since we are definitely promised that "This same Jesus, which is taken up from you into heaven, shall so come in like manner,"[5] we have every reason to believe that just as He appeared thirteen times to His disciples of old after the resurrection,[6] so will He appear to His true disciples of today "in like manner." Therefore, as we go about our daily tasks many may expect to hear the comforting "All hail," such as was given to Mary as she sought Him at dawn. And if we worship Him in our hearts and hold to His "feet"—hold fast to Him in understanding—as did she, we will surely receive His assuring, "Be not afraid." Even when the doors are shut where His faithful ones are assembled in the upper chamber in His name, He will stand in their midst and each heart shall hear Him say "Peace be unto you." And many whom the Great Law will not permit to "tarry until He cometh" will be vouchsafed a vision of Him long before He manifests on Earth in the flesh.

But there is much preparation necessary ere the world is ready to receive Him. And in a far more definite sense than many can now understand, those who are ready to receive Him will be gathered together with one accord in certain places to meet their Lord. And they shall hear Him speak, each in His own tongue in which he was born. To those whose hearts are filled with love and understanding this will be no miracle, for long ere the many cataclysmic changes in

---

[5] *Acts*, I, 11.
[6] See *The Key of Destiny*, Curtiss, 140.

both humanity and the planet have been finished they will have learned to know and understand. And through true spiritual co-operation they will have prepared a place for Him on the regenerated Earth where all can worship with one heart and one mind.

Let no one who reads this lesson ask, as did the disciples, "Lord, is it I who shall be there?" But rather answer in the fullness of their hearts, "I surely will be there in spirit and in truth. For I shall no longer tarry in the market place idle all the day because no man hath hired me. I will go to work at once to prepare for His coming, knowing that be I early or late in His vineyard, if I serve in truth and sincerity according to my abilities, I shall receive the reward of seeing Him face to face, even as will those who have borne the heat and labour of the day." Yet, the longer and the harder we have worked for Him, the better do we understand His mighty love, hence need no greater reward. For each day brings its own blessing and each accomplishment its joy. Even the long weary waiting for His coming perfects our Souls in realization and love until we seem to be one with Him in spiritual co-operation, He in us and we in Him. We feel His presence and know His voice. To us there is no waiting, for He is with us always, even unto the end.

CHAPTER V

MAN AND THE ZODIAC

PART I. THE TWELVE SIGNS

"The planets are not merely spheres twinkling in space and made to shine to no purpose, but they are the domains of various Beings with whom the uninitiated are so far unacquainted, but who have, nevertheless, a mysterious, unbroken and powerful connection with men and globes. Every heavenly body is the temple of a God, that these Gods themselves are the temples of God, the Unknown. . . . There is nothing profane in the Universe." *The Secret Doctrine*, Blavatsky, I, 632.

"An immaculate white disk within a dull black background . . . . represents Kosmos in Eternity, before the reawakening of still slumbering Energy . . . . the same disk, but with a central point Space and Eternity in Pralaya, denotes the dawn of differentiation. It is the Point in the Mundane Egg, the Germ within it which will become the universe." *The Secret Doctrine*, Blavatsky, I, 31.

In addition to that which we have said elsewhere as to the relation of man to the zodiac, the stars, planets, angels and the Garden of Eden,[1] we wish to add the following further explanations. That which we call God or the great First Cause is universally represented in symbology as the Central Point or Creative Dot in the Circle of Manifestation, the germ within the Mundane Egg from which the manifested universe unfolds and the center around which it revolves. This Divine Dot may be compared to an arc-light which radiates outward to a circumference, forming a circle of light which is but a manifestation of the potencies of its central point.[2]

In the Vedic philosophy the manifestation of the divine

---

[1] Look up these terms in the index of our various books, especially *The Key of Destiny* and *The Truth About Evolution and the Bible*, Curtiss.

[2] For details see *The Key to the Universe*, Curtiss, Chapters I to V.

Creative Dot is described in terms of the human form, thus: "Heaven is his head; the Sun and Moon his eyes; the Earth his feet; Space his ears, and Air his breath." Following this same symbology man, made in the image of God, may be called the circumference or limit of a special outshining of his Spiritual Self or Divine Dot. Each human being would thus be a condensed and limited expression of one of the seven differentiated aspects of God, as manifested through the seven-fold Elohim or Cosmic Rays through which the Divine Light of the Central Point or Godhead shines forth. Hence in each individual the Spiritual Sun, shining through the Higher Self—man's individualized center or Divine Dot—becomes in its turn a primal point or a focus through which the Divine Light shines out to the circumference formed by the limits of man's bodies, his environment and his sphere of influence.

The Higher Self thus radiates throughout its circle of manifestation the divine qualities and attributes received from the Spiritual Sun to the best of its ability, according to the development and purity of man's bodies and the clarity of his reflecting power. Therefore, man's circumference or his sphere of influence contains—at least potentially—all the godlike power, beauty and holiness of his Divine or Higher Self, as well as that possibility of perfection which inheres in the Divine Dot of which he is an emanation, altho more or less distorted by his density, lack of response to the Inner Light and his imperfections as a reflector of that Light.

But with all his imperfections man is and must be to some degree a reflector of the universal God-consciousness shining through the limitations of the human personality, even though the light he radiates may be clouded by much that is crude and imperfect. Yet, standing as he does as the chosen avenue of the Divine Light, he must ultimately know as he is known and radiate even as he is the result of the radiation of the Divine Light, altho he may have to pass through much sorrow and self-created suffering, much destruction, labor and rebuilding ere he learns to profit by his mistakes. It is precisely because man thus inherently possesses the attributes of the Divine, focused in his seven sacred centers, that he is called the microcosm of the macrocosm or a Cosmos in miniature, an epitome of the universe, "A sentient microcosm, pulsating in silent harmony with the more stupendous macrocosm."

Therefore all the phenomena of the Cosmos[3] are connected with and reproduced in man. But if man determinedly refuses even to try to correlate with, unfold and manifest his innate God-powers, and chooses for his own gratification to live only in the outer consciousness of his animal self, that he may give free rein to the indulgence of his lower appetites and desires, then the centers which connect him with the seven planets of our solar system remain either undeveloped or their development remains subconscious or below the threshold of his consciousness, and he remains unaware of them and their influences. Thus, altho the brain of such a one may be highly developed, he remains little more than an intellectual animal. For his consciousness reaches no higher than the lower realms of the mental world and is used merely to make money his God, to indulge his appetites, to strut before the world for admiration and to glory in his ability to rise above his comrades, no matter how shameful and cruel the means used to attain these ends.

We all know that when a ray of white light is passed through a prism it breaks up into the seven colors of the spectrum. "As below, so above." The Divine light—which is God—ere it reaches the limit of its special creation or circumference—man—shines through the Prism of Dif-

---

[3] Astronomically speaking the Cosmos consists of the Sun, Moon and planets of this solar system. "Our whole planetary system moves in a retrograde direction through the twelve signs of the Zodiac, which like a gigantic ring encircle our Cosmos with numerous other solar systems. All these solar systems revolve around one Central Sun, which is supposed to be in the constellation Pleiades (Alcyone)."

ferentiation and is manifested as the seven Divine Rays, the Elohim or the seven Planetary Deities, which are the prismatic centers through which the white Light of Divinity passes to be differentiated into the seven aspects through which God manifests in the objective worlds. To illustrate: If we had a lighthouse surrounded by seven windows, the glass in each window being of one of the seven colors of the spectrum, the rays of the pure white light in the center would not only send out light of a different color through each window, but the colors would take different directions as they radiated out to the circumference. And as the potency of color is known, each color would have a different activity and sphere of influence, also an overlapping region where it blended with the colors on either side.

If we hold such a picture in mind we can apply it to the Cosmos—God in the center of the seven prismatic expressions (the Elohim) which stand round about His throne, and humanity at the circumference—and thus get a better comprehension of what the zodiacal and planetary forces are. For altho God is reflected in all parts of the circumference, each part receives directly but a portion of that Divine Light, colored and differentiated according to the particular place on the circumference which he occupies. Moreover, since the colors are ever circling around the Center and since mankind (the circumference) is divided into twelve "tribes" or twelve "projections of the Christ Spirit and its twelve differentiations or subsisting intelligences upon the plane of physical existence," man receives not alone the influence of his Parent Ray, but of all the other Rays as well.

The "twelve tribes" are therefore the twelve aspects of the power of God sent forth in humanity to accomplish their ultimate work of evolution in each age. "It is not by accident that man, struggling in this life, inwardly and outwardly anxious, lifts his heart up to the stars which seem unmoved, inexorably fixed, untouched by all that stirs down here. Indeed, their rest and calm come back to him. Their quiet and their fixedness make him quiet and fixed. Does not man know that just as his wheel of life revolves from cradle to grave, the planets do from coming into being until setting? . . . But above all, he, looking at the stars from below, is conscious of the fixedness in their revolution, the certainty in their whizzing, the law in their fieriness. The law which bears all these things bears him also. . . . This great thought that nothing proves to be chance, is the thought which makes man quiet when regarding the starry sky above him." [4]

The biblical allegory of Adam and Eve and the Garden of Eden is an exemplification of all that we have said above, for while this allegory has its interpretation in the body of man, as we have explained elsewhere,[5] it also has its cosmic application and is outpictured in the zodiac. Looking at the zodiacal map, such as the one opposite page 30 in our *Key of Destiny*, we find Paradise or Eden is the path of the Sun during the summer season from Aries to Libra after it has moved eastward from the winter solstice (Capricorn, the manger) to the spring equinox (Aries, the resurrection). This point in Aries is called "The Gate of Paradise" and is formed by the horns of the Ram. In the early spring the ram goes before the flock and with his powerful curved horns tears up the thick underbrush of the past season and "opens the gate" or makes a path so that the sheep and lambs can find and feed upon the tender grass underneath. Hence Aries is sometimes called "The outstretched arms of the Christ" (♈), a symbol of the Good Shepherd, who points out the path and leads His flock to the green pastures. In this Eden we next find Taurus the bull, bearing upon his head the solar symbol (♉), who toils for us that we may plough the ground and plant the seed or "work in the vineyard of the Lord."

---

[4] *Astrology, Its Technics and Ethics*. C. Aq. Libra, 30.
[5] *The Truth About Evolution and the Bible*, Curtiss, Chapters VIII, IX. Also see the index in our other books.

In the dual sign Gemini, "the Portal of the Temple," we find that dual Soul, Adam and Eve. In Cancer we partake of the nourishing milk in the breasts of Mother Nature (the sign Cancer rules the breasts) on which the dual Adam and Eve must feed, at first. But as soon as we begin to partake of the fruits of the Garden we are confronted with die serpent, for we cannot be "Born again" of a virgin (Virgo) and reach balance in Libra (the Balances) until we have been tempted. The serpent is said to be "more subtil[6] than any beast of the field." Altho it is absurd to class the serpent among the beasts, yet in the field of the zodiac it is among the beasts of that cosmic field, for it is none other than the constellation Hydra (the Serpent) which extends across the heavens from Cancer to Libra. It thus covers four signs, which is one third of the zodiac, and hence is that same "dragon" referred to in *Revelation*, xii, 4, whose "tail drew the third part of the stars of heaven and did cast them to the earth." We cannot complete the tests, work out the results and acquire the wisdom of the serpent as long as we remain in Eden (or evolving from Aries to Libra), hence we must descend into the lower or physical world and put on "coats of skin" or bodies of flesh. Astronomically, therefore, the "fall" occurs when the Sun reaches the autumnal equinox in Libra (the point of Balance) and begins to descend or fall into the southern hemisphere, the "pit" or the winter half of the year.

After the experience in Cancer, whose influence tends strongly toward sensation and thus makes it the scene of our temptation, we enter the fiery sign Leo, the Lion. Here the Fire of Divine Love touches our heart and develops our love and compassion, and also arouses its lower pole, sex; for without the development of these qualities we cannot attain our spiritual birth in the next sign, Virgo, and be born of the Virgin, and reach the point of balance in Libra,

---

[6] See meaning of subtil in *The Key to the Universe*, Curtiss, 31.

where we can be guided henceforth by the characteristic of that sign, Intuition. For after we have received our spiritual birth it is upon our awakened Intuition that we must depend during the rest of our journey through the period of darkness while the Sun is below the equator. We thus unfold and progress through these signs, following the same events that Nature passes through during the seasons as the Sun journeys eastward through the "garden *eastward* in Eden," until we have entered into "the covenant of grace" (Libra) at the end of our summer period.

Some astrologers hold that Adam and Eve symbolize Gemini, the Twins. Hence, as they fall from Eden and sink below the western horizon, the constellation Perseus (the Angel with the Flaming Sword) appears in the East to guard the gates to Eden until we have passed through all the experiences of the lower physical world (the winter period of the Soul) and have conquered death and reached our resurrection and are ready to re-enter Eden, thus completing the cycle of manifestation or out-going, the "Cycle of Necessity," and becoming one with our Father-in-Heaven.

In common with the symbology of all spiritual truths, we must find them manifested on all planes. Hence, could we not find their expression both in the zodiac and in man, we would be justified in doubting their spiritual origin and universality. Applying this symbology to man[7] we find that, in the path of the Spiritual Sun as it finds expression through us, Eden is the perfect spiritual body which we inhabit while existing in the higher realms, but out of which man cast himself when he disobeyed the command not to eat of the fruit of the Tree in the midst of the Garden,[8] and followed after the desires of the flesh instead of those of the Higher Self. In this personal application of the allegory

---

[7] Look up "Eden" in our *The Voice of Isis, The Key of Destiny, The Message of Aquaria* and *The Truth About Evolution and the Bible*, Curtiss.

[8] See *The Voice of Isis*, Curtiss, 244.

the Angels who guard the gates of Eden are the Lords of Karma, whose flaming swords "which turn every way" will keep mankind from entering into the higher spiritualized body—where he shall eat of the Tree of Life and live for ever more—until through great toil and labor and by the "sweat of his brow" he has purified himself and lifted the curse which his disobedience brought upon himself and all the lower kingdoms.

The Lord God who walked in the Garden was not God the Father, but the embodiment of the Law of Good. This is made plain by the fact that when Adam and Eve ceased to live in harmony with that Law that mighty Angel could no longer see them, and could commune with them only when they answered the vibrations of His call. Up to the time of their fall into matter they were spiritual and semi-ethereal beings, who had "walked and talked" or lived in perfect harmony with the higher aspect of the Law, but by their disobedience in eating of the forbidden fruit they "hid themselves," i.e., their vibrations were so lowered that the Angel could not see them.[9] Hence the Angel was obliged to call "Where art thou?" to which Adam answered, "I was afraid, because I was naked." Only then did the Lord (Law) make for them "coats of skin"; in other words they became completely clothed or incarnated in bodies of flesh on the physical plane, just as at this point the Earth became clothed with thorns and thistles (antagonistic and opposing forms of life) because of man's misuse of his creative powers. And as a result of his disobedience, in sorrow has man eaten of the fruits of the Earth ever since.

Ever since the disobedience of the early Races, who listened to the beguiling of the serpent-force which led them into the black magic which resulted in the sinking of Atlantis, man has forgotten that the serpent was in reality Saturn, the Tester, one of the sons of God, who had to de-

---

[9] See *The Ministry of Angels*, Curtiss, 4.

termine how man would use his newly acquired creative powers
before he could be allowed to go on. "The so-called temptation
was but a test as to man's ability either to use or abuse this divine
gift. . . . The power was given him not as a temptation, but as a
step in evolution through which he must pass in perfect purity—
Man has chosen to become 'as gods,' knowing the evil through
the misuse of this power, but ere the cycle closes, he must become
'as gods' to know the good."[10]

---

[10] See *The Voice of Isis*, Curtiss, 246-7

CHAPTER VI

MAN AND THE ZODIAC

PART II. THE CONSTELLATIONS

"Humanity and the stars are bound together indissolubly, because of the *Intelligences* that rule them." *The Secret Doctrine*, Blavatsky, II, 368.

"Just as we imagine the coming into being of the material centers of power of the planets, by contraction of matter around a center, so we may imagine the human body as having arisen by the condensing of the more ethereal vehicles of the Ego." *Astrology*, C. Aq. Libra, 225.

"There is one glory of the sun, and another glory of the moon, and another glory of the stars; for one star different from another star in glory." *I Corinthians*, XV, 41.

It is well in this chapter to answer the criticism of certain astronomers that students of astrology frequently seem to confuse the zodiacal *signs* with the *constellations* having the same name, and use them as synonymous terms, while as a matter of fact the constellations are neither equal in size, as are the signs, nor do they coincide exactly with the 30° of each sign. On this account the Sun could not remain in each constellation the same length of time in passing through them as it does in each *sign*. Were the ancient Chaldean (later called Babylonian) understanding of astrology more widely known today there would be less confusion in the use of such terms. But, like all scientific subjects translated into foreign languages, unless the translator is also a student of the subject and thoroughly familiar with its technicalities and their mode of expression, many inaccuracies, misconceptions and vague expressions are bound to occur and thus mislead those who study such translations.

The Chaldeans, when speaking of the influence of the signs, referred to the mystic potencies of the constellations contained in the signs, rather than to the physical or astronomical forces of the particular stars composing their constellations. That these characteristic influences were well known to the ancients is evidenced by the seemingly casual inquiry of Job: "Canst thou bind the sweet influence of the Pleiades, or loose the bands of Orion?" This teaching the Hebrews evidently got from the Chaldeans, for their reputed founder, Abraham, is represented as coming from Ur of the Chaldees. Therefore, since the constellations vary widely in size and in the number and brilliancy of the stars composing them, the twelve *groups* of stars comprising the zodiac cannot be divided into twelve *equal* parts covering 30° each as are the signs, although the constellations do, with some overlapping, fall fairly within the limits of the signs.

Furthermore, in Chaldean astrology—as well as in the more ancient Wisdom Religion—it was an axiom that the macrocosm, or the universe, and the microcosm, man, were epitomes each of the other, one not being a copy of the other, but both being the result of the outshining of the Divine Dot in the center of their respective circles of manifestation. Hence to know man the ancients studied the constellations and their influences, and vice versa, to know the constellations they studied man. For the various organs or viscera of man are but the counterpart in him of the constellations ruling the zodiacal signs, and the influence of the organs in man's body is similar to the influence of the corresponding constellations (organs or viscera) in the body of the Heavenly Man of the zodiac, and vice versa.

Just as the stars of heaven are grouped in certain forms called constellations, grouped together because each group is the radient or distributor of a characteristic force and performs a definite function in the universe quite different from the stars in other groups—the individual stars corresponding to the cells of the organ or group, so in the body of man we find certain cells, specialized in form and function, grouped into tissues and organs which express a characteristic force and function. Each such group, organ or constellation of cells is necessary to the health, life and perfect functioning of the body as a whole. Each organ is separate and distinct, yet they all correlate with and reinforce each other in perfect harmony, just as the constellations influence, sustain and help to hold in mundane manifestation the body of the Heavenly Man, the Cosmos.

Scientists tell us that we must regard the body "as a collective organism consisting of a huge colony of micro-organisms becoming capable of a common life by common and mutual arrangement and differentiation of function, and by toleration and utilization of each other's peculiar products." In this co-operating colony of organs we find the heart as the central organ. And although the liver, lungs, brain, stomach, etc., are much larger in size and contain a vastly greater number of cells, nevertheless the influence of the heart on the organism is far more important, for without its force and function none of the other organs could live and carry on their functions, while many of the other organs may be removed and the body still live on after a fashion. Similarly, although the adrenal glands are very tiny organs resting upon the upper end of the kidneys, without the hormones which they elaborate and contribute to the blood stream the tonicity of the arteries, and therefore the circulation of the blood, could not be maintained. This shows that the importance of the organs does not depend upon their size. In fact, we see that this is a law of Nature, for nothing is really great or of vital importance except as measured by the quality of the function it contributes to the welfare and evolution of the whole.

This is as true of the stars—in which the tiny group of the Pleiades contains the heart center (Alcyone) around which the whole Cosmos revolves—and of society, in which we see the great masses of the ignorant and unevolved led and guided—and we are sorry to say often wrongfully exploited—by the enlightened few. Yet the few who lead in the various fields of the world's advance—science, industry, art, religion, etc.,—accomplish more for the advancement of the whole by their activities or functions in the body politic than do the combined activities of the great masses who are thus led. Nevertheless, all classes are needed, just as are all the organs of the body and all the constellations of heaven, each to perform its own function in its own place and manner, yet all co-operating with each other, the few to plan, lead and direct, the mass to execute or manifest the plans for the good of all.

True democracy and co-operation must therefore follow the pattern written by the hand of God both in the stars and in the body of men. And only when the leaders of mankind awaken from their selfish aims to this fact and are willing to copy that Divine Plan, can the nations truly cooperate and function together harmoniously and fulfil the angelic prophecy, "On earth peace, good will toward men." When we speak of organs in the body of society we mean types of thought or ideals or groups of persons who hold similar ideals, each individual finding his own work and most perfect expression within the organ or group to which his thoughts and ideals affinitize him.

The physical Sun is the heart of our solar system and like the heart of man it sends out a stream of the Divine One Life—which it receives from the Spiritual Sun—to all the members of our solar system. As it makes its yearly journey through the circle of the zodiac this stream of Divine Life-force—the Cosmic Christ-force—both focuses its force in the signs and constellations and also gathers up their specialized influences and cleanses them, just as the blood in man, as it passes through each organ, both nourishes it and gathers up its products, eliminating or transmuting the destructive elements and utilizing the constructive forces and radiating the latter to the circumference of the body and of the aura. The zodiac may therefore be likened to a gigantic switchboard upon which the twelve differentiated aspects of the Christ-force—the One life—are focused and through which these specialized aspects are radiated to the Cosmos and to man. For man, being the microcosm, has within him focal points through which the forces of the signs and constellations contact and influence him.

The zodiac is divided into twelve signs because twelve is the number of the Manifested Universe.[1] Since a circle contains 360°, as the Divine Dot of God Consciousness (focused *physically* in the Sun) unfolds into a circle of Divine Light, it must be expressed in twelve divisions, for the Divine Trinity—God the Father, the Mother and the Son—must manifest its three-fold power in the material universe in each one of the four elements, earth, air, fire and water ($3 \times 4 = 12$), through which the Godhead must find material expression, thus showing that the Divine cannot manifest in matter completely except in a twelve-fold manner.

Therefore, when man has completely developed and expressed the Trinity (body, mind and Spirit) within his circle of manifestation—the microcosmic zodiac of his personality— or has balanced all the microcosmic forces which he receives from the zodiac and which he is destined some day to correlate and radiate in perfect equilibrium, he will have developed within him the twelve avenues through which the God within him will find complete manifestation (Mastery). But at present, since each individual expresses but a part of the forces he receives, "and that imperfectly—although he receives the forces from all the twelve signs—his aura is not a perfect sphere, and we speak of him as a Leo, a Taurus or an Aquarian, etc., according to the predominant force he expresses (usually the force of the sign in which he is born), as revealed by his horoscope.

But ultimately each one must balance all the forces in him-

---

[1] See *The Key of Destiny*, Curtiss, Chapter V.

self during his many incarnations on Earth. To do this he must be born under the influence of each of the twelve signs until he learns their lessons and correlates with and balances their forces. This will require at least twelve incarnations in each sign, but when he has completed this cycle of 12 × 12 he becomes one of the mystical 144,000 who were the first— because they have consciously striven and made definite efforts to advance faster than the slow stream of evolution of the masses—to be sealed with the seal of Christhood and become ready to re-enter Eden or the perfect spiritualized body out of which they were cast because of their mistakes when they descended into the cycle of material incarnation. But the great mass of mankind, who make no conscious effort to advance, may require several hundred incarnations in each sign, since most of us do not learn our lessons the first time we go over them, but go over and over them many times before they are mastered.

There can be no effect of spiritual force manifested in matter without, firstly, a radiant focal point or spiritual center of force— which being spiritual is invisible—and secondly, a visible circumference of matter as the limit of the circle of its radiation. This circumference will naturally divide into twelve regions, corresponding to the twelve signs, because the twelve streams of force from the spiritual center must each find focal points and register in a corresponding and suitable environment. The New Jerusalem or Sacred City is therefore represented as having twelve gates, at each of which a sentinel stands to guard the portal so that no thing unworthy or inimical to the safety, harmony and peace of the city may enter.

There are also twelve vital salts in the body which, carried to the tissues and organs by the blood, are necessary to the health and functioning of the body, just as the cosmic currents of force or "blood of the Cosmos" carry the twelve influences of the zodiac through the body of the Heavenly Man. This cosmic stream of Divine Life-force is called the blood of the Cosmic Christ, which both nourishes and cleanses, just as does its counterpart in man, the physical blood. It is to this spiritual "blood" or Christ-force[2] to which so many references are made in the New Testament, especially as to its power to cleanse from sin; for only as we imbibe or are literally bathed in the stream of this radiant Cosmic Christ-blood can we be cleansed from our sins or impurities of mind and body. We therefore seek the truth of the mystical injunction, "Except ye eat my flesh and drink my blood there is no (spiritual) life in you," although it is a most revolting and cannibalistic idea if taken literally.

We are also told to "Feed on Him in thy heart with faith and thanksgiving," *i.e.*, through a definite effort understand what the "blood of the Christ" is, and so let the understanding of its mystical Divine Presence within us give us the life that is one with all manifestations of life in ourselves and in the Cosmos. Thus will this understanding feed and nourish our Inner Self even as the blood of the body feeds and sustains the physical body and its functions.

As we cannot accomplish all this at once, nor perhaps in one incarnation—although in some incarnation we must complete it—as we feed or meditate upon the idea and seek to understand and assimilate it we find the mind of our divine Higher Self radiating through and permeating more and more our lower human mind and consciousness. And since it is in our Higher Mind that the results of all experiences in all lives are stored up, as we correlate with the Higher Mind we are enabled to go back in consciousness through past lives and gather the stored up lessons of the experiences of the past, much as the Sun recedes backward through the constellations (through precession) and gathers up their forces. Thus do the great Lords of Karma bring about the adjustment of all conditions, both in the Cosmos and in man; for they make man face conditions until he learns just wherein he has failed and how to start out on a new cycle

---

[2] Review the lesson on *The Eucharist*, Curtiss.

in a New Age of cosmic unfoldment with new ideas and increased powers. This also accounts for the apparently sudden changes in the mind of mankind at certain cyclic periods. Just so in the individual. As he comes into closer and closer union with his divine Higher Self he is more and more washed in the blood of the Christ and enabled to take up the conditions and Karma of the past with greater comprehension and greater power and thus work with the great Law of Karma to straighten out and adjust the legacy of the past in the life of the present. But since it is only through the consciousness of the Higher Self that the experiences of the past can be understood and utilized, let no one attempt to penetrate, through the use of mere psychic powers, the veil that is mercifully drawn over the past, for the knowledge so gained is usually misunderstood and misleading and often is disastrous. It is far better simply to rely upon the Divine Law to bring to us that which is necessary day by day, knowing that when the time is ripe and it is best for us to know, all things now hidden will be revealed.

CHAPTER VII

THE LORD FROM HEAVEN

"The first man is of the earth, earthy; the second man is the Lord from heaven. . . . And as we have borne the image of the earthy, we shall also bear the image of the heavenly."*I Corinthians*, XV, 47-49.

"The Progenitors of Man, called in India 'Fathers, Pitaras,' or (lunar) 'Pitris.' are the 'Creator' of our bodies and lower principles. . . . The Endowers of man with his conscious, immortal Ego, are the 'Solar Angels.' . . . The esoteric name of these 'Solar Angels' is, literally, the 'Lords.'" *The Secret Doctrine*, Blavatsky, II, 92.

Change is essential to all growth and progress, even the changes of disintegration—whether of old forms, customs, habits or thoughts—that new and better types may manifest. The sweet and helpless babe, passing through great changes in outward form and appearance, becomes the stern and relentless man of affairs. The tiny sprout becomes the sapling and the giant tree, often—as with the eucalyptus tree—changing the shape and colour of its leaves and its manner of growth at different ages.

But when we are asked to apply this same Law of Change to mankind and to the Earth, many in amazement shrink back with fear at the rumors of unrest and the seeming disastrous changes, in thought and belief as well as in conditions, which are revealed as necessary and inevitable in the growth and progress of humanity and the globe.[1] But if we once understand that all change and progress take place according to the divine, cyclic Law of Manifestation[2] we need not fear the outcome, either for ourselves or for humanity

---
[1] See *Coming World Changes*, Curtiss.
[2] See *The Voice of Isis*, Curtiss, 192.

as a whole. What we should do is to open wide—through aspiration, prayer and meditation—that inner door of our consciousness which unites the human and the Divine, that we may understand the Divine Plan and teach humanity to work in harmony with it.

In the quotation at the head of this chapter St. Paul epitomizes the distinction and the relation between the physical-intellectual human personality—the man of earth—and that immortal Spiritual Self which seeks expression on Earth through the personality. "The first man is of the earth, earthy; the second man is the Lord from Heaven." And it is the pressure of this Inner Man, the Lord from Heaven, for ever greater recognition and expression in this new Aquarian Age, that is the cause back of the great unrest and the great seeking for new and higher manifestations of Truth in all avenues of expression in the world today.

Quite naturally some seekers go to the extreme, some cults holding that since there can be no imperfection in God and since man is a son of God, man as he manifests today is necessarily perfect and divine, and that his obvious defects and limitations are only errors of thought. But St. Paul reveals no such limited knowledge of the Law and makes no such mistake in philosophy, for he clearly distinguishes between the imperfect man of flesh and the perfect Man of Spirit, and reveals to us the method of their correlation. To understand this relation we must remember that during the early Races man was far from being as perfectly developed and intellectual as he is today, and that he is still unfinished and evolving. For the body was created by a lesser hierarchy—the Lunar Angels—of Creative Beings, and many experiments and mistakes were made and discarded in their efforts to build up a material organism which would ultimately embody the Divine Ideal and become a fit instrument through which the Spiritual Self could find expression in this world of matter. For to express in any world the Spirit must have an instrument composed of the substance of that world

which it must learn to use and control.[3] And it was only when this
primitive animal organism—symbolized by the Adam who was
created out of the dust of the ground—had reached the human
stage, that the higher Creative Hierarchy—the Solar Angels—
were able to endow him "with his conscious, immortal Ego," so
that he only then became "a living Soul," *i.e.*, a human body plus
the incarnation of an immortal, spiritual, individualized Ray of
the Divine, called both by St. Paul and occult philosophy "the
Lord from Heaven."

Is it any wonder then that the Spiritual Man has not been able to
manifest more of his divine perfection through a bodily organism
which is still so imperfect and unevolved and which responds so
sluggishly to the guidance of that inner Spiritual Self? Is it any
wonder that thought alone cannot bring this imperfect organism
to instant perfection? Yet, this human body is the kingdom which
the Lord from Heaven must learn to rule and perfect until the
"celestial body," of which St. Paul and occult philosophy speak,
can be manifested through the physical. The word "Lord" is used
by both the authorities quoted to signify one who has been given
a kingdom and the power and authority to rule it, and for which
he is responsible; for the Lord from Heaven was sent from God to
this Earth to help on and perfect its evolution and rule it through
perfected Man.

As the mind of primitive man developed and expanded, his
body became more nearly perfected, refined and sensitive; yet it
also reacted more strongly to his states of mind, his emotions and
the thought-forces which he created as his intellect developed.
And as many of those forces and creations were inharmonious and
destructive, his body has reacted in sickness and disease. From
the days of the most primitive "cave man," the development of
man's mind has enabled him to help on the evolution of himself,
the Earth and all its kingdoms. He learned how to use fire, how to

---

[3] See *The Voice of Isis*, Curtiss, Chapters XII and XVII. See also *The Truth About
Evolution and the Bible*, Curtiss.

cultivate the soil and improve the crops, how to breed higher types of animals, how to harness the streams, tame the lightning and later create higher types of thought (altruism, literature and greater expressions of beauty, art, music, etc.), all contributing to a greater manifestation of the Ideal, altho all his creations still bear the imprint of his limitations and mistakes.

All these changes have followed in great cyclic waves of civilization, alternately manifesting in a crest of achievement and advance toward the Ideal, and then as a trough of reaction during the so-called Dark Ages. But today the great changes which all mankind more or less vaguely feel impending; without clearly understanding, will not be simply the result of the next upward surge of the waves of evolution and civilization, but will be the result of a mighty tidal wave due to a very particular cycle; for it will be the gathering up of the lesser waves of many separate cycles, all of which now culminate together to usher in the new Great Cycle of the Aquarian Age. And altho we are now passing through the stormy season on the sea of life which ushers in a new springtime for humanity and are now deep in the trough of the sea, when the coming mighty tidal wave breaks, many, many old things will be swept away—physically, mentally, politically, industrially, socially, etc.,—and all things be made new: new not so much outwardly as new in man's understanding of and attitude toward them, because that which has long been misunderstood or hidden from his consciousness shall be revealed. And this revelation will be possible because of man's increasing response to the inspiration and guidance of the Lord from Heaven within.

The fundamental reason for this inner quickening and changing of the thought of mankind is that the culminating together at this time of many cycles permits the manifestation and reappearance of the great Cosmic Lord from Heaven, the Solar Logos, the Divine Ruler of Mankind, the mighty Avatar or Son of God, with His holy angels, whose advent is expected so soon, under various names and conditions, by nearly all the races of mankind. His near approach quickens and gives greater power to the individualized Ray of the Divine in each Soul, the mighty I Am Presence or the personal Lord from Heaven, and stimulates it to seek greater manifestation in the individual through whatever avenues of expression it has been able to develop in the human personality.

But the potency of the spiritual force of the Cosmic Lord from Heaven also stimulates all the unconquered opposition of the man of flesh to the reign of his personal Lord from Heaven. Hence we have the strange paradox that while we see around us a greater desire for brotherhood and co-operation between nations, a greater revival in religious and spiritual matters and psychic investigation of the unseen, a greater expression of altruism and sympathy for the unfortunate, a greater outpouring of philanthropy, charity and help from fortunate persons and nations to those in distress, than the world has ever seen before, amidst all this we also see a greater materialism, a greater lawlessness and selfishness, crime waves, racketeering and general loss of respect for all law, authority and restraint, and a greater individual and national ambition and pride of separateness (nationalism) than the world has ever known heretofore.

But just as the solid and seemingly impervious and unalterable barriers of ice and snow of winter are melted and swept away as the Sun of springtime rises higher and higher, so will the rising of the Spiritual Sun, the Cosmic Lord from Heaven, melt the barriers of opposition, separation, inharmony and strife among the classes and nations and usher in a new spiritual springtime of peace, harmony and cooperation among the various classes, nations and races of mankind. For those who refuse to respond to this new outpouring of the Sun of Righteousness—whether individuals or nations—will be swept away in the coming cataclysms,[4]

---

[4] For details see *Coming World Changes*, Curtiss.

together with the great forces of evil created by man which have accumulated as the debris of humanity's past winter period.

This is not a picture of disaster and hopelessness, any more than the freshets of any springtime necessarily spell disaster and hopelessness; for St. Paul tells us plainly that the Lord from Heaven shall triumph and "As we have borne the image of the earthy, we shall also bear the image of the heavenly." How thoroughly we have borne the image of the man of earth! How it has dominated and been allowed to rule us, permitting only a vibration now and then to reach us from the Lord from Heaven! And because of this, how we have been taught to despise the man of earth and have struggled to kill him out! But we now see that, as an instrument and necessary vesture of the Soul, the man of flesh must be purified and trained to respond obediently to the Lord from Heaven, and ultimately be redeemed and fully spiritualized by Him; for "flesh and blood cannot inherit the kingdom of God; neither can corruption inherit incorruption."

We therefore should not make the mistake of denying our obvious faults, mistakes, incompleteness and limitations, nor need we affirm that we are now perfect or able to manifest perfection; for we know that our bodies and minds will not be fully evolved before the end of the present Fifth Great Race— we are now just entering its sixth sub-race—and our spiritual development cannot be fully perfected before the close of the Sixth Great Race millions of years hence.[5] Even though we do not know exactly what we shall be in those far distant days, we can say with the Psalmist, "I shall be satisfied when I awake, with thy likeness," *i.e.*, with the likeness of our individual Lord from Heaven. Hence we will not all be alike, but each will be the perfect expression of the individual Soul which God intended us to be.

---

[5] For details see *The Voice of Isis*, Curtiss, 230–9

But we should realize that we are constantly evolving toward that perfection more rapidly now than ever before, and *our pressing, personal duty now* is to prepare ourselves for greater service in this coming New Age. Our steadfast aim should therefore be to open the door of spiritual understanding—the Door of the Silence—and realize the perfection and power which the Lord from Heaven— our own Higher Self—is trying to manifest through us now, that through this realization the radiations of the spiritual life-force and the Christ-consciousness of that Spiritual Self may more fully penetrate into and permeate every particle of our human personality and thus more rapidly drive out all opposition, inharmony and imperfection and embody those Divine Radiations within our very flesh. As we thus express more and more of the inner Spiritual Man we will grow more and more into the image of the heavenly man and thus make possible the manifestation through us of the Lord from Heaven.

When this has been accomplished we will no longer have to lament with St. Paul: "When I would do good, evil is present with me"; for the Lord from Heaven will have given us the victory over the man of earth, and we shall be able to say: "I delight in the Law of God after the inward man."[6]

Therefore, when we hear of wars and rumors of wars and have to face change, disturbance, upheavals and cataclysms, either in our own conditions and lives or in those of the world at large, our hearts need not be troubled nor our faith in the Divine Overshadowing be weakened, for we know that all these things are but passing phases of the great cleansing and preparation so necessary for the coming of our Lord from Heaven. Those who are of the earth, earthy, or who cling to the things of Earth must perish with the Earth, but they who have separated that which is earthy within themselves and have placed it under the dominion of

---

[6] *Romans*, VII, 21-2.

the Lord from Heaven will live thereafter with their Lord.

No tribulation can affect us if we trust and believe and try to correlate with our Lord from Heaven within and endeavour to manifest Him without. Let us kneel, therefore, in glad and humble adoration before his Shining Presence and be baptized with the spiritual waters of His divine Life and Love and Beauty, and realize that all is well.

It will be a great help to this realization if we repeat the *Prayer to the Divine Indweller* as given by us elsewhere.[7]

"Come, O Lord of Life and Love and Beauty!
Thou who art myself and yet art God!
And dwell in this body of flesh,
Radiating all the beauty of holiness and perfection,
That the flesh may outpicture all that Thou art within!
Even so, come, O Lord. Amen."

---

[7] *The Message of Aquaria*, Curtiss, 477. *Prayers of the O. C. M.*, Curtiss, 6

CHAPTER VIII

THE SOUL-LANGUAGE

"For then I will turn to the people a pure language, that they may all call upon the name of the Lord, to serve Him with one consent." *Zephaniah*, III, 9.

"My lips shall utter praise, when thou hast taught me thy statutes. My tongue shall speak of thy word; for all thy commandments are righteous." *Psalms*, CXIX, 171-172.

"Oh that men would praise the Lord for His goodness, and for His wonderful works to the children of men. . . . Then they cry unto the Lord in their trouble, and He bringeth them out of their distresses. He maketh the storm a calm, so that the waves thereof are still." *Psalms*, CVII, 21, 28-29.

In the biblical story of man on this planet one of the early symbolic pictures represents all mankind as being of one speech, gathered into one place, and as saying, "Let us build us a city and tower, whose top may reach unto heaven; and let us make us a name, lest we be scattered upon the face of the whole earth."[1] This story allegorizes firstly the innate tendency of mankind to seek approbation and recognition. So ingrained is this desire that it is one of the great, almost unconscious, well-springs of human endeavor and is largely responsible for that laudable ambition whose effort to excel is one of the important factors in the progress of mankind. In fact, it might almost be ranked as the third great human hunger, following closely upon the hunger for food and sex expression. So fundamental is this tendency that it is exhibited alike by the child who cries: "Look at me! See what I can do!", the strut of the general clad in a glittering uniform and decorated with medals, and on up to the king upon his throne.

---

[1] *Genesis*, XI, 4.

This desire for personal recognition springs not from mere vanity, as it would seem at first sight, altho it often reinforces and encourages it, but from a vague realization of the Soul's essential divinity and the necessity of the human personality to reach up to and become worthy of recognition by, and ultimately become one with, the Soul, the Spiritual or Higher Self. Not understanding the source and purpose of this innate desire or urge upward man naturally uses all his physical powers and all his mental faculties to build a great tower of personality not, as it should be, that such a perfected personality shall be a more perfect instrument through which he can reach up to heaven, gain greater understanding of God and realize man's oneness with the Divine Self, but merely to gain human—instead of spiritual—recognition and make a great name for himself.

This tendency was acquired even before he put on "coats of skin"[2] and incarnated in a body of flesh; when he was still an ethereal being, long before he was born on Earth. In fact, his ability to recognize and manifest his oneness with the Divine while still incarnated in the flesh in this lowest physical world was one of the great lessons he had come to this planet to learn. Therefore, having passed through certain ethereal and spiritual stages of evolution on other planets, the Lord or the Divine Law decreed that he must learn the lesson of unity in duality, *i.e.*, both by incarnating in separated sexes and by learning to differentiate the human and the Divine in himself and give perfect service to both. He must learn to recognize, give absolute allegiance to and use the powers of the Divine Self within him, and also learn that as a man it is his duty, under the direction of his Inner Guidance, to develop all his human faculties and functions and thus perfect his personality, instead of starting with the personality and hoping to develop a Spiritual Self. In other words, he must recognize that he is essentially a spiritual being made in the Image of God,[2]

---

[2] For explanation see *The Truth About Evolution and the Bible*, Curtiss.

endeavoring to manifest through a physical body, and not a God masquerading in the image of man.

This dense physical planet is the school-ground whereon man must learn primarily to conquer and use constructively both his physical and his God-powers; his creative powers of spirit, mind and body, as well as his physical powers, within the limitations of Earth conditions. Only so can he conquer his physical limitations and win his spiritual freedom; for both must be perfected because both are but opposite sides of the shield given him for his salvation.

After the dramatic lesson of the Tower of Babel, man should have learned that he cannot climb to heaven and "be as gods, knowing good and evil," through physical and mental prowess alone. But the vast majority of mankind have not learned this lesson as yet. In fact, humanity is only beginning to find out, through sad experience, that all things and conditions can and should be used for good and as God intended but that even good things can be turned into evil if used to oppose the Divine Law or for mere self-indulgence and the aggrandizement of the personality.

Man has had to learn through repeated failures that his human body and his mental faculties are not all-powerful or even completely satisfying; that they are but "of the earth earthy," capable of both good and evil *according to their use*. It is his Inner or Spiritual Self that is the Lord from Heaven[3] one with the everlasting Father, and it is through the power of this Spiritual Self or Image of God[4] that he must learn to rule the personality and all its thoughts, desires and acts, and thus conquer this world of materiality; a new and important world wherein mighty lessons must be learned. For he must learn to find in this world all the physical helps needed for his evolution and perfect manifestation here on Earth, just as he must find the spiritual helps in the higher realms.

---

[3] See Chapter VII herein.
[4] See *The Truth About Evolution and the Bible*, Curtiss, Chapter XIX.

The allegory of the Tower of Babel[5] tells us that the Lord came down and confounded the speech of those who were building the tower. The various races of men were never intended to speak the same physical language, for they were evolved, not in one spot or from one primordial pair,[6] but as independent races scattered over the Earth under varied conditions. Language is developed as a method of expressing thoughts, desires and instincts under the conditions of a certain locality and of a certain race-type. Physical man looks outward at physical problems and must express his reaction to the problems of his environment. Therefore, it is inevitable that different Races see things from different angles, hence express them differently. This is a wise provision; for the mortal man is limited, and varied aspects give a more perfect picture of the whole. But the inner Spiritual Man is not limited. The same Spiritual Essence animates all humanity. Hence we must recognize the great truth that while outwardly humanity expresses the seven diverse race-types[6] of thought, the God-consciousness within all has the power to unite all types of thought into one unified spiritual consciousness. This is the law of "unity in diversity," a lesson of great importance for mankind to grasp, especially at this particular era of changing planetary conditions.

We have already laid before our students an outline of the great changes that are pending in this world of ours.[7] Especially have we emphasized the power of man to minimize the destruction and suffering due to these changes, *provided he will unite to that end* in the use of his spiritual forces and in the use of the powers he can invoke from the higher worlds which surround him. But to do so he must listen within to the one Soul-language of the Inner Self which speaks silently yet distinctly in the hearts of all who

---

[5] *Genesis*, XI.
[6] See *The Voice of Isis*, Curtiss, Chapter XVII.
[7] See *Coming World Changes*, Curtiss.

will listen. But if man persists in identifying himself exclusively with the outer physical personality and its diverse and separative languages he will find his way of looking at things so confounded that, like the builders of the Tower of Babel, he will find that the cataclysmic changes will be the necessary instruments of the Great Law to scatter rather than unite all mankind, so that they will be obliged to leave off building their towers of personal conceptions of world conditions. The Lord "bringeth them out of their distress," not because our prayers have induced Him to change His mind, but because we have learned to work with His forces according to His laws; because we have learned to speak with one tongue, the Soul-language.

Broken law inevitably brings about unbalanced conditions, and a rebalancing must necessarily take place, either constructively by consciously working with the Law before the unbalanced tower topples, or destructively after the toppling over takes place. The world will continue to "reel to and fro" or have its cyclic changes in a more or less disastrous fashion until a sufficient portion of mankind has learned the great lesson of uniting in speaking the one tongue, the Soul-language. It is those who call upon the Divine Law in this language who will be "brought out of their distress." The great lesson then for humanity to learn is that while the language of physical man may be ever so diverse, the language of the Spiritual Man—the Soul-language—is one and must ultimately become the language of all in guiding their relations one with the other.

Let us then begin to learn this lesson at once. During the coming days let us concentrate upon realizing (*i.e.*, making real) that we are both body and Soul, and that each of them can speak, yet each awakens quite different vibrations and causes different reactions. Think of the Soul, not as some part of us that we must "save," nor yet as a great Being who watches our every act and thought in a critical attitude and marks down each mistake in a great book to be corrected through bitter struggle and much suffering by the personality. Think of the Soul as an individualized divine Ray of God and one with Him, which has come down to Earth and voluntarily clothed Itself in various vestures until it manifests in the physical body, that it may inform, inspire, guide and help the man of flesh until he can understand this mystery of the Divine manifesting through the human. Thus will we learn what we truly are, and how to look within for the God-powers given us with which to accomplish the manifestation of our True Self in the flesh. Until this is learned mankind must ever be in turmoil.

Once we understand this mystery, whenever we are confronted with a task which to our outer consciousness seems impossible, we will call upon our spiritual consciousness, the Higher or mighty I Am Presence, for illumination and help, realizing that the Soul has the power to guide us even in the physical and seemingly little things of life. As we *practice this realisation of the presence* of the Divine within we will soon be surprised to find that by calling upon the Inner Self we can accomplish anything that the Great Law brings to us as our duty or as the next step in evolution and progress.

Many earnest seekers have been taught that they must find this help and guidance through the powers of their own mentality, but after many heart-breaking disappointments they find that while the mind has marvellous powers it is often confronted with problems it cannot solve of itself. Then it must appeal to the spiritual guidance of the I Am-consciousness and make itself but a humble instrument so that the Soul can use all the faculties of the mind and all the functions and powers of the body to manifest Its will and accomplish Its desired ends.

Since all Souls are individualized Rays of the one Spiritual Sun raying out in all directions and gathering all the experiences and forces of the planet, all Souls meet in oneness at the Center where Divinity is found. When our minds grasp this picture we can understand how God and

His Christ can be everywhere and manifest unto all beings at the same time. Just as the physical Sun gives its light and heat and all its powers to everything it shines upon, and without being diminished itself, so can the Spiritual Sun shed all its powers upon and illumine every heart, all at the same time, with that "true light which lighteth every man that cometh into the world."

True religion is but the organized expression of the tuition or Soul-language which each Soul receives from the Divine. Yet, alas, because of the tendency of the unenlightened mortals to consider the physical body supreme—since it correlates with physical conditions, can be seen, etc.,—the tuition from within (intuition) becomes materialized or disregarded entirely. Each religion expresses this intuition in different terms, for each has different conceptions of the Divine Realities, yet the outer expression is not the true religion, but its inner meaning is. All awakened Souls feel the inner tuition and recognize that it comes from some mysterious source, yet words are so inadequate that among all peoples religion has to be expressed in parable, allegory, myth and marvellous tales. And each thinks its own expression the only true interpretation of the Realities, hence condemns all others who use different expressions, ceremonies, symbols and allegories.

Thus religion has grown more and more sectarian and more and more mental, and the Soul-language has been more and more ignored. Even those who have heard the Inner Voice and would fain teach mankind in the simplicity of the Soul-language find that they must use the familiar expressions. For the Soul must speak to the mind through its familiar channels to illumine it and enable it to grasp and understand the true inner meaning or Soul-language. Therefore, there must be those who are true priests and teachers, God's messengers to man, who are capable of understanding the Soul-language and of translating it into the language of the daily life. For a deeply learned priesthood, compelled to express religion in a way foreordained by man, with a definite vocabulary and recondite expressions, has tended to create a great gulf between the affairs of everyday life and the great inner urge which each Soul is ever sending forth for Its expression. And because the inner Soul-language often disagrees with the outer orthodox interpretations set up by man, many try to silence or turn away from the Inner Voice and refuse to listen to the Soul-language.

Is it any wonder then that we find the world today facing the cyclic changes now taking place with no united common spiritual unity, no understanding of how to unite its Soul-powers to adjust itself to outer conditions? If humanity will not remove the causes of inharmony, then the Great Law must sweep away the disturbing factors ere humanity can enter upon a new and better day. To counteract inharmony and evil man must gain wisdom and brotherly love; must learn to listen to and use the Soul-language. And if he finds it not in religion because, like the builders of the Tower of Babel, he has listened to and followed the many outer voices and silenced the Voice within, then the tower of his mighty civilization must remain incomplete or perhaps fall and its builders be scattered.

The call of the Christ forever is, "Suffer the little children to come unto me, and forbid them not: for of such is the kingdom of God." By "little children" was not meant those young in years, but those young in spirit, teachable, ready to listen to and obey the Voice of the Christ within. Some Souls may be so oppressed by worldly conditions or business affairs that they have little time for study, and having been taught that only the learned can interpret religion or the Soul-language, they feel that they must accept what is given them by the authorities, even though the Inner Voice is always asking questions which their authorities cannot answer. It is all such who like little children are bidden to

"Come unto me." And they are glad to follow the Christ when the truth is given them in the Soul-language which they can understand.

The little child is the type of simple trust in the Father; trust in the knowledge that the Inner Man is made in the Image of God. And even though the manifestation of that Image be today but as a little child, yet if brought forth in the midst of the teachers and elders—the mental faculties and orthodox outer conceptions—it will confound them with its wisdom and the simplicity of the Soul-language. The little child also symbolizes the new-born, yet rapidly growing, realization that in the midst of all the confusion of the outer world there is this Image of God, and all who listen to its Soul-language "shall not perish, but have everlasting life."

Be not disturbed, therefore, though the Earth shakes; though empires crumble and civilization fails. The Lord Christ has sent forth His call that He may gather all His children who will, into the nest of His love and there shelter them under the wings of His protecting care. No cataclysm is too great if it destroys the tower of Man's pride and self-sufficiency and opens his ears to the Soul-language of the Christ and brings Him to the recognition of humanity. Already the angels' song is thrilling through the world today. "Behold! He is risen!"

> "O King of Kings, above all earthly powers!
> Help us Thy children in these our darkest hours.
> Thy radiant Light, Thy mighty Love, now showers down.
> Rich be the hearts this Love shall bless and crown.
> No longer in a manger laid
> Now in transcendent glory He
> The debt of sin hath paid.
> Down from high heaven the gladsome chorus rings.
> To waiting hearts its joyous promise brings.

Hark! Hark! Beloved, hear the heavenly songs!
To Him the blithesome joy of this New Age belongs.
Glad at His feet, behold all offerings laid:
Offerings of Love, of service, of sin's redemption paid. "
                              Harriette Augusta Curtiss.

CHAPTER IX

TRANSMIGRATION

PART I. THE DOCTRINE

"According to the Egyptians, 'At the end of 3,000 years, sometimes more and sometimes less, after endless transmigrations, all these atoms (of the mummy) are once more drawn together and are made to form the new outer clothing or the body of the same monad (the real soul) which they had already clothed two or three thousand years before. . . . Life is ever present in the atom of matter, whether organic or inorganic; . . . . when life-energy is active in the atom, that atom is organic; when dormant or latent, then the atom is inorganic.'" *Five Years of Theosophy*, Blavatsky, 531-534.

"Thou takest away their breath, they die, and return to their dust. Thou sendest forth thy spirit, they are created: and thou renewest the face of the earth." *Psalms*, CIV, 29-30.

Many of the processes of evolution in Nature are very slow in their outworking and often cover vast ages, not only in the laying down of geological strata, but also in the progressive adaptation and unfoldment of life-forces and forms to outer conditions. This slowness of evolution is due both to the density of the materials in which the life-forces must manifest and to the fineness of the forces and vibrations working upon those materials to fashion them into more advanced forms of expression.

When left to the slow progress of mass evolution alone, the process of man's evolution (unfoldment and spiritualization) is almost as slow as the laying down of the sedimentary rocks and their subsequent upheaval during vast geological ages. But we know that ultimately those seemingly unalterable rocks are uplifted out of the darkness of the ocean depths into the light of day; out of the mud and slime of the quagmire into the purifying light of the Sun; out of the dense and rigid conditions of their materialization into the region of freedom in the air. Thus what was once the bed of the ocean may now form mountain peaks which seem to touch heaven and are crowned with a mantle of eternal snow: which bear aloft many forms of vegetable life—flowers, shrubs and trees—and also many forms of bird and animal life.

Following the same Law of Eternal Change and progress, just so will the forces of spiritual evolution ultimately raise the mass of mankind up out of the dark waters of ignorance into the light of understanding; up out of the quagmires of sin and disease into the sweet fresh air of health and happiness; up out of the dense and hampering conditions of materialistic thoughts and conceptions into the bright illumination of the Spiritual Sun, and ultimately into the freedom of Divine Realization.

Through the light and warmth of the Spiritual Sun, shining within man as the I Am-consciousness, he will be able to see and realize the light of Divine Illumination and the warmth of Divine Love, and realize that he is indeed a Son of God. So will man be raised up in his spiritual unfoldment until he, too, touches the skies of heavenly consciousness and is crowned with the clear white mantle of eternal purity. Thus will he lift up with him the countless millions of cells and atoms and other lower forms of life which are a part of his outer personality.

This is the picture. This is the hope of mankind. This is the eternal promise of the Father. This is the Law. But since the mass evolution of mankind is almost as slow as the geological evolution of the planet, are we content to wait for that slow, even if inevitable, process which requires ages of incarnations and the countless buffetings of karmic conditions for the fashioning and perfecting process? Or shall we not realize our power here and now consciously to correlate with the streams of Divine Life and Love and Consciousness so freely poured out for us? By such correlation we shall grow as the flower grows, pushing up our tender sprout of divine realization above the limiting physical conditions until we put forth the blossom of I Am-consciousness and the fruit of Immortality.

This is our goal. This is our destiny. It is for us as atoms of God to transmigrate through all these lower conditions as rapidly as possible, but now willingly and unresistingly following the Light of the Spiritual Sun, and drawn by the law of spiritual affinity into the bosom of the Father to be one with Him here and now forevermore.

The origin and destiny of the Soul, and the reason for its appearance on Earth has, throughout the ages, been a theme of vital importance to humanity. But we can have no satisfying philosophy of life and the Soul unless the doctrine of reincarnation is one of its fundamental postulates. But many persons refuse to investigate the doctrine of reincarnation because they have confused it in their minds with the mistaken exoteric Hindu doctrine of the transmigration of the Soul through the bodies of lower animals. This doctrine of transmigration, arising through a misunderstanding of the law of reincarnation and through ignorance of the details of its processes, has quite naturally given to the Western world a great disgust for any doctrine even remotely suggesting that the human Soul incarnates in lower animals, and so prevents the rational study of reincarnation.[1]

As a matter of fact, transmigration is quite distinct from reincarnation, for reincarnation refers to the repeated incarnations of *the same immortal spiritual entity or Soul*, while transmigration refers only to what becomes of the atoms of the various bodies occupied by the Soul after they are thrown off from the body or after the Soul has left them entirely through the gate of death.

Transmigration into lower animals could not apply to the human Soul—the three higher principles *Atma, Buddhi,*

---

[1] For a general study of the subject see *Reincarnation*, by Walker, also *Reincarnation*, by Atkinson.

Manas[2] —as there is no animal form lower than the human which could contain a human Soul; no form which has the organs, centers and functions necessary for the incarnation and expression of a human Soul. And since the lesser can never contain the greater, no animal form less developed than or below the human in evolution could possibly contain a human Soul. So we may dismiss such a doctrine from our minds as basically and scientifically unsound. How, then, did such a misconception arise and become a doctrine of large, but ignorant, masses of people?

The confusion probably began, firstly, by a misinterpretation of a certain passage in the *Laws of Manu* (Sec. xii, 54-5) which states that "a Brahman-killer enters the body of a dog, bear, ass, camel, goat, sheep, bird," etc, and secondly, to a lack of understanding of two very simple facts. The Brahmins have applied this passage to themselves and, by a play on words, have allowed their followers to assume that the passage alluded to those who killed a member of the Brahmin caste. But the word used is not Brahmin-killer, but a Brahman-killer. The word Brahmin refers to a member of the Brahmin caste, while the word Brahman, in this connection, refers to man's seventh or spiritual principle, the immortal Monad. Therefore, "he who kills or extinguishes in himself the light of Parabrahm, *i.e.*, severs his personal Ego from the Atman (or seventh principle) .... becomes a Brahman-killer. [3]

In other words, instead of aiding the union of the personal consciousness and the lower principles, with the Higher Self or Father-in-Heaven—through prayer, spiritual aspiration and a virtuous life—it is possible to cut the lower personality off from contact with die Higher Self and thus condemn every atom of his lower principles to disintegrate and become attracted to—by the magnetic affinity created by his lower passions—and assimilated by the bodies of cor-

---

[2] See *The Key to the Universe*, Curtiss, 255.
[3] *Five Years of Theosophy*, Blavatsky, 537.

responding lower animals. But *it is not the Soul* or its emanations that are thus drawn into animal bodies, only the atoms of man's lower bodies and principles.

The first of the two simple facts referred to above is that man tends to become and look like that of which he thinks most persistently. If he is a glutton and thinks chiefly of food and how much of it he can gorge and enjoy, such thoughts imprint themselves upon him and he grows to look bestial and even like a hog, both in form and feature. If his major trait is cunning he may take on a fox-like look; if avaricious or miserly he may have the appearance of an eagle or a vulture, etc. We are all familiar with such types of humanity.

But more important still in forming the misconception as to transmigration is the second fact that on passing out of incarnation our astral bodies take on still more definitely the impress of our characteristic thought-forms. Therefore, after death, in extreme cases, the hog-like man may actually assume a still more hog-like appearance than while on Earth; the cunning man that of the fox; the avaricious that of a vulture, etc. Thus, one who was sufficiently clairvoyant to see such animal-like astral forms might easily conclude, unless properly trained, that such persons had become or would inhabit corresponding animals in their next incarnation, which of course is not possible, as we have seen above.

A third fact leading to the confusion is that the atoms of man's bodies, once they are released—either gradually during life or rapidly after death—and allowed to disintegrate by the withdrawal of the cohesive force of the animating Soul, do return to the dust from whence they came and are thus taken up and built into various forms of plant and animal life and thus do transmigrate through many different nonhuman forms.

Among the Egyptians it was taught that a mummy, in spite of all the chemicals used in its preparation, nevertheless goes on throwing off invisible atoms—altho not as rapidly as when the corpse is allowed to disintegrate normally— and that these atoms enter every form of vegetable and animal life by which they may be taken up according to their affinity. The Egyptians taught that this process went on for approximately three thousand years more or less, at the end of which period the atoms, having transmigrated through innumerable substances and forms, were once more drawn together magnetically to help make up a body for the incarnation of *the same Soul* which they clothed in the previous incarnation. A corruption of this doctrine was one of the reasons why the Egyptians mummified their dead, as they were allowed to believe that the Soul would return to animate the same body it had left at death, which of course was not possible.

This form of reincarnation was the belief of the masses, the *exoteric* doctrine for those too ignorant to understand the philosophy of the more subtle changes. But it was not the *esoteric* doctrine held by the Priests of Isis, the true Initiates, whose real doctrines were even more veiled from the ignorant masses than those of the Chaldeans. In fact, there were three doctrines or sets of teaching in vogue at that time, *i.e.*, that of the Initiates, that of the priests of the outer temple and that of the ignorant masses who were allowed to worship certain animals and birds as divine, much as the members of certain Christian sects today are allowed to worship the cross, saints' pictures, bones, relics, etc., all of which tends to arouse either disgust or pity in the minds of the more enlightened.

But today the researches of science are enabling anyone of ordinary intelligence to understand the truth back of the vulgar superstitions of the ignorant masses. We now know that no matter, force or consciousness that has ever existed can cease to exist. Things which seem to have been destroyed only change their form, their essential constituents remaining and reappearing under other forms. A log of wood when burned disappears as a form, but every atom can be traced, weighed, measured and chemically accounted for in the water vapor, carbon dioxide and other gases and volatile oils thrown off and in the ashes which result from the burning. And all these atoms can be taken up by and built into other forms of life such as grass, vegetation, trees, etc., and reappear as other logs, animal bodies, etc. "E'en wasted smoke remains not traceless."

In fact, this scientific law of the indestructibility of matter, force and consciousness has always been one of the basic laws of occult philosophy long before it was confirmed by science. Our planet itself is composed of the atoms and forces which once composed the previous chain of globes which preceded the formation of the Earth-chain, namely, the Moon-chain,[4] while our bodies now contain particles and forces which we failed to spiritualize and redeem while on the Moon-chain, as well as those used by us in former incarnations on this planet.

The Egyptian doctrine, therefore, when properly understood, agrees both with the most recent experiments in the radio-activity of matter and with occult philosophy. It also agrees with the account of creation in our own *Bible*. For if we properly understand that account[5] we will find it quite as esoteric as the Egyptian teachings and quite as thoroughly misunderstood by the ignorant mass of Christians as were the teachings of the Priests of Isis by the ignorant mass in their day.

The Fundamentalists would have us believe that, because the incarnation of the Spiritual Man in the body of flesh took place at the time God is described as breathing into the animal body the breath of life, there was no such thing as evolution as applied to man. This shows how little they understand their own *Bible*, for it specifically points out that there were five great "days" or vast ages of creation and evolution *preceding* the creation of man, during which the

---

[4] For details see *The Voice of Isis, Curtiss*, Chapter XV.
[5] See *The Truth About Evolution and the Bible*, Curtiss, 102–3.

successive lower forms were evolved—and in the exact order
claimed by science—before man appeared at all.

In *Genesis* i, 9, "God said, Let the waters . . . . be gathered
together . . . . and let the dry land appear." Then "God said, (i,
11,) Let the earth bring forth grass, the herb yielding seed, and
the fruit tree yielding fruit after his kind . . . . and God said, (i,
24,) Let the earth bring forth the living creature after his kind,
cattle and creeping thing, and the beast of the earth after his kind,"
etc. And only in the sixth day of planetary evolution are we told
that "God formed (animal) man out of the dust of the ground."
As a matter of fact, it required countless ages for the atoms of
matter to be built up into more and more complex forms and
associated with higher and higher manifestations of life, as they
passed upward through the successive kingdoms, ere they were
fit to be associated with the Spiritual Man by being incorporated
in the body in which he was to incarnate. For until they were so
prepared, by the development of their successive spirillae, He
could not utilize them in His body.

Altho animals are composed of the same chemical elements as
are the rocks and minerals they cannot live on rocks and minerals
or utilize them directly—with certain exceptions such as salt,
etc.,—until those materials have been built up into the colloid
forms of a lower kingdom, the vegetable, and thus be prepared
for their nourishment. No more could the Spiritual Man use the
atoms with the lower rates of vibration until they had passed
through countless lower forms and thus been prepared for His
assimilation and use. While the animals are also animated by the
universal One Life-force like man, they do not have the capacity
of assimilating the higher octaves of spiritual vibrations, for their
atoms are many octaves of vibration below those which animate
man, unless man deliberately lowers his vibrations to those of the
animal kingdom by his low desires, thoughts and acts.

Thus *Genesis*, by confirming both modern science and

occult philosophy, proves itself to be one of the most esoteric and occult books ever given to man. In fact, it is but a condensed story of the gathering together of the materials of the former chain of globes[6] and their bombardment by the life-atoms until the life-force evolved from those materials first the simple and then the more and more advanced forms, until finally there were evolved human forms or "coats of skin" into which it was possible for the Spiritual Man of *Genesis* i, 27, to incarnate here on Earth. When the Lord God breathed the breath of life into the nostrils of this animal man he then became "a living Soul," because *only then* had the Spiritual Man incarnated in him. It is this animal body, and not the immortal Soul, that is referred to in the words: "Dust thou art, and unto dust shalt thou return."

It is through incarnation in such evolved human bodies—and not in the lower animals—composed of the atoms and forces we had not finished spiritualizing either on the Moon-chain or on this Earth that we must reassume and finally complete that process until, through the unfolding and use of greater spiritual powers, we ultimately build up a completely spiritualized body in which we can dwell on any plane without having to die and leave the body behind as dust.

The Egyptian doctrine of the life-atoms emanating from a mummy for three thousand years, therefore, has a certain scientific basis, for we know that even certain minerals—the radium group—require nearly three thousand years of continuous emanation before they lose more than half their weight, approximately the same time given by the Egyptians as elapsing between incarnations.

According to the laws of chemical affinity certain atoms combine only with atoms with which they have more or less affinity. If a substance contains atoms held loosely within it by slight affinity and other atoms having greater affinity

---

[6] For details see *The Voice of Isis*, Curtiss, Chapter XV.

are brought near, the loosely held atoms will leave the first substance and rush to the one with the greater affinity. Often this process is so rapid and powerful as to cause disintegration of what are apparently the most solid substances, as witnessed in the action of acids upon steel or granite or the instant disintegrations of gun-powders which cause explosions. And if chemical affinity is sufficient to produce these tremendous results with the hardest substances, surely magnetic and spiritual affinity are amply sufficient to draw together the atoms which are strongly affinitized to a certain Soul. For it is the occult doctrine that as the Soul descends into incarnation it awakens the permanent atom[7] on each plane, and through this gradually draws to itself many of the atoms which belonged to it in past lives. This process is not completed at once, but goes on throughout each life as former atoms are released from other forms and made available for us.

(To be concluded)

---

[7] For details see *The Key of Destiny*, Curtiss, 17.

Chapter X

TRANSMIGRATION

"Occultism teaches that the life-atoms of our Life-Principle (prana) are never entirely lost when a man dies. That the atoms best impregnated with the Life-Principle—an independent, eternal conscious factor—are partially transmitted from father to son by heredity, and are partially drawn once more together and become the animating principle of the new body in every new incarnation. . . . As the *individual* Soul is ever the same, so are the atoms of the lower principles (the body, its astral, or life-double, etc.), drawn as they are by affinity and karmic law *always to the same individuality* in a series of various bodies." *The Secret Doctrine*, Blavatsky, II, 709.

"And the Lord God formed (evolved the body of) man out of the dust of the ground, and breathed into his nostrils the breath of (spiritual) life (the Spiritual Man); and man became a living soul. *Genesis*, II, 7.

During the latter part of the last century, in the days of gross materialism in science, the definition of the atom was "the smallest particle of matter that could exist alone; the ultimate indivisible particle of matter." But from the astounding discoveries of this century concerning radioactivity we now know that the atom is not indivisible; indeed, that the atom is not matter at all as we are accustomed to view it. The atom is now defined as "a center of force, a phase of electrical phenomena, a center of energy, active through its own internal makeup, and giving off energy, or heat, or radiation."[1] This atom or "center of force" is made up of a central positively-charged nucleus, called a *proton*, surrounded by a cluster of negatively-charged corpuscles called *electrons* and neutrons, which revolve around

---

[1] *Standard Dictionary.*

the nucleus in orbits corresponding relatively to the orbits of the planets about the Sun of our solar system, proving that the same Grand Plan of Manifestation exists from cosmos to atom.

These combinations of electrons or atomic clusters impress our senses with the various characteristics of matter according to the arrangement of the various electrons in the cluster. And just as the arrangement or aspects of the planets at the time of birth indicate the main characteristics which the incarnating Soul must manifest or encounter, so, if we could view the predominating arrangement of the electrons in the atoms of our bodies and correlate them with the planetary aspects, then would astrology be the exact science it was of old, instead of the art it is today.

Like the planets of our solar system, the atoms have their cycle of activity or *manvantaras* and their cycles of disintegration and inactivity or *pralayas*. As each planet begins its period of manifestation, the same old atoms of which it was composed during its previous *manvantaras* or cycles of objective manifestation, are once more attracted around its nucleus, first as fire-mist, then as astral substance and then as the mineral kingdom or "dust of the ground." Thus is the physical planet as we know it materialized out of its invisible laya-center. As the various forms of life appear, the atoms of the mineral kingdom are built into these forms, first transmigrating into the vegetable kingdom, then into the animal and finally are so advanced that they can be used to make up the body of man.

Just as the nucleus of each atom exercises a selective action and attracts to itself only such electrons as are affinitized to it, so does each cell of the body and each form of life attract to itself—through affinity—those atoms in its environment which will best contribute to the manifestation of that particular form. The body-cell selects the particular substances it needs from the food given it; the plant selects from the mineral kingdom—also from the air and water—

the particular atoms needed by its species; the animal selects the particular plants or animals best suited for its food, and man selects from all the kingdoms as food—through the selective action of taste and appetite—that which contains the atoms necessary for his particular stage of unfoldment. If man was careful to follow the guidance of the subconscious mind of his animal-soul as to food, and eat it properly—masticate it thoroughly in reasonable amounts—and did not insist that everyone else should follow his tastes, idiosyncrasies and theories, there would be no such thing as indigestion and few intestinal diseases.

Just as the positive, radio-active nucleus of the atom is constantly bombarding and impressing upon the electrons which make up its cluster or body the characteristics of its own emanations, just so does the radio-active nucleus of life-force or "soul" in each form of life—Vegetable, animal and human—impress its characteristics and stage of evolution upon all the atoms composing its body, thus raising those atoms to its vibratory rate and stage of evolution. The atoms, therefore, advance in evolution according to the stage of evolution of the forms of which they are a part. Also, advanced atoms transmigrating into lower forms help to promote the evolution of those forms. Thus does the Law of Compensation adjust and compensate for the sacrifice of one form of life to another.[2]

Through the life-force's gradually raising the vibratory rate of the atoms in the higher forms, it becomes possible for still higher and finer and more intelligent forms to be built up and evolve—such as the dog, horse, elephant, etc.,— capable and worthy of associating with man. Finally, atoms are evolved which are so impressed with the vibrations of intelligence of the highest forms through which they have transmigrated that they are fit to be used in building up a brain for man which is capable of responding to the vibrations of the higher mental world—even as the animals re-

---

[2] See "The Law of Sacrifice," *The Message of Aquaria*, Curtiss, 254.

spond to the lower—and ultimately to spiritual aspirations and longings for something more than the material world can supply. Only when such a form was evolved through the ages could the Spiritual Being which is the Real Self, created in the image of God,[3] descend from the higher worlds and incarnate in it. Again we see how impossible it would be for the human Soul to incarnate in any animal form *lower* than man. It is through this human body and not that of a lower animal that the Soul must continue the unfolding of its spiritual qualities and powers in the world of matter, and through it work out the unadjusted Karma generated during previous incarnations on this and other planets.

The study of reincarnation teaches us that not all Souls born here on Earth began their evolution in matter on this planet: only those who emanated from the Planetary Ruler of the Earth. It is only these latter who are properly called Earth-children.[4] These are less unfolded spiritually because they have had less experience in material conditions on this or other planets, hence are largely concerned with the lower and more material interests in life. These make up the majority of mankind. But vast numbers of Souls also came from the Moon-chain and lesser numbers came from other planets to learn the lessons of Earth.

After having learned many and deep lessons during the period of rest (*pralaya*) between planets, the Egos from the Moon-chain incarnated on this new planet, Earth, to continue the mastery of the problems and forces left unconquered on the previous planet, and also to teach and help onward those less advanced than themselves. Thus everywhere do we see continual unfoldment, evolution and advance. Even the globe itself belongs to a higher octave than the globes of the previous Moon-chain.

Naturally there are millions of atoms upon which each

---

[3] See *The Truth About Evolution and the Bible*, Curtiss, Chapter XIX.
[4] See *Coming World Changes*, Curtiss, 60–1.

Soul has placed the radio-active imprint of its stage of unfoldment. In the early days of mankind, when the animal form was untrained and incapable of responding consciously to the indwelling Soul, the animal selfishness, passions and desires predominated and impressed their vibrations upon the atoms of the body. As these atoms were thrown off they were built into the lower kingdoms and thus carried with them the vibrations of cruelty, enmity, impurity and antagonism with which the largely-animal man had impressed them. Need we be surprised, therefore, to find that, instead of all the lower forms of life co-operating with man in peace and harmony, there are many forms in each kingdom— poisonous minerals and gases, pathogenic bacteria, poisonous plants, blights and fungi, insects and animals, etc.,—which are antagonistic to man? As we have said elsewhere:

"The curse which God is represented as placing on the lower kingdoms when man was turned out of Eden was in reality a prophecy of the Karma which man must continue to reap from the lower kingdoms because of the forces he places upon them, his resulting suffering and death slowly bringing about an awakening to his true heritage, *i.e.*, his power as Priest to bless all kingdoms. And verily just as the curse has operated and still operates today, so shall the blessing, until some day man shall find himself King and Ruler over all the kingdoms of the Earth."[5] Since by man came evil, sin, sickness and death into the world, even so by man must come the redemption of the Earth from all such disintegrating and antagonistic forces. Hence, the sooner man begins to learn this mighty lesson of *personal responsibility* for the conditions of his life *and environment*, the sooner will both humanity and the lower kingdoms attain their true place in the Divine Plan.

The millions of atoms upon which the Soul has placed the imprint of its perfections and imperfections must be taken up again and again and be built into its new bodies during

---

[5] *The Key to The Universe*, Curtiss, 177.

many incarnations, each time taking them at least one step upward as it advances through experiencing the Karma and conquering the conditions encountered, on the path of spiritualization. For as man advances and radiates higher forces, he raises the vibratory rate of the atoms which he embodies. If the qualities which the Soul is unfolding at a particular time attract atoms whose transmigrations have been largely through forms in the vegetable kingdom, such atoms naturally bring a preponderant essence of that kingdom, and such a person would naturally crave a largely vegetarian diet. If one's evolution needs and attracts atoms whose transmigrations have been largely through animal forms they would bring the vibrations of that kingdom, and such an one would naturally desire and need the vibrations of animal food, milk, butter, cheese, eggs, etc., which often bring the animal vibrations almost as much as meat. But most of us are unfolding more than one important quality and have many atoms from all kingdoms, hence need, enjoy and thrive best upon a mixed diet. Hence, there are no two persons exactly alike or who continuously need exactly the same food combinations.

When there is any great change, either gradual or rapid, in the character of our unfoldment or in large numbers of our atoms, our desire for certain foods changes, often quite suddenly. In such cases the desire of the animal-soul (subconscious mind) for a change of food should be followed, *but controlled* by reason. But to force one's self to subsist on a particular diet that is not appetizing or satisfying, just because someone tells us it will advance us spiritually, is only postponing our taking in the transmigrating atoms for which we are responsible and to which we are attracted by our natural appetites and which are waiting to be redeemed and spiritualized by us; for some time later on in our evolution we will have to go back and take up those atoms, perhaps at a time when it will be very much more hampering to do so than now at their normal time for such transmutation. One thing we should keep clearly in mind. *Spirituality does not come from the stomach*! It comes from the heart. Our food should be that which satisfies our taste and appetite and which makes our bodies *positive* and full of energy and efficiency and our spirits happy. Physical food feeds the physical body, not the Soul.

If our diet leaves us pale, anaemic, negative, irritable, "cranky" toward others and lacking in energy and positive magnetism, then obviously it is not the right diet *for us*, no matter what the theories of other people.[6] But in any case we should not let our food occupy too great a part of our attention or thoughts, but keep it in its proper place as a *mere detail* of our physical supply. In no case should we allow thoughts about food or the vibrations brought to us from either vegetable or animal kingdom to dominate us, but should place upon every atom we take in the key-note or impress of our present stage of spiritual unfoldment and make all subservient to our uses and welfare.

Just as the Sun, as the positive nucleus of our solar system, attracts the planets necessary for the manifestation of its system and holds them under the radio-active bombardment of its rays, and just as the protonic nucleus of the atom attracts the electrons necessary for the manifestation of its cluster and holds them under the bombardment of its radio-activity, so does the Soul, as the positive nucleus of man, attract the atoms necessary for the manifestation of its body and hold them under the bombardment of the refining and spiritualizing influence of its spiritual radio-activity. As we have said elsewhere: "No entity can attain Mastery and final liberation until all the atoms for whose expression he is responsible have been redeemed. This includes all the atoms thrown off from all his various bodies during all his incarnations, as well as all the entities

---

[6] The whole problem of diet is covered in "Thou Shalt Not Kill." *The Voice of Isis,* Curtiss, 393.

he has created either with his physical creative force or by the creative power of thought."[7]

The fact that we draw to ourselves a vast number of atoms which we have used in past lives is one of the reasons—but only one of several—why we in this life look and act so much as we did in the last life. This resemblance is so great that in most cases if our friends could see a picture of us in our last incarnation they would instantly recognize it as our picture or at least enough like us to be readily taken for a brother or sister. This also helps us to understand why we bring over so many strong inborn traits, peculiarities, aversions and affinities, not exhibited by the other children of the same family and therefore not merely inherited from our parents, and otherwise inexplicable.

We bring over so many influences from the past that it is no wonder that many persons claim to have been persons of importance in the last life. But these claims can readily be verified or disproved by a careful comparison of the pictures, and especially of the distinguishing traits of character, of the great personage claimed with those of the claimant. While the circumstances of the present life may be entirely dissimilar, the stage of Soul development, or the lack of it, and the most prominent traits of character, together with the *capacity and powers*, of the past life will show clearly in this life, *no matter what the environment*. Abraham Lincoln was born into an environment in which all outward aids were denied him, but he demonstrated his greatness of Soul in spite of his hampering environment. Unless the innate traits do show clearly and confirm the claim made, the claimant is surely mistaken,[8] even if told it by someone in the astral.

For instance, the atoms which belonged to our brain in the past and which may again be built into our brain in this life, altho modified by the physical heredity of the family

---

[7] *Letters from the Teacher*, Curtiss, I, 76–7.
[8] See "Memories of Past Lives," *The Voice of Isis*, Curtiss, 269.

in which we now incarnate, would nevertheless enable us to exhibit mental qualities and powers similar to those in the past. A reincarnated Caesar would not exhibit the traits of a Nero, and vice versa. The reputed reincarnation of a Pharaoh (Akhenaten) in the person of a young English engineer[9] can be proved, not by spirit messages or by automatic writing produced by him while under the control of some disembodied entity, but by carefully comparing the traits, habits and capacities of the two.

The brain is but the instrument of the mind, hence can be played upon by the lower mind and made to cater to the passions and appetites of the animal-soul, or it can be made to respond to the guidance of the Higher Mind, the mind of the Spiritual Self or Soul. If we refuse to permit our brains to be occupied exclusively with the affairs of the lower mind, and refuse to build into them only the atoms cast off from our former brains, then the Higher Mind will have a chance to build in new and higher atoms in addition to those from the past; new atoms capable of responding to more spiritual vibrations. This will enable us to grasp more and more spiritual ideas, until ultimately we can consciously respond to the overshadowing Higher or Spiritual Mind, and receive the guidance and outpouring of the spiritual ideas with which that mind constantly bombards us in an effort to inspire and awaken in us some conception of the God-consciousness, and also an eagerness to strive for its realization and attainment. For the emanations from the higher mental and spiritual worlds, as well as those of the physical and astral worlds, are continuously bombarding us. But they can be assimilated and built in only to the extent that we prepare the soil by spiritualizing our physical atoms and purifying our minds until we can tune in to their octave of vibration and affinitize with them. For man, unlike the lower animals, has free-will to select that to which

---

[9] See *The Occult Review*, August, 1926.

he will respond, instead of responding automatically or reflexly to everything that contacts him.

While intensive study of higher things enables us to attract to us the most highly evolved atoms of our past which are in our environment, and build in new atoms from this and the higher worlds, nevertheless it is only the assimilation of atoms and forces from the spiritual outpouring of the Christ that is the greatest factor in our spiritual advance. To advance harmoniously, body, mind and Soul, we must continually build in the highest atoms we can draw to us from each world. Just as the physical atoms of the Earth remained in *pralaya* and dormant in the mineral kingdom until lifted up by the cohesive power of the life-force and built into the higher forms of life—from vegetable up to man—so the spiritual atoms and centers in man remain dormant until awakened and animated by the bombarding currents of the spiritual life-force of the Christ, who thus literally stands at the door of our hearts and knocks.

Man's ability first to sense his great possibilities, then desire their attainment, and then consciously work toward it, enables him to transmute the atoms he builds in from former lives and from the lower kingdoms and to dominate them—no matter what their transmigrations have been— and make them subservient to the key-note of the higher ideals which he has set for his life's attainment.

Just as the physical Sun will ultimately rejuvenate and transmute devastated areas into usefulness and beauty, so will the Spiritual Sun ultimately transmute the evil and devastating vibrations and experiences in us into usefulness and beauty. This process of continuous transmutation, if persevered in, makes it possible for man's body to become so purified and spiritualized as literally to be a temple of the Living God through which he can manifest his Real or Higher Self as the Lord from Heaven and rule himself and all the kingdoms of the Earth.

Since man has the power to select and attract finer and

more spiritualized atoms and forces from the higher worlds, and also of transmuting the less evolved atoms he builds in through Karma and otherwise, he is in very truth the Lord of the Earth, as indicated in *Genesis*, ii: 15. For not only through scientific plant and animal breeding, but also through broadcasting into the lower kingdoms of the atoms he has transmuted, and their countless transmigrations through the various forms, he can so uplift and improve the lower kingdoms as literally to remodel the Earth and the products thereof and redeem it from the curse of inharmony and disease which his previous misuse of its substance and forces placed upon it.

This is a great duty which he must accomplish ere his "cycle of necessity" in Earth conditions is completed and he is free to progress to higher worlds. But this he will accomplish only as he advances and spiritualizes himself through the radio-activity of the Cosmic Christ-force. Often after death those who have wantonly killed birds and animals for mere sport and not from necessity or for some constructive end, learn the lesson of cruelty and in the next incarnation are born with an innate revolt against all unnecessary suffering and become supporters of, if not enthusiastic workers for, the prevention of cruelty to animals. For ultimately, just as God looked upon everything that He had made and pronounced it very good, so must man be able to do likewise, ere the Earth can be redeemed from man's curse and again become the Eden of peace and harmony it was when given unto man to dress and to keep.

How true and grand in its comprehensiveness do we find the simple language of the *Bible!* The more we unfold and grow in comprehension, and the more we understand the details of the Grand Plan of the universe, as set forth in the cosmic philosophy of Christian Mysticism, the more do we admire and wonder at the simple language which includes so much in so few words! Most of us are but children in spiritual things and as well might we criticize and take exception to the A B C's and the multiplication table as to condemn the grand allegories of the *Bible* or the older religions and the philosophy of peoples who have gone more deeply into the philosophy of life. Since there are many types of mind, many forms of presentation are necessary to explain to all types the one fundamental truth that man himself is responsible for the conditions which surround him here on Earth, and that because of this responsibility, by him must all be redeemed, *i.e.*, through his correlation with and radiation of the Cosmic Christ-force.

We are so used to thinking of our spiritual life and its heavenly reward as pertaining to some far off future, that we are apt to overlook one of the most vital of truths, "As a man thinketh in his heart, so is he." This influence of thought is not confined to the Spiritual Man or even to the mind, but reacts upon the body as well. Nor are the spiritual virtues all that we incarnated to unfold and manifest. If we look from a new angle of vision at the injunction, "Seek ye first the kingdom of God, and his righteousness; and all these things shall be added unto you," we will see that instead of crying out like children for some Divine Being to save us from the results of our mistakes and sins and bring about the conditions we desire, we must realize that by our thoughts and actions and by the radio-active effect of our lives, we must perfect and spiritualize the streams of atoms as they transmigrate through our bodies. Then as they fly away and bombard all things in our environment and are built into the lower kingdoms, according to the infallible law that man must reap whatsoever he sows, they will send back to us the harmonious co-operation and the spiritual forces with which we have impregnated them. This is the problem of redemption, as we explain in the next chapter.

"By redeeming our own body, that much of the Earth is uplifted and spiritualized. And that is the only way the Earth can be redeemed; for every vibration of spiritual force to which the human monad responds, sends an answering wave of force through the whole cosmos. Thus, by man and through man, shall the Earth be redeemed."[10]

"When it is once grasped that the working out of a personal salvation is the only way really to help the world, the man who neglects it is a retarder of the public good."[11]

---

[10] *Letters from the Teacher*, I, 209–10, 44.
[11] *Ibid.*

CHAPTER XI

COSMIC CAUSES OF WORLD CONDITIONS AND THE REMEDY[1]

PART I. PLANETARY AND KARMIC FACTORS

Mr. Chairman, Members of the Orlando Chamber of Commerce, and Friends:

For the first time in our twenty-four years on the lecture platform we ask permission to read our address. This is due to the fact that we propose to make certain concrete suggestions and prophecies, some of which may be of an unusual and startling character. Under such conditions we naturally wish our carefully chosen wording to express exactly what we mean, so that we will not be misunderstood and misquoted in a sensational way, as has already been done by certain newspapers.

The fact that the present world conditions of financial depression, unemployment, crop failures, floods, famines, and political unrest affect practically all countries and peoples, shows that the causative factors lie far below the surface appearances. Some writers have attributed present conditions to "the breaking down of the foundation of things upon which civilization has been built." Even if that were true, why should those foundations crumble just at this particular time after having withstood the varying conditions

---

[1] An address br Dr. F. Homer Curtiss of Washington, D. C., President of *The Universal Religious Foundation, Inc*. and Co-founder of *The Order of Christian Mystics*, delivered before the Orlando (Fla.) Chamber of Commerce on March 29, 1932 and broadcast over station WDBO of the Columbia network.

of the past two thousand years? Others see the depression as the result of the literature given to the world by Nietzsche and his followers. But even that has little effect outside of Germany. Others hold that the sudden liberation of the lower passions of selfishness, greed, self-indulgence and lust for power and pleasure following the World War has been the causative factor. While all these things may be factors in present conditions, they are really only symptoms rather than causes, and they are relatively limited and *do not cover the facts*. Hence they are no adequate explanation for why the tribulations now being suffered by all mankind should come just at this time. Therefore, we mystics claim that the causes must be sought in a far wider field of causation, namely, cosmic causes which naturally affect all mankind in varying degrees.

Now a mystic is generally supposed to be a very impractical person who, if not exactly mentally unbalanced, is at least a dreamer and a visionary. In view of the prevalence of this misconception we are greatly pleased to see so many men of large business interests present with us today. Their presence here shows that they belong to that broadminded class of business men whose advanced thinking along other than strictly business lines is responsible for the great change in the attitude which practical men of affairs are now taking toward such intangible factors as psychology, business morals, good-will, co-operation and mutual helpfulness which are now recognized as important factors in the success of modern business enterprises.

The mystic has been considered impractical because in the past he has devoted himself largely to religious ideals and to visions in the higher realms of manifestation and to the realization of states of consciousness far above the physical. And to that extent he does seem to be impractical. But we only need to remind you of some of the great dreamers and visionaries—from Joseph in Egypt and Jesus of Nazareth, down through the ages to Joan of Arc, Martin Luther, John

Wesley, and Abraham Lincoln, to mention but a few whose so-called "impractical" visions have changed the course of history and revolutionized human society—for you to realize the role that the mystic has played in the practical affairs of the world.

This astonishing result is due to the fact that a mystic is one who is not content to accept surface appearances, but sees behind the outer phenomena of physical manifestation the unseen and mystical causes which produce them: the realities which exist in the unseen. All life is a mystery: the mystery of causation and manifestation. For *all manifestation comes from the unseen.* Science has proved that there is no life, consciousness, creative power or ability to plan, design, originate and execute in matter itself. Matter is merely the substance with which unseen forces and unseen intelligences use to build up vehicles of manifestation. Hence science has abandoned the doctrine of materialism of the nineteenth century for the doctrine of dynamism. Yet seeds germinate: forms appear from the unseen, apparently self-generated, flourish for a limited cycle, then disintegrate and disappear, leaving behind as their only trace the ash or material particles of which their forms were built up,—a mystery indeed; a mystery of causation, plan, purpose, design, manifestation, and result.

We therefore see that all forms, including the physical body of man, are but outer shells or instruments through which some unseen and mystic cause, "the thing in itself," manifests in the physical world. Everywhere we see the inner mystical causes moulding the outer manifestations. Ideals govern ideas. Ideas mould thoughts, and thoughts find expression in words and actions.

Everything in the universe finds expression in rhythmic waves of cyclic expression: periods of outgoing into manifestation followed by periods of indrawal into obscuration, as we see illustrated in the cycles of day and night and the miracle of spring and fall. But there are still greater cycles:

those of nations and races, of centuries and ages, in each of which humanity must inevitably reap the results of the causes it has created and set into operation in previous cycles, just as surely as the farmer must reap the results of the seed he has sowed, whether or not he has sown tares and thistles instead of wholesome grain. Jesus stated this law when He said: "As a man soweth so also shall he reap. . . . For not one jot or tittle shall in any wise pass from the law until all be fulfilled."

History therefore tends to repeat itself in greater or lesser cycles. Nations, peoples and races tend to pass through similar conditions, especially toward the close of their greater and lesser cycles. And just as at the close of the cycle of the year all Nature passes through the disagreeable and trying conditions which result from the storms which close the cycle of summer, so do nations and humanity as a whole have to pass through similar conditions of stress and strain at the close of their respective seasons or cycles. This is due to both planetary and to national causes. Through their cyclic revolutions the planets periodically tend to return to their former relations to each other and to the Earth and therefore tend to subject the Earth and its humanity to conditions similar to those which these relations set up in the past cycles.

Humanity as a whole is now in the throes of such a great cyclic reaping. We are now experiencing the culmination of several lesser national and racial cycles which at this particular time coincide with the still greater 2160 year cycle called an Age, namely, the closing of the old Piscean Age and the beginning of the new Aquarian Age. In addition to this, many years ago (1917)[2] we predicted that the Earth was likely to encounter a dark, invisible planet whose emanations would poison the atmosphere and upset the nervous systems of great masses of peoples, making them hyper-

---

[2] In *The Philosophy of War*, Curtiss.

irritable, suspicious, quarrelsome, and even frantic and homocidal. Now comes astronomer Boothroyd of Cornell University with a recent newspaper announcement that we are now beginning to enter a cloud of *invisible cosmic dust* which he calls a "dark nebula," which he says will become so dense that it will ultimately interfere with the amount of light which we receive from the Sun, and will mark the twentieth century as the "age of darkness." Thus, to the planetary and karmic influences already mentioned, do we have added *actual physical particles* of poisonous cosmic dust for humanity to contend with. Please understand us clearly on this point. We do not claim that this "poisonous star dust" has caused present day conditions, but it may have been a *predisposing factor* of importance.

This statement has been misquoted in front page sensational headlines by certain papers[3] in such a way as to make us say that this poisonous star dust is responsible for all the ills of present world conditions. But as you will note, that is not our statement. You have just heard us say that present world conditions are the mathematical *results of the inharmonious, evil and destructive causes man has generated* during the past long cycle of the Piscean Age, and that these must either be redeemed by mankind or be experienced by him through physical manifestations of an inharmonious or destructive character. The poisonous star dust is but *one factor* in this reaping, a physical vehicle by means of which the past creations may be precipitated upon humanity, just as the adverse planetary conditions form other factors working toward the same end.

Astronomers tell us that all these things indicate that the planets are returning to the same relative positions and subjecting humanity to the same combinations of forces and "cosmic rays" as they did in the days of Noah and later on in the days of Lot. And naturally we find human society

---

[3] *Orlando* (Fla.) *Morning Sentinel*, March 30, 1931.

in a similar state of unrest, inharmony, selfishness, lust, crime, war and bloodshed. It is therefore high time, if we really have learned anything from those former catastrophes, to pay attention to the modern mystics and prophets who are able to discern behind the outer forms of our present chaotic conditions the *mystical causes* which are producing them. For if humanity does not accept the warnings and *apply the remedy* which the prophets set forth, we must expect to reap results similar to those which followed the ignoring of the warnings of Noah and Lot. That is the law.

Astrologers tell us that the Sun is in a very adverse aspect to Saturn, Uranus and Jupiter. And as Saturn is especially afflicting Uranus, it tends to retard all progress. Such combinations have a very adverse influence both upon finance and labor, as well upon agriculture. Hence we are now experiencing planetary influences which tend to bring about "hard times," unemployment, financial depression, and panics, as well as political unrest and unusual droughts, floods, crop failures and famines. These generally adverse world influences will not cease until Saturn passes out of the thrifty but earth-bound sign Capricorn into the airy but erratic sign Aquarius on November 20, 1932, altho conditions were modified for the better by the benign rays of Jupiter, the Planet of Finance, when it passed out of Leo into Virgo on August 11th of 1931.

But according to the Pyramid Measurements, whose prophecies as to the exact days for the beginning and ending of the World War and subsequent events have proved so remarkably accurate, we need not look for the end of these "Days of Tribulation" before September 15-16, 1936. The length of first Low Passage of the Pyramid, allowing one inch to a year, gave the exact dates for the most terrible catastrophe in human history, the late World War, beginning August 4-5, 1914 and ending November 10-11, 1918. On the latter date we entered the period symbolized by the Great Antechamber of the Pyramid, the chamber between the First and Second Low Passages and symbolizing the "Truce in Chaos" between the two Tribulations.

The Second Low Passage indicates that the Second Tribulation began May 29, 1928, and will extend until September 15-16, 1936. This Second Tribulation is indicated as the "Tribulation of the Elect," during which they will adopt, adapt and lend themselves as living materials for the building up of His kingdom. According to Mr. Davidson:[4] "The First Low Passage is in limestone, and signifies a period of chaotic conditions of a physical nature. The Second Low Passage is of granite, and signifies a Tribulation of a different nature (apparently spiritual), with burdensome conditions due to chaotic factors emerging and continuing over a prolonged period. . . . The closing date of the Second Low Passage, September 15-16, 1936, is a date which is tremendously interesting to all, and involves the closing of affairs of this state of world conditions along with the problems of the actual Second Coming of Christ and the establishment of a new race of people and a new system of living. . . . In every direction we now see threatening chaos. Upon every horizon is observed fundamental reaction. Mystery seems to surround natural tendencies. Human nature is stormy. Peculiar gravities pull at situations—religion, statecraft, philosophy, manners and customs. Herculean efforts are made to veer the ship—reforms, punishment of high crime and low, prohibition, League of Nations, disarmament agreements—but in vain. . . . *Away down deeply, something fundamental and foundational is sensed—blurred and out of focus as yet, but looming, prodigious and portentous.* . . . Before the goal is reached many will look back with understanding to the sequence of now apparently unrelated events in physical phenomena, trade, commerce, finance, economics and international relations, and will then realize the truth of the Pyramid message." According to these prophecies (which are not ours)

---

[4] *Liberation*, January 1932, 319–20, 334.

September 15-16, 1936 is the date set for the phenomenal appearance of the Christ upon the Earth in the flesh to inaugurate the reign of a New Age of peace and harmony and to lay down the laws and policies for the Aquarian Age of love and brotherhood.

(To be concluded)

CHAPTER XII

COSMIC CAUSES OF WORLD CONDITIONS AND THE REMEDY

PART II. THE REMEDY

If these are cosmic and karmic conditions from which the whole world is now suffering and which are still impending, what can we do about them? As the cycle of the Piscean Age closes and the results of man's unredeemed wickedness becomes concentrated in the last few years of the cycle, it must manifest destructively, both by interfering with and deflecting the magnetic currents by which the crust of the Earth is sustained and by unusual storms, floods, droughts, plagues and pestilences. Thus we may expect widespread cataclysms expressing through all four kingdoms of Nature-forces, namely, earth, air, fire, and water. According to the Rev. Walter Wynn,[1] whose astounding pyramid prophecies have come true to date, these days will mark the last battle of Armageddon and the fulfillment of the biblical prophecy: "Immediately after the tribulation of those days shall the Sun be darkened and the moon shall not give her light," because of the terrific volcanic eruptions whose dust will so fill the air and sweep around the world that they, together with cosmic dust of the "dark nebula," will interfere with the light of the Sun, lower the temperature and markedly change the climate of the globe.

But instead of being entirely pessimistic, we teach that if mankind can generate and broadcast sufficiently powerful currents of righteousness, justice, international friendliness, brotherhood and co-operation, such constructive forces will

---

[1] *Liberation*, Jan 1932, 321.

neutralize the destructive forces and leave little to be adjusted cataclysmically. Much has been done toward this end recently by the many international conferences of premiers and statesmen, good-will airplane flights, meetings of business associations and peace societies, etc. But all this constructive force thus generated can be dissipated by one war of aggression and land-grabbing, such as is now going on in China, which leaves us about where we were before, if not a bit worse off.

But cosmic and planetary and karmic influences are not fate. For an ancient axiom tells us that "the stars incline, but do not compel." Also we are told to "rule our stars," instead of passively and helplessly giving way to their influences. That is, we must take advantage of their influences to attain our ends, just as the mariner takes advantage of favourable winds or adjusts his sails to adverse winds so that he uses their opposing power to push him on toward his predetermined port. In other words, we must learn to turn every adverse condition or force into constructive channels. And with this cosmic background in mind, let us see how it applies to present day conditions.

The remedy must be applied upon the plane of the causes, namely, in the mind and heart of man, to control his reactions to and the use he makes of the planetary and karmic conditions. But how can the mind of man affect these conditions? One of the strangest phenomena of the World War was the sudden collapse of the Central Powers. This was due, not to any serious lack of men and munitions, but to a so-called "loss of morale," both in the trenches of the Central Powers and among their people at home. Why was this? In 1916 our *Order of Christian Mystics* inaugurated a world-wide prayer service each day at noon, praying that righteousness and justice should prevail. And as we have students in seventy foreign countries, and as it is noon somewhere every minute of the twenty-four hours, the forces generated in all those countries were joined with ours and *circled the globe continuously* every minute of the day and night.

This idea of community prayer was taken up by many churches and other organizations and as a result a tremendous psychological and spiritual force was generated and set sweeping through the mental world in great currents of thought-force which naturally affected every mind at all sensitive to its radiating wave-length. It therefore operated against continuing the war and neutralized the war-thoughts spread by the smaller number of militarists and ambitious politicians and nationalists. These great international prayer currents became more powerful and potent from day to day as the *futility of the terrible carnage of war* was brought to man's realization, so that finally the war psychology was neutralized and overcome by thoughts of peace, and the sudden collapse from the so-called "loss of morale" took place. Now if psychological and spiritual forces generated *en masse* upon an international scale and *consciously directed* to a definite end could stop a World War, so can they stop a world depression.

First, let us take the stock-market collapse. While there were economic factors back of it, the precipitating feature was psychological, namely, FEAR. The bad aspect of Saturn to Uranus, the planet of sudden changes, and especially Saturn's adverse aspect to Jupiter, the planet of finance, was a predominating unbalancing influence toward unreasoning and frenzied speculation. It even upset the judgment of financiers and managers of big business. For they are largely responsible for allowing stocks to be traded in far beyond the point where they could possibly pay interest or dividends upon the price paid. In other words, the bad planetary influences against the planet of finance warped the usual good judgment of all but a few financial leaders, and their warnings were not heeded. Even the Federal Reserve Board was swept by the same force until too late to stem the tide.

But why did it not continue? Why the sudden collapse? It was due to a sudden wave of change from Uranus and a wave of fear from Saturn which the financial and stock-market leaders allowed to go on to a panic. Therefore Saturn's chilling and congealing influence upon Jupiter, the planet of finance, naturally produced "frozen assets" as a psychological result of fear. There was just as much money in the world as ever, since it had not been suddenly destroyed or buried. But those who had it and controlled it were afraid to put it into circulation. For instance, there were some *thirty-five billions* on deposit on the savings banks alone, the greatest amount in the history of the country. Between September 1st and 15th (1932), newspaper reports tell us that more than *twelve hundred millions* were paid out in cash in New York alone in interest and dividends by the great corporations. Not a paltry *two hundred million* England wished to borrow, nor the *four* hundred millions Germany wanted, but *twelve hundred* millions. The U. S. Treasury loan of eight hundred millions was over-subscribed six times and at the low rate of 1 3/4 %. Hence never was money so cheap when once the influence of fear was overcome by confidence.

Turning to the constructive side of the picture, what are some of the remedies the "impractical mystic" sees for such conditions? Firstly, our whole financial system must be so revised that a few groups of uncontrolled banks and corporations cannot tie up the assets of the Nation for selfish purposes and without regard for the good of the whole. Secondly, *all deposits* must be either *insured* or in some way *guaranteed*. The savings of a man's lifetime of industry and frugality must be made absolutely safe in some way for his use in time of need. If the banks do not voluntarily work out this problem from within, it will be worked out from without, even if it comes to the point where *the Government should take over the entire banking system* as it has the postoffices, perhaps keeping some of the present officials as managers, but at reasonable salaries instead of exorbitant ones now often paid. We have been advocating this for years and we are glad to say that steps have already been taken in this direction by the Glass bill and the one now before Congress to insure deposits.[2] We are not financiers and we do not care how details are worked out, but we can see the results if conditions are not adequately remedied.

Men of great wealth and those in control of great wealth must stop and realize that they cannot take their wealth with them after death any more than Kreuger and Eastman did. They can take only the memory of how they used the funds that were entrusted to them by the Great Law to administer for the greatest good of all. They will then realize that *they are but temporary custodians or trustees* for the Great Husbandman to Whom they must ultimately give an account. Therefore they must neither waste the funds in riotous living, nor bury them in a napkin for their own selfish uses, but put them out to *constructive use* in such a way that they will benefit the greatest number, *including the spread of spiritual and moral principles* and a real understanding of the mystery of life and why we came here to Earth and what we can take with us when we return to our true home in the higher worlds.

Even if the stock market collapse and the entire business depression was but one phase of a deliberate conspiracy among Jewish international bankers for the ultimate destruction of Christian civilization and Christian governments, as claimed by some authorities and as some Jewish periodicals boast, nevertheless such conditions only emphasize the necessity for either closer governmental supervision or entire governmental control of the financial structure of the country.

As to hoarding, long before President Hoover's campaign against it, *we had advocated the spending of cash now* for every *permanent improvement* and construction needed and

---

[2] Later this bill was passed, insuring deposits up to $2,500.00.

also for investment. For now the dollar will buy more than ever before. And as President Hoover has said, a dollar spent now will release ten dollars in credit.

Next let us look at the business depression. The stock market collapse was a factor, it is true, but that should have been limited largely to speculators who paid far more for stocks and bonds than they were worth or who sold something they did not own (short selling) and hence should suffer for it. That is a practice which should and must be stopped. And we are glad to see that it is now before congress for investigation and remedy. Therefore let your Representatives and Senators hear what you think of it as soon as possible. But in spite of the collapse of the stock market the factories and mills and mines are still here and just as efficient as ever, but each had gone ahead independently increasing production without regard to consumption or demand, and so they were forced to waste their assets in trying to create and force artificial markets and demands for their unwise over-production. But the Manufacturers Association or some similar body recently reported that over-production could not be assigned more than 25% of the causes of the depression. The others resulted from fear, frozen assets, greed, and cut-throat competition.

Nevertheless there must be some kind of organization for planned production which will *control production* in due relation to consumption. Whether this will be done by regional monopolies for each product or by control boards which will license manufacturers and assign to each the amount of production needed by their specialty, these are details which can readily be worked out when their fundamental necessity is grasped. We are glad to see that this process is already being put into effect voluntarily right here in Florida—as it has long ago been put into operation in California—with the organization of its Citrus, Grape, Celery and Potato Growers and Poultry Raisers associations.

But especially must agriculture in general be put on the

same or similar basis as manufacturers, and not be at the mercy of auctions for the sale of their products. What manufacturer could long stay in business if he shipped his goods to the big cities and took whatever they would bring at auction? Neither should agricultural products be at the mercy of such a system, but *should be paid for either at the farm or f.o.b.* at the nearest shipping point. This method is already being put into effect for certain crops which are now bought and paid for either on the trees or in the field. But before this process can be more widely extended there must be some method either of voluntary or compulsory *regulation of production to demand*. Also the price must be determined not by auction but by a fair profit to the producer.

Now what is the remedy? *Production must be geared to consumption* either by voluntary co-operation within each industry or by limited regional or national monopolies under state or governmental regulation. Big business must also learn that *business exists to serve* the needs of the people, with only a reasonable compensation for that service, and not that the people exist to be exploited up to the limits the traffic will bear. If real co-operation and co-ordination and control of supply and demand is not instituted from within, it will be from without. Since we have been advocating these ideas we are glad to see the Swope plan and others of a similar nature now being seriously considered.

As to unemployment, again we must realize that according to the great underlying law of brotherhood and co-operation the *state and society exist to serve man* and not man for the state or society. In other words, some plan must be devised whereby every person shall be guaranteed some avenue of productive employment according to his abilities. Properly arranged, this need not eliminate private initiative and responsibility nor put a premium on laziness and inefficiency nor put the unemployed working man on a dole. Those are details of management which the experts in various lines have plenty of brains to work out. Much has been done in a preliminary way by profit-sharing, unemployment insurance, industrial indemnity, old age pensions, etc. But *this must be extended* in a comprehensive and inclusive system.

Until this is accomplished, after the unemployed have sought for every avenue of activity, even if it be not to their exact taste, they should take the mental attitude that *they will not be unemployed*. If they cannot work for others let them work for themselves. They should busy themselves in some constructive activity of body or mind. Let them make repairs to the house or the car, mend the fence, paint the garage or the roof, dig in the garden, or if such activities are not open to them, they should do something for a neighbour or for some one else. Let them even offer to work for their keep and let the balance of payment wait for six months or a year. Many a business could use extra men if the major part of the payroll could be postponed for a few months. In any event, *such an attitude of mind* would tune the worker in with the constructive currents of the cosmos which have brought all forms in the universe into manifestation, and as they flow through him in some activity, it will not be long ere some remunerative avenue will open for him. In any event it costs nothing to try it and see.

To sum up: what the mystic sees coming is that mankind must learn that the *ultimate good of the whole is the basis of all progress and prosperity*; that true *brotherhood and co-operation* is the basis of humanity's happiness and success; that while nations and races may have definite boundaries, as do the various organs of the body, they must not be allowed to become *selfish barriers* which prevent the organs of the body politic from co-operating with one another for the good of the whole of humanity, by which co-operation alone their own individual good is assured.

And finally, after we have recognized the effect on our civilization of the foul ulcers of narcotic addiction, white-slavery and organized vice and their diseases, also drunkenness and organized crime, and have *cleaned them up*, we must realize that the destructive forces of *national and international non-co-operation and selfishness*, which inevitably culminate in war, is the great cancer which is sapping the vitality from every organ of the body of humanity, and that if these conditions are not corrected by the enlightened intelligence of the practical men of the world, *they will be operated upon by the great cosmic Law of Adjustment* in such a cataclysmic way that the terrible suffering which will result will break down the barriers between nations and open the eyes of mankind to the fact that only through the cohesive and regenerating power of love, brotherhood and co-operation can the body of mankind survive. Only as we seek to manifest the Christ-consciousness within in our daily dealing with each other and realize that we are indeed "our brother's keeper" can humanity be saved from reaping destructively the results of the inharmonious and destructive forces we have generated.

We mystics may not be practical,[3] but we do see fundamental causes of world conditions and glimpse their results if they are not corrected and neutralized. And we would not be doing our duty if we did not give our vision to the world, in spite of the ridicule and abuse of minds whose consciousness cannot expand to grasp ideas that are beyond their immediate environment. It is therefore a great pleasure to speak to a body of business men of so wide a vision as to be willing, not only to invite us to present our visions of coming events, but to give us such careful and considerate attention and such a courteous reception. I thank you.

---

[3] Every one of the recommendations prophetically presented in this speech, made during the Hoover administration in 1932, has been adopted, either directly or in a modified form, by the Roosevelt administration in 1935.

CHAPTER XIII

THE MYSTIC ROSE

"I (the Real Self) am the rose of Sharon, and the lily of the valleys."
Song of Solomon, II, 1.

> "Look to the Rose that blows about us, — 'Lo,
> 'Laughing,' she says, 'into the World I blow:
> 'At once the silken Tassel of my Purse
> 'Tear, and its Treasure on the Garden throw. '"
> *The Rubaiyat of Omar Khayyam*, XIV.

There are no words which can exactly express Divine Realities because those Realities exist in the higher dimensional worlds, the worlds of four or more dimensions. A four-dimensional idea can be expressed in this three-dimensional world only by a symbol, analogy or allegory which manifests something of the qualities of the Reality that is being presented for our comprehension. For countless ages and in many lands the rose has been used as such a symbol; to symbolize Divine Love, because of its ravishing perfume, its cheering beauty, and its other innate qualities which help man to forget the commonness and sordidness of everyday life.

The object of evolution among all forms is the perfect manifestation of the highest type-form of each species.[1] Such a state of perfection is called Mastery in each species. This state we are told has already been attained in many kingdoms. Among the various earths the diamond has reached this perfected state of Mastery. Among metals it is gold. Among trees it is the oak, and among flowers it is the rose. Among animals it is man. Among mankind it is the spiritually illumined Initiate. Doubtless man could have

---

[1] See *The Truth About Evolution and the Bible*, Curtiss, Chapter III.

learned his lessons and ultimately have achieved Mastery in a world devoid of beauty, but to be surrounded by the wondrous beauty of those kingdoms whose highest forms have attained Mastery not only affords him example and encouragement, but gives eloquent evidence that God is Love.

The rose symbolizes Divine Love and the spiritual unfoldment of mankind because it pictures forth the various stages of the mystical unfoldment of Divine Love within the heart of man which are evidence that man is made in the Image of God; that Image or Higher Self of man which is destined ultimately to blossom as a Mystic Rose and manifest in the heart and life of each human personality.

While the rose is said to be the most beautiful and mystical of all flowers and to reach its perfection only in Paradise, yet even its simplest and least cultivated blossom never fails to awaken in the most untutored heart a wave of joy at its beauty, and at least a temporary, even if unrealized, vibration of aspiration and hope for a manifestation of that Divine Love which is God. This response brings at least a dim realization that if God manifests through Nature in such beauty and fragrance, no one should think that He could forget or overlook even the poorest and humblest of His own children, but manifests in the heart of each in the beauty of holiness and the odour of sanctity.

Primarily the rose symbolizes the oneness underlying the many, or unity in diversity. It has many individual petals, yet is one blossom. Each petal has its own individuality, yet each draws its life from the one source. Its petals have no rootlets, yet are firmly joined to a common center. Humanity may, therefore, be likened to the petals of the Rose Divine. Each Soul has its own individuality, yet each has its roots in the common spiritual center and draws its life from the one great spiritual Source. All are equal in the possibility of expressing the aspect of the Divine that is within, but each varies according to the degree of his manifestation of that Inner Self. In the personality the number and beauty of the qualities unfolded like petals and the perfume of the life mark definite stages in the manifestation of the Mystic Rose within.

Some roses, like some Souls, are more advanced than others and manifest in greater beauty and perfection, and exhale a greater quantity and rarer quality of perfume. Many Souls have opened but a few petals like the wild roses which require a whole hillside of blossoms to express the beauty and perfume that is concentrated in the many petals of the American Beauty and other advanced roses. Yet no matter how primitive a blossom, how few its petals or how faint its perfume, its blooming brings joy and beauty to someone and its presence transforms the poorest dwelling or the most desolate garden. No matter how undeveloped and far from our ideal the manifestation of our Mystic Rose may be, our life and environment are transformed and beautified according to the degree that we express Divine Love, be we but simple wild roses or advanced cultivated ones.

Many Souls who are still on the lower rungs of the ladder of evolution, and whose lessons lie largely in the material world, are like the rose bush which has as yet put forth only leaves and thorns. Such need the storms and lessons of the outer life to teach them that intellectual attainments and worldly successes alone—mere leaves and thorns—no matter how brilliant, pointed and shining, are not the ultimate attainment or blossom of life. Many such are now realizing this and are beginning to put forth buds, although as yet there is little understanding that a blossom is forming, and no conception of the beauty and perfume of that which is to come. Yet if they keep on striving to assimilate the experiences of life, their bud will surely come to bloom in due season. Some, however, reach the bud stage but fail to go farther because of some blight of selfishness or canker of impurity within. These are roses which need severe pruning. For all advanced roses reach their richness and beauty of perfection only after repeated pruning, many bitter experiences and the constant attention of a wise gardener.

There are as many varieties of roses as there are types of humanity, yet like each type of humanity, each rose has within it the possibility of manifesting an outpouring of Divine Love and beauty which shall awaken in humanity a mysteriously touching inner gladness. For there is not a single type of rose which does not bring delight and which is not loved by someone, because it embodies some aspect of beauty which touches the heart and correlates with a similar stage of unfoldment of some Soul. As wild roses require many masses of blossoms to fill the air with perfume and many seasons and much transplanting and culture to transform them into roses of greater beauty and perfection, so do the blossoming of simple human virtues among the ignorant masses of mankind bring joy and happiness to many. Yet it will require many incarnations and much patient striving ere their Mystic Rose can come to perfect bloom. Only as each rose grows in its own place and expresses its own aspect of beauty and gives forth its own perfume, can all parts of the world be beautified and the hearts of all types of humanity be touched and uplifted.

The blossoming of the rose must not be forced if it is to endure, but must unfold according to the nature of its species. The bud must not be pulled open from without, but must follow the Law of Manifestation, *i.e.*, that all growth must come from within outward. The buds of the rose may be likened to the mystical centers in man's body which, in some incarnation, are destined to unfold and shed their perfume in his life. If their unfoldment is forced they are apt to develop abnormally and confront the student with forces and problems he is not prepared by normal growth to master. Only when we have been firmly rooted by experience in the soil of Earth conditions and our buds begin to open normally, because we are responding to the Sun of Righteousness and are absorbing the waters of Divine Love, can these centers blossom in our lives as true spiritual unfoldment or petals of our Mystic Rose within.

When a rose is analyzed it is found to consist of an outside protecting sheath—the green calyx—which surrounds the petals composing the corolla, while within is a golden center composed of stamens. From this standpoint the calyx corresponds to the physical body which is so necessary to enclose and protect our mystic centers, while the petals correspond to our inner spiritual faculties and powers. But as long as the petals remain tightly closed and undeveloped no one can perceive the beauty or enjoy the perfume of the rose that is to be. Only as we open our higher faculties and begin to bloom spiritually, can we really express the beauty of the indwelling Soul or exhale the perfume, which is its spiritual essence. Our petals may be few and small, as in the wild rose, or many, as in an advanced rose, but each petal unfolded is a thing of beauty, and the perfume is delightful, even if faint.

The golden center is found in the heart of all roses, just as the golden Light of the Christ-force is found in the hearts of all mankind. This golden center represents the Divine Flame; for the curved, yellow stamens are as perfect a pattern of a flame as Nature can outpicture. They also act as wireless antennae which catch the vibrations or key-note of the perfect pattern or Ideal Type[2] which each particular rose is intended to manifest, and register those vibrations in form and colour instead of sound. They also transmit the special characteristics of each rose to the seed as it adheres to the stem after the petals have fallen. Through our spiritual stamens or the upreaching aspirations of our hearts, we catch the key-notes of the Flame of spiritual life of our Ideal Type or Higher Self and register them in the beauty of our lives and transmit them to the permanent atoms upon which our future incarnations are built.

Just as the unfolding of the petals into full bloom

---

[2] See *The Truth About Evolution and the Bible*, Curtiss, 34.

to the Flame of Life or the manifestation of the Spirit of the Rose, by causing the growth and expansion of the golden center, so is it that only as the heart awakens and begins to unfold and the sacred Flame streams forth from the Divine Self, can our spiritual petals come into full bloom and the Soul-essence, or the perfume of Divine Love, be shed abroad upon all we contact.

If a petal lets go its hold upon the golden center it falls to the ground, for there is nothing to hold it fast save its own power of cohesion. And no matter how fresh and beautiful the petals may be in themselves, they are a part of the rose only while they cling to their proper place around the center. Like petals, we absorb our spiritual life from the Sacred Flame within our hearts. And only as we voluntarily cling close to the inner Flame of the Christ-force can we bring forth the beauty and sweetness which must manifest as we unfold the blossom of the Mystic Rose within. Therefore, must we *deliberately and continually choose* to dwell, in thought and with faith and thanksgiving, upon our Mystic Rose, if we are to make it the visible manifestation of the Christ within us. And no matter how wonderful the petals we may unfold, if we do not retain our touch with the heart-center and draw our life from the Christ within, we can never express the Rose of Divine Love, for our petals will fall to the ground or manifest only in their earthly aspects. But when all have been manifested to perfection we will drop all our outer expressions and withdraw from Earth conditions and manifest in the higher worlds.

Considering the Mystic Rose as the Real or Divine Self, the blossoms, as they unfold season after season, may be likened to the personalities through which the Flame of our Soul-life finds expression age after age, all of which are required to complete the full blooming of the Soul on Earth. After each blossom or personality has drawn from the Mystic Rose as much of its Soul-qualities as it is capable of expressing, or if for any reason it no longer clings to the heart-center, it falls to the ground. But even though it disappears and seems to die, yet it has built its experience into, and added its strength and beauty of expression to the one Eternal Root, the Mystic Rose which is our Real Self, from which new and more perfect blossoms will put forth in each incarnation.

Every rose has its thorns, some more, some less, which are necessary to protect it from those forces which would consume it or prevent its manifestation. Thorns and leaves represent our outer characteristics while the petals represent our inner spiritual gifts. Uncultivated roses run largely to bush and leaves and have few or primitive blossoms. But with cultivation the rose gradually modifies its thorns, increases the number and beauty of its petals and the amount and quality of its perfume. In our earlier or wild-rose stages of spiritual unfoldment, we may have but a few primitive blossoms and little perfume, and may retain many harsh thorn-like expressions, but as we deliberately make an effort to cultivate our spiritual petals, as persistently as a gardener works over a rose, and try to radiate more and more of the perfume of love, our blossoms will be more beautiful and more numerous, and the need for harsh defensive expressions will grow less and less until all our force of growth will be continually concentrated upon blossoms which shall manifest the beauty and sweetness of our Mystic Rose, the Real Self.

No matter how wild and uncultivated a rose may be: no matter how unimportant, unnoticed or neglected we may seem to be, we can each bring forth some flower of Soul unfoldment. When sad or despondent or when discouraged with the stony soil of our environment and our seeming lack of growth, we should visualize the Mystic Rose within and inhale its perfume. Cling to the thought that if God can make roses bloom on a barren hillside or even in a desert, if we try to correlate with our inner Mystic Rose, so can

He bring forth some beautiful Soul-quality to bloom in our lives, no matter what our environment.

If we realize that we too have a golden heart where the Divine Flame manifests as life, love, cheer and beauty, we can send up our stamens of aspiration no matter how gloomy and sunless the day, and draw down and absorb the warmth of Divine Love which shall enable us to put forth blossoms instead of thorns in our life. Therefore, day after day let us concentrate on the Mystic Rose within and the ideals we desire to have bloom in our life and let the undesirable qualities fall from us like faded petals, because we no longer hold them to us or give them life-force by our attention or by thinking of or expressing them.

While we must all manifest in the environment and through the body in which we have chosen to incarnate, nevertheless we can choose our path and guide our course through those conditions *if we will*. But we must cultivate each ideal and vital principle which we have thoughtfully chosen to guide our lives until they become beautiful petals in the unfolding of our Mystic Rose, that we may express on Earth that Image of God in which we were created.

God intended this Earth to be a perfect Eden, a perfect garden of roses, yet He will not compel His children, because He has given us free-will. Nor would He be wise to force even the beauty and joy of His Love upon an unreceptive or unwilling heart. He has planted the Mystic Rose of His life and love within our hearts, but there is something *we must voluntarily choose to do to* bring it into manifestation. Unless we purposely cultivate our Mystic Rose it may bring forth only leaves and thorns. For when untended even the finest roses may become only cumbering, tangled thickets or even like noisome weeds, when despoiled by insects or covered with mould.

Realize that the students of this Order are not merely a band of occult students selfishly seeking only their own enlightenment and psychic unfoldment, but are meant to be an enlightened regiment of trained warriors, understanding the conditions which confront humanity and determined to do all in their power to shorten the dark days of tribulation that are now upon us.[3] They stand hand in hand and heart to heart to make their garden of roses radiate such a beauty of holiness and such a perfume of Divine Love that it shall help to illumine the minds of mankind, cleanse the Earth and counteract or neutralize many of the destructive conditions which humanity is bringing upon itself[4] as the old Piscean cycle draws to a close, and which must be cleared up and eliminated, ere the new Aquarian Age can fully manifest. Thus can this Order become a mighty rampart of protection and also a giant broadcasting station to help prepare the minds of mankind and also Earth conditions for the coming of the Divine One. Realizing the mighty Power that is back of us and which is seeking expression through our united efforts and thought force, we can say with David: "Though an host should encamp against me, my heart shall not fear: though war should rise against me, in this will I be confident"[5]

Think of *The Order of Christian Mystics* as a garden of roses, a Garden of the King's Delight. Realize that each one who finds in it his true Soul-home has been selected and transplanted into it from his former spiritual environment by the Great Gardener to see if all can grow together in this especially prepared soil and under His personal care. Here we must forget self and our own development in the greater work of helping humanity to meet the "days of tribulation" which are now upon us; for we have been transplanted into this Garden of Souls because we have eagerly responded to His call to do the will of Him who hath chosen us.

As we all grow together we shall make this Order a spiritual Garden of Roses whose beauty shall attract the atten-

---

[3] See *Coming World Changes*, Curtiss.
[4] *Ibid*.
[5] *Psalms*, XXVII, 3.

tion and touch the hearts of all who are ready, and whose perfume shall fill the air with the emanations, the very Presence, of Divine Love, bringing comfort to the sad, peace and rest to the weary, cheer to the discouraged, and beauty and love to all.

Chapter XIV

THE GREAT AND THE SMALL

"Though thy beginning was small, yet thy latter end shall greatly increase." *Job*, VIII, 7.

"Oh, how great is thy goodness, which thou hast laid up for them that love thee; which thou hast wrought for them that trust in thee before the sons of men." *Psalms*, XXXI, 19.

"Wisdom is the principal thing; therefore get wisdom: and with all thy getting, get understanding." *Proverbs*, IV, 7.

"He brought me to the banqueting house, and his banner over me was love." *Song of Solomon*, II, 4.

The mighty Law of Life is moving, ever moving, to its destined fulfilment. Out of Love and Wisdom did it come forth, and back into Love and Wisdom must it indraw all things. It moves on the wings of silence, for all things that are divine and destined ultimately to manifest, move silently, growing after the Divine Pattern, building in atom by atom the Divine Substance which is forever changing, ultimately glorifying earthly things into their heavenly pattern. Alas, however, man, who was breathed forth in God's image, has so distorted and hidden his heavenly pattern in physical matter of the earth earthy and fashioned his thoughts after the desires and ideals of the man of earth—each following his own ideas as to what pattern he thinks will appear most attractive—that the heavenly pattern is often scarcely recognizable.

But as the great Wheel of Life turns steadily onward and upward the time draws near when mighty changes must come both to man and the planet, because the Earth never goes back over the same path nor should man, if he learns his lessons. For while the Earth rotates on its axis as it revolves around the Sun it is also moving onward through space with the rest of the solar system. So should it be in man's spiritual life. That which is up today shall be down tomorrow, and that which is down shall be up, yet each time in a different region in space and subjected to different combinations of forces and conditions. When all things seem topsy-turvy; when those things we have considered great shall be seen as of small account and those that we have thought small shall prove to be great, it is because of the perspective in which we then view them. It is therefore well for each Soul to know that there are certain realities which are eternally great, no matter how seemingly small they may appear at times, and certain weaknesses and human mistakes which are always small in the sight of God, altho they may loom large to us at times. For God is Love, wise Love or Wisdom-Love. And His banner of Light is over us, even though we cannot see it because of the clouds of our own misunderstanding.

There is not one of us who has not the great things, the eternal things of the Real Self within, and who has not also the small things, the transient things of the personality to manifest. By small we do not mean minute or of little consequence, for at times they fill our whole consciousness and horizon. We mean small in the sense of being so little worthwhile, so petty, so non-essential that they are not worthy of a place in our consciousness or life, yet have a lesson for us to learn. If we know positively that in a definite length of time certain things which now seem important and which we are manifesting in our lives would then appear, even in the eyes of our worldly friends, as too far beneath us, too small to be given such importance or even to be taken notice of, how quickly would we try to transmute them, to turn our minds from them and change our conduct! Therefore it is wise for us to examine our lives and our acts, our ideals and our thoughts, and determine just what qualities we desire to manifest and what we should transmute; just how we would like our name to go down to posterity; just what kind of a character we would like to manifest as our own.

We know that every Soul that is reborn on Earth is born with certain characteristics or inherent faculties and traits which are its very own and which distinguish it from all others. And some of these are great. In fact, there is something noble and true in the things which have persisted; in the things which we have built up life after life, age after age. But as we enter into this life, in certain nations, in certain environments, in certain families, we take on at least a colouring from the national and family heredity and from the conditions and things with which we are associated. All these are not really our own. We may think they are ours and we may need the experience which they will bring, but they are not a part of us. Yet they are responsibilities which we have assumed and things we have predicated ourselves to inherit as a part of the price of our earthly incarnation.

Everyone born of woman is born to a certain greatness, for the greatness is inherent in the Real or Spiritual Self. In many the expression of this greatness is latent, for they have not realized it nor striven to manifest it. But it is this innate power of the Spiritual Self which we must seek to awaken into manifestation and cultivate. Let us say to ourselves: "The little petty things that have occupied so much of my attention and that I have expressed so often that my friends are familiar with them are not really myself, do not come from my Real Self, are but imperfections of my personality. They are but the karmic dust which still clings to me." What then is karmic dust? It is something from out the past which we permit to cling to us, which we have not permitted the greatness within to wipe away. Therefore we have to meet it again and again and suffer from it until we conquer it.

What are the forces of selfishness and vanity, of greed

and lust that sweep over us at times and carry us from the Path of
our destined greatness; that plunge us into the slough of despond?
They are but the dust of the ages which we have left behind; the
residue of the things we have apparently conquered, yet whose
dust remains to follow us like a cloud in the shape of temptations
which blind us to the guidance of the Real Self. They appall us
because they seem to be a part of us, yet they are only the dust of
those things from which we have not fully separated ourselves.
This is why those who boldly step out upon the Path are often
assailed by clouds of evil temptations seemingly greater than
before they started to climb the Mount of Attainment, just as the
traveler who is determined to win the goal is covered with the dust
of the road he travels in proportion to the rapidity of his progress.
They assail us today because we are progressing, but have not
absolutely annihilated them. But they are only dust which, with
God's help, we can shake off if we will. They are the petty things
which must give place to the great.

The whole world is now being brought to the banquet of the
Soul which Divine Love has prepared for us in our Father's home
from the beginning of time. Surely those of us who are tired
of feeding on the husks with the swine and who have perhaps
been led—either by our own doubting heart or by misdirected
teaching—to believe that these husks and these swine with whom
we wrangle for the gratification of the petty things of life are all
that God has prepared for us. Surely if we stop to listen we can
hear afar off the angelic chorus of joy and thanksgiving of Those
who have found their way back to their Father's home. We may
even hear the loving words of our Elder Brothers asking us: "Why
sit ye here all the day idle? Why grovel ye among the swine? Arise
and follow us into the banqueting hall of your Father."

For a time we may listen rejoiced, but when we find that
we are far from Home and the Way is long and weary and

requires much exertion and persistent plodding, we are apt to say: "Here I at least have husks to eat. How can I trust to empty promises which I have heard repeated over and over until I am weary of them? I can see little change in my environment or in me, nor do I see any wonderful changes or great advantages in those who have left the husks and started out to travel I know not where, ragged, footsore and weary and covered with dust. Why should I give up the little enjoyments of my present life for empty promises of greatness to be attained in the far distant future?" This is the argument of the petty human personality which is unawakened to a realization of the Great Self which is striving for expression and which is calling it Home to the banqueting house of the Father'.

Those who respond to the call and start out on the journey may see the bogs to be crossed, the heights to be scaled and the dust of the road, but they are upheld by faith; for they have had the vision of the Father's home and are sustained by the realization of their Sonship and the welcome that awaits them, even though often forgotten when footsore and weary. And, who knows? Around the next turn in the Path they may see one of the Father's servants (the Masters) coming toward them with the Robe of the Household and the Ring of Sonship.

Many earnest and sincere students who have gained from books and teachers and mystical lore much wisdom, but without real understanding, grow discouraged and despondent and lose faith if the Great Teachers, the Masters of Wisdom, do not at once acknowledge their sincerity and in a miraculous manner fulfill their desires and supply the petty needs of the personal self, which are nearly always physical — abundant supply, success and worldly recognition, etc. Ofttimes they ask for these things that they may do what they believe to be the Master's work. But in their seeking for wisdom they have not gained true understanding or they would realize that the Master's work is expressed in the words: "Seek ye first the kingdom of God, and his righteousness; and all these things shall be added unto you." For the Father waits to give them as soon as we prepare ourselves to receive and use them aright.

If we forget the injunction: "How great is thy goodness, which thou hast laid up for them that love thee; which thou hast wrought for them that trust in thee before the sons of men," and grow weary of the Way and of the long wait while our understanding is developing; if we forget our innate greatness and argue ourselves into an inferiority complex or disbelieve in the promises which are constantly repeated to man all down the ages by Those who have attained to their fulfilment, how patient must our Elder Brothers be with us! Realize if you can the divine patience and love of those Great Souls who, because They sought for and gained real understanding, have been appointed by the Father as His servants to help every child who sets out upon the Path to the Father's home. For They are near every struggling Soul, holding over us God's Banner of Love. They are never faint or weary, but lead us ever onward until They bring the impatient and disbelieving children into the banqueting house where they never more shall lack any good thing.

But ere we can reach our journey's end we must get understanding. We must realize that we can and must live in His banqueting house here and now; that we do not have to wait until we suffer and die before we can find the Father's house. The personality and its needs is but the outer earthly covering of the Real Self, the divine Immortal Soul which is one with God, who is Love and Wisdom personified. This is what so few of us have realized and understood, because we have put the man of flesh first and have learned either to ignore or look upon our mighty I Am Presence as but a beautiful mystical dream, so ethereal that only after death can it be fulfilled and only in the far distant future when we are done with the things of this physical life.

But if we understand the true place of our Lord from Heaven and realize that the personal man of earth must be His servant, then we will say: "There shall be no more of this. I will no longer let the small things of the personal self obstruct the great things of the Real Self. The things of the past shall no longer stifle me, for I will shake them off like the dust of the Path." Some day, when the time of our Great Initiation comes, we will be able to look back and see how much of our littleness, of our bad tempers, of our thoughtless unkindness's, of our cruelties and impurities we have left behind; will see how much of them have crumbled to dust, yet how much of the dust still remains. But since that great day is not yet here for most of us, we can only prepare for it by trying to live more closely to that which is our Real Self, that Greatness which has brought us forth from among the swine and their husks, which has set our feet upon the Path.

Instead of thinking of how small we are, of how many faults we have, of how few our number is, let us remember how great we are within, how strong we are, how loving we are! Then let us utilize that strength and manifest that love! When we feel tempted to be petty, to be little, to be anything less than the ideal we have chosen, let us say to ourselves: "Is this I or is it only something I have taken up along the way, some dust of the past that clings to my garments?" Then let us say: "O Divine Indweller, draw near and let Thy greatness manifest through me. Let Thy radiant shining make white and spotless my garments of mind and body. Let me be washed in the blood of the Lamb that I may be filled with the Divine Life of the Christ."

Then will we hear the Voice of the Christ speaking to us from out the Silence: "My beloved ones, I need your help. I must have you clothed in the beauty of holiness. I must have you stand before the world as My chosen ones. I know the time is coming when you will conquer all. Why not conquer now? Why not push aside the littleness that you find clinging to the Greatness which is you? Have Wisdom: it is yours for the asking. Have discretion: it is freely found within you. Have power: My scepter is stretched out for you to take. I ask you to represent me before the world. Can you not hear My Voice? Can you not understand the yearning of My Love? Can you not make the effort now? Must I wait and wait and wait? Must it be that each lesson you learn, each failure you put behind you, each mistake you overcome, must require the experience of great suffering before you can understand it? Before you are willing to let go the little and manifest the Great?

"Do not wait for the chastisement of many sorrows to bring you to wisdom, to give you understanding. Nothing holds you back if you will to go forward. Nothing can cling to your robe or soil your garments if you make up your mind to be clothed in My garments of Purity and Truth. Therefore I say unto you, Come unto Me. Rest in the thought that Love is mighty; that Wisdom is infinite; that Understanding is transcendent; that this great storm of physical life which beats you hither and yon is but fleeting; that the Greatness which is You can conquer; that you will no longer be buffeted and tossed and covered with the dust of ages, for you shall enter the banqueting house at your Father's home where even now you dwell in your Soul consciousness."

Chapter XV

THE LORDS OF KARMA

"In the beginning was God. From Him proceeded the Lord of Life, the embodiment of the Divine Law, from beginning to beginning, everlasting." *Harriette Augusta Curtiss*.

"The refusal to admit, in the whole Solar System, of any other reasonable and intellectual beings than ourselves on the human plane, is the greatest conceit of our age." *The Secret Doctrine*, Blavatsky, I, 157.

"Be not deceived; God is not mocked: for whatever a man soweth, that shall he also reap." *Galatians*, VI, 7.

That which we know as time has many changing manifestations, altho in reality there is but one eternal, changeless now. In those early ages referred to as the infancy of humanity, we are told that the Lord Christ walked in His Garden and talked with man and taught him the great mystery of creation and the great miracle of redemption.

As we have explained elsewhere,[1] the Garden in Eden symbolizes the pure, etherealized, super-physical body of man through which the inner Spiritual Man, made in the Image of God, must learn to manifest in this world of matter. It was while his consciousness was functioning in that pure ethereal body that man walked and talked or consciously contacted the Divine. But later on, as man descended more and more into dense physical conditions, he began to listen to and follow the dictates of the physical desires of his evolving animal body and mind instead of following the dictates of the inner Spiritual Man.

The results of that disobedience to his Higher Guidance exiled man from Eden. And we are told that an Angel

---

[1] *The Truth About Evolution and the Bible*, Curtiss.

with a Flaming Sword was placed at the four gates of Eden to prevent man's return. In the individual this Angel symbolizes the inner Spiritual Man whose Sword is the Shekina or the radiant purity and glory of the spiritual or Christ-consciousness which bars man's re-entry into the realms of spiritual consciousness until he masters and uplifts the selfishness and desires of the flesh and once more listens to the Voice of the Lord God, or obeys the Law of God given him through his Inner Guidance. It is this Inner Guidance which continually strives to awaken in man a memory of his Divine Self and its spiritual consciousness. It also impresses upon him the sense of right and wrong, the failure to follow which brings remorse.

Cosmically the four mighty Angels with the Flaming Sword which guard the gates are the four Maharajahs or the Four Lords of Karma[2] who stand at the four corners of the Earth as the Protectors of mankind and also as the Agents on Earth of the seven cosmic Lipika, the Adjusters of cosmic Karma. "The Lipika . . . . are the Recorders, or Annalists, who impress on the (to us) invisible tablets of the Astral Light, 'the great picture-gallery of eternity,' a faithful record of every act, and every thought of man; of all that was, is, or ever will be, in the phenomenal Universe. . . . As it is the Lipika who project into objectivity from the passive Universal Mind the ideal plan of the Universe, upon which the 'Builders' reconstruct the Kosmos after every Pralaya (a night-period of the world), it is they who stand parallel to the Seven Angels of the Presence, whom the Christians recognize as the Seven 'Planetary Spirits,' or 'Spirits of the Stars,'"[3] referred to in the Ritual for the Spirits of the Stars of the Roman Catholic Church. The four angelic Lords of Karma are therefore the Agents of the Lipika to administer the decrees of Karma to this Earth and its humanity.

---

[2] For a fuller exposition see the chapter on "Karma" in *The Voice of Isis*, Curtiss, 114.
[3] *The Secret Doctrine*, Blavatsky, I, 130.

We must never think of the Lords of Karma as Nemesis, as Satan or as avengers or tempters, but rather as Divine Beings who temper karmic justice according to the conditions, strength and degree of unfoldment of each Soul; for They have the power to hold back much of our Karma and portion it out according to our strength to overcome the adverse Karma or to enjoy the good Karma we have created.

Neither should we think of the Lords of Karma as heathen deities belonging to some other religion, for They are often referred to in our own *Bible*. Not only are They the four great Angels who guard the gates of Eden, but it is They who are the Recorders who keep the Book of Life (*Revelation*, xx, 12-14) out of which all are judged "according to their works." Also in *Malachi*, iii, 15-18, it is explained how sometimes even "they that work wickedness are set up; yea, they that tempt God are even delivered" until the Book of Remembrance is opened, whereupon each receives his just reward. Having learned our lessons, "Then shall ye return, (reincarnate) and discern between the righteous and the wicked, between him that serveth God and him that serveth him not." Without the Law of Karma, giving to each that which is due him in absolute justice, God must be looked upon as a capricious monster without either justice or compassion. But understanding this Law, God is seen to be a just, all-wise and compassionate Father who treats us more wisely and lovingly than any human parent could.

The only explanation which those who oppose the doctrines of reincarnation and Karma have to present is the stultifying idea of a heaven of innocuous bliss for the good, and the horrible, unjust, materialistic and soulless doctrine of an eternal hell-fire for those who made mistakes. But how much more like a loving Father who "would not that any perish (instead of the great majority), but all have eternal life?" is the explanation given by reincarnation! Under this law mankind, like disobedient children, have an opportunity to reap and experience the conditions they have set up for themselves and others—even through sorrow and suffering—until they learn from their mistakes, instead of being utterly condemned to eternal punishment and without an opportunity to correct them and turn their evil into good. For suffering of itself cannot adjust Karma. It can only teach the Soul to recognize the mistake and therefore develop the quality whose lack made the mistake possible.

World Karma, racial Karma, and the Karma of the community in which we live can to some extent be helped by us, for we would not be in a nation or community where karmic catastrophes were manifesting, if we had had no share in creating them. Hence it is in our power to help to lessen them and do something now to help others who are suffering from them.

If we had to reap in this incarnation all the Karma we have created in the last incarnation, there would be little time or strength left to take up new lessons or advance along other lines than those followed in the past. For humanity as a whole, the Lords of Karma "fulfil the will of the Gods (or Karma) by means of storms, tempests, transitions of fire and earthquakes; likewise by famines and wars."[4] Nevertheless, in Their great compassion They portion out to us as individuals only that which They see will be best for us to experience in each incarnation, and thus allow us ample time to interpolate those new experiences which the exercise of our free-will may determine; that is, those which are within the general limits of our karmic destiny.

For humanity in general there are seven great classes of Karma, namely, world, racial, sub-racial, national, community, family and individual Karma, all of which are inextricably interwoven and in all of which the individual participates as part of the various groups of which he is a member. It is important that we recognize these classes of

---

[4] *The Secret Doctrine*, Blavatsky, I, 313.

Karma, else we are apt to grow discouraged when general karmic conditions hold us down, altho we are doing our very best and cannot think why we have to participate in them.

For the individual there are three general classes of Karma, "*Sanchita* karma includes human merits and demerits accumulated in the preceding and in all other previous births . . . . The actions formerly done, serving as seeds to grow in the countless births; the store of former actions preserved . . . . That portion of the *Sanchita* karma destined to influence human life in the present incarnation is called *Prarabdha* karma . . . . The actions of this incarnation which give pleasure or pain in this life alone.

"*Agami* karma is the bodily actions good and bad—done after the acquisition of discriminative knowledge. It extends over all your words, thoughts and acts . . . . as well as whatever results your thoughts, words and acts produce on yourself, and on those affected by them . . . . Each action may in itself be as slight as can be conceived, like the minutest filaments of cotton—such that hundreds of them may be blown away by a single breath; and yet, as similar filaments when closely packed and twisted together form a rope, so heavy and strong that it can be used to pull elephants and even huge ships, so the articles of man's karma, however trivial each of them may be in itself, would yet, by a natural process of accretion, combine themselves closely and form a formidable Pasa (rope) to pull man with, *i.e.*, to influence his conduct for good or evil."[5]

Before incarnation the Soul is aware of its own Karma and what must be done to work out that portion of it which is assigned to it in the new incarnation. It therefore works under the direction of the Lords of Karma to prepare such a body and such conditions as will afford the best opportunity to accomplish its main tasks and also learn its new lessons in the new incarnation. The Lords of Karma should

---

[5] *The Theosophist*, VII, 60, quoted in *Cosmic Fire*, Bailey, I, 470-1.

therefore be looked upon as loving Helpers whose part it is to help man work out and fully learn the needed lesson from every act, thought and experience. It is They who often flash us a warning not to repeat old mistakes, sometimes giving us a memory picture in dream or vision of a similar event in the past in which we failed. Yet, since we can see no outer reason for the feeling that we are about to make a mistake, and have not been taught to listen to our Inner Guidance, we often disregard and disobey these plain warnings.

It is the Lords of Karma who may be said to arrange events like stepping stones over which we may cross the fierce torrents of our own disobedience and mistakes, that we may reach the goal of attainment set for each incarnation. Were it not for the inspiration and encouragement of these great Helpers we would often return to our Father empty handed and without having progressed, and so have to go over and over the same ground again in subsequent incarnations. For They are ever urging us on to overcome obstacles and redeem our mistakes and fearlessly face the Flaming Sword, which for the individual is entrusted to our Divine Self who will never let us enter Eden or even rest until we have redeemed our mistakes and learned the lessons necessary to manifest that Divine Self on Earth.

Since this Divine Self is made in the Image of God its task is to evolve an instrument or personality which will express that Image in the flesh. This great task we can accomplish far more quickly and harmoniously if we recognize the goal to be attained and, under the guidance of the Divine Self, take our Karma into our own hands and voluntarily work it out instead of compelling the Lords of Karma to force it upon us in sorrow and suffering because of our refusal to admit it and our rebellion against it. This does not mean that we should call down all our past Karma in an effort to work it out quickly. To do so is to be overwhelmed with more than we now have the strength to bear. We should simply recognize conditions as they are presented by life and pray for understanding and help to master them.

If certain events in our Karma seem to repeat themselves it is simply because we have failed to learn the lessons they have brought to us the last time their problems were presented. We are like children detained after school to make up our back lessons. The experiences of life point out to us just how much or how little we have followed the Divine Guidance of our Higher Self and built into our understanding and character the vital experiences our Karma has brought to us. For the cycle of each life is not a closed circle around which we go again and again endlessly, but is a spiral path[6] which as a whole is forever climbing, in spite of little dips or relatively low spots here and there.

As the various points are reached on each round of the spiral we meet the same tendency, urge or force that helped us to conquer, or else we meet the dips or blank spots where the lack of a certain quality or unfoldment caused us to stumble and fall — individually, nationally, racially, etc., — while on the last round. Yet each time we are on a little higher level, from which we can see more clearly, and where, because of even a vague memory of the past, we have the fuller understanding and the greater strength gained during the last cyclic round, so that this time when disappointment, sorrow or temptation comes we *can* conquer *if we will*. For now we can say to ourselves: "Altho I have created these experiences and failed to conquer them in the past, I know that I have the help of the mighty Lords of Karma and the strength of my own Divine Self and the Christ within to conquer this time. But I must hold fast to the hands (powers to accomplish) of the Christ held out to me and not slip and fail again." For the Lord Christ is closest to us in times of temptation and trouble. All we have to do is to open our hearts and ask His help, and then take His hand and follow His guidance.

---

[6] See "The Spiral of Life," in *The Message of Aquaria*, Curtiss, 196.

We must never blame the Lords of Karma for depression, sorrow or misfortune or think of ourselves as the helpless victims of the ebb and flow of a karmic tide which is a fate that we cannot resist and which is bound to sweep us off our feet. This is not true. When temptations come, when mistakes creep in, when failures seem immanent, we should realize our own inner strength and the help that is ours for the calling, and determine to conquer these things now, once for all. After we have used this idea as a sort of talisman to turn sorrow into joy, we can look back and see that we conquered because we listened to our Inner Guidance, held fast to the hand the Christ held out to us, and refused to give up until the victory was won.

Karma is not merely an abstraction, but is a Cosmic Power in the universe, the squaring force which upholds and strengthens that which is destined to take place, both for the Cosmos and for the individual. The destiny of the Soul is the ultimate unfoldment of the Image of God here on Earth and the re-entry of the individual consciousness into Eden, but the Path which the individual chooses is left to his own free-will. This is the vital distinction between destiny and the erroneous doctrine of fate or predestination.

In the Path our Soul has chosen, the Lords of Karma place those things which each particular individual must face and experience in order to take his next step in progression and unfoldment. To one is given poverty, to another riches—a very severe test—to another insincere friends, or fame, or disappointment, or an ailing body, etc. But all are needed for the perfecting of the Soul to whom they come.

We should therefore recognize and thankfully bless the Lords of Karma who patiently wait for us to recognize the Law and accept Their help as the arbiters, adjusters and fulfillers of the Divine Law, which is ever adjusting all things to help on man's spiritual unfoldment and perfection. We should *gladly accept*—as new opportunities to overcome, learn and advance—everything which They place in our Path of Life. For Karma should not be looked upon as a punishment or even a burden to be borne, but as the messenger of the King, who proclaims: "Behold, here is an opportunity given you to bring forth that which the Lord of Life has whispered to you as a possibility."

We should never say that we would do so and so "if we only had the chance." We always have the chance, the chance to accomplish the next thing, learn the next lesson and take the next step that is the best for us. And in proportion as we listen to our Inner Guidance and work with the Lords of Karma, the way will open step by step. If we see a step which our Inner Guidance plainly shows us must be taken, yet which seems closed to us, let us look deep into our own hearts and lives and see what it is in us *or what is lacking* in us that prevents its attainment, *not demanding* that it shall come to pass, *but praying to be shown* what it is that prevents its manifestation or attainment; for our Path is barred until we recognize and remove it.

As time rolls on in its ever-circling flight and we reach a point where the Lord Christ is once more preparing to walk in His Garden and talk with man, the great Lords of Karma again bring to mankind an opportunity to take a great step upward and onward. But this step can be taken only as man recognizes the great mistakes of the past and helps to adjust their consequences. This he can never do by denial or by shutting his eyes to obvious facts. Only by recognition and acceptance of conditions can he master them.

We have elsewhere[7] detailed some of the cataclysms and horrors which humanity must face and pass through in the great karmic cleansing and readjustment which is now upon us, during which the negative, destructive and other evil forces will have great power and strive frantically, knowing well that their day will be short. But we have also called attention to the gathering of the angelic hosts who are the

---

[7] *Coming World Changes*, Curtiss.

reapers of the good and whose spiritual powers will be poured out upon humanity in such wonderful demonstrations of the Shekina that even the materially minded will have to acknowledge them. But when we sense this spiritual outpouring or see this Divine Light reflected on Earth we must not cry out: "All is well! Let us go with the crowd and be happy lest we be a kill-joy." For *all is not well* until the readjustment is finished and the force of evil has been overcome by the power of the living Christ and His angelic hosts. This is as true of the Karma of the individual as of the seething turmoil of the world Karma of today.

Let all those who desire to work with His hosts to help the Christ redeem the atoms of good set free by the crash of empires, the sinking of continents and the wiping out of whole communities and nations, put on the whole armour of Christ,[8] lest the froth and foolishness of passing physical pleasures and self-indulgence now being churned to the surface under the name of enjoyment, sweep them from their moorings. For we cannot pass safely through the terrible days of cleansing with which the Lords of Karma must face humanity unless we stoutly cling to that which we know to be sacred; unless we *persistently maintain our standards of right and wrong, of personal conduct and morality*, in spite of being laughed at as "old fashioned". The "fashion" of a period, whether of clothes or of morals, cannot alter the fundamental laws of life. To them we must steadfastly adhere in spite of the riotous clamor of those who cry: "Let us eat, drink and be merry, for tomorrow we die." For we know that we do not die. We only withdraw for a time from the whirl of sensuous physical life, and later have to come back and "pay the piper" for the mad dance in which we have indulged.

Altho the events of life may be reviewed and their lessons learned and great progress be made after we leave the physical, yet the karmic *adjustment must be made on the plane*

---

[8] *Ephesians*, VI, 14–17.

where the causes were generated. And it is the Lords of Karma who face us with the results of our past acts and thoughts while on Earth that in meeting them this time we may prove that we have learned the lesson by conquering them and so no longer need to be tested by similar experiences. If we have really learned the lesson the conquering will be so easy as scarcely to be a test at all. This explains why the same temptation will be difficult for one to overcome and easy for another.

As we peer through the gathering mists of time and feel the chill of the coming tribulations, let us realize that as we open our hearts to the Light of the Christ and feel the glow and warmth of His presence within us. His radiant aura that enfolds us will prove an impenetrable, protecting "Ring Pass Not" around us, no matter what may be transpiring in the physical world. Within the sacred precincts of His aura we again find ourselves "hid with Christ in God" in the mystical Garden where the Lord Christ walks and talks with us as of yore; where He whispers: "Well done, thou good and faithful servant . . . . enter thou into the joy of thy Lord."

CHAPTER XVI

REDEMPTION

"I beseech you therefore, brethren, by the mercies of God, that ye present your bodies a living sacrifice, holy, acceptable unto God, which is your reasonable service. And be not conformed to this world: but be ye transformed *by the renewing of your mind*, that ye may prove what is that good, and acceptable, and perfect, will of God." *Romans*, XII, 1-2.

"Therefore, if we sacrifice knowingly and willingly, the redemption is accomplished without the suffering which the crucifixion brings about for those who resist and refuse to work with the Law." *The Key to the Universe*, Curtiss, 141.

In a previous chapter[1] we have tried to open in the hearts of our readers the little door which admits them into the spiritual consciousness where only the Soul-language is spoken. And we sincerely hope that many have at least glimpsed or felt the warmth of the vibrations from the radiant Light which streams out from that little door and makes a pathway over which, even in their physical consciousness, they can ascend into the mystic inner shrine of the heart. For there the Lord Christ waits for His children to come unto Him and receive the blessing of His recognition — the crown of their lives — and absorb the Divine Love so freely showered down on all who come thus unto Him.

What is the result of the absorption of the radiations of this Divine Love and this blessing which has awaited us so long, hidden in the inner chamber of the heart, but which can fully bless and enrich the life only when recognized and assimilated? For only those who persistently follow up the first faint glimmerings of the Light on the Path which ever

---

[1] *The Soul-language*, Chapter III.

shines in the darkness of their outer lives, can find the little door and ultimately enter the inner shrine and worship in its holy precincts.

The result of the absorption of the radiations of the Christ-force is redemption, both of the mind and of the flesh. As we have already pointed out: "Without this redemption, and a comprehension of what is meant by Divine Love, the student, no matter how much occult theory, fact or knowledge he may store up, will still wander in the outer darkness and never find or recognize his Father's face. Once grasp this truth with Soul knowledge, not mere intellect, and you will find that you have hold of your Father's hand and nothing can ever separate you from Him, for the Comforter has come who will abide with you forever. Only thus will you find the key that unlocks all mysteries, that overcomes sickness and conquers death, and that ultimately places your feet upon the highest mount of attainment."[2]

What then is redemption and how is it accomplished? For centuries the materialists in religion—the literal interpreters—have taught that our redemption resulted from the physical crucifixion and death of an innocent victim nearly two thousand years ago. And our hearts have melted with pity and our tears have flowed in sorrow at the terrible picture of the Crucified One hanging on the cross in bitter and helpless agony. How our minds have revolted at the injustice of the conception of His having to pass through such agony for us centuries before we were born! And how we have secretly rebelled at accepting it! Yet in the past we were almost compelled to accept it as "one of the mysteries of God which we could not hope to understand," as we were told. But in this New Age, when we are gradually proving that "Nothing is secret, that shall not be made manifest; neither anything hid, that shall not be made known," the enlightened mind and the awakened heart can no longer accept such medieval and materialistic interpretations of cos-

---

[2] *The Voice of Isis*, Curtiss, 410.

mic truths; for we are beginning to understand the angel's words: "He is not here: for he is risen."

The literal meaning of the word *redeem* is to buy back, ransom or release from bondage. The old theological doctrine is that all mankind are in bondage to sin because of Adam's fall of original sin. This was a *mere theological speculation* which in time has become a dogma. But it is essentially ridiculous in view of modern scientific investigations, even if we take Adam to represent all humanity and not one man. We are, indeed, all under the bondage of sin, but it is not the result of Adam's so-called sin, but of our own, both in this life and in the past. In other words, we are constantly generating and radiating emanations and vibrations of all kinds—physical, mental, pranic, astral, spiritual—by emotion, thought, word, deed, etc. And being the creators of these emanations and vibrations, we are not only responsible for them, but being magnetically en rapport with them we must react to them and their results until we have neutralized or redeemed them.

If they have been constructive and harmonious, as their return waves come back to us our reaction will be constructive and harmonious and we will be happy, healthy, joyous, etc. But in proportion to the inharmony, impurity and destructiveness of our creations our reactions must necessarily range from mere inharmony to actual suffering and even disease. We should remember that disease is not a decree of God or a condition imposed upon us as a punishment by something or someone outside ourselves. It is an inharmonious manifestation of the life-forces generated because we have in some way violated the laws of health. Yet every phase of disease was prepared for and the remedy made ready by Nature and waiting for the time of its need long before man incarnated on Earth. For nothing is lacking on this planet for man's health, happiness and evolution. It is only man's failure to ask of God for His guidance as to how to find, understand and utilize that which has been prepared for him which keeps him from finding and making use of the help which God has provided.

The Law of Manifestation requires that, "Whatsoever a man soweth, that shall he also reap" and "One jot or one tittle shall in no wise pass from the law, till all be fulfilled." Thus do we suffer under the bondage of the inharmonious creations (sins) we ourselves have sent forth, and also under the collective creations of the race of which we are a part and which we, in this and past lives, have helped to create. And we must so suffer in and with the race until we learn to transmute and thus redeem such creations. We are brought face to face with such creations and given an opportunity to redeem them, according to our capacity and strength, by the Great Law as Karma, which "tempers the wind to the shorn lamb."

But if we must redeem our creations and thus become our own redeemers, why are we told that Christ is our Redeemer and that we must cast our burdens upon Him? How can the blood of Christ redeem the sins of the world? Or is this a false teaching? Is it but a myth or an allegory? Can it have been meant to deceive? By no means. This seeming paradox is a cosmic reality, forever true in the life and experience of every awakened Soul. But it must be interpreted through the Soul-language in the Light which streams from the little door that opens into the higher or spiritual consciousness.

The difficulty arises through a materialization of the Gospel story and a failure to distinguish between the Cosmic Christ-principle and the personality of the Master Jesus who manifested an individualization of that Principle to a superlative degree. This Cosmic Christ-principle is the Universal Sun or Life or creative aspect or Son of the Godhead, the source of the spiritual life of mankind just as the physical Sun is the source of the physical life in all the kingdoms of Nature. St. Paul makes this distinction very plain when he speaks of his followers as little children "of whom I travail in birth again *until Christ is born in you.*" Also Jesus said: "Except ye eat the flesh of the Son of man, and drink his blood, ye have no life in you. Whoso eateth my flesh, and drinketh my blood, hath eternal life." Manifestly such statements could not be made about any human personality, but must refer to the Cosmic Christ—or Divine Life-force.[3]

The explanation of the paradox is that while man must be his own redeemer *he cannot accomplish his redemption in his own strength* or with his own unaided mortal powers. He must call upon, correlate with and use the radio-active power of the great cosmic current of Christ-force to accomplish the transmutation of evil into good, just as the plant must call upon the actinic and chemical rays of the Sun to transmute refuse and manure—also inert inorganic matter—into living tissue. Therefore it is literally the Christ-force which redeems us, but only as we correlate with it and use it and make it truly manifest in us.

While this Christ-force is universal and pervades all kingdoms, unless man places himself en rapport with it he can utilize it only unconsciously and therefore only to a limited degree. But if we consciously strive to correlate with it in our spiritual heart it will send the spiritual currents of the Christ life-force throughout our bodies and minds and manifest in our lives. This is the significance of the passage in *St. John* i, 11-13, where the Christ-force is referred to as personalized. "He came unto his own (humanity), and his own (humanity as a whole) received him not. But *as many as received* (by correlating with) him, *to them* he gave *power* to become (*i.e.*, by transmuting and redeeming their sins) sons of God (*i.e.*, Initiates). . . . Which were born (the spiritual birth) not of blood, nor of the will of the flesh, nor of the will of man, but of God."

It is, therefore, not enough for us merely to repent of our mistakes and misdeeds and be forgiven; for we are for-

---

[3] See chapter on "Jesus and the Christ" in *Letters from the Teacher*, Curtiss, Vol II.

given seventy times seven. There must be a positive, constructive factor *voluntarily introduced by ourselves* if we are to regenerate our creations and counteract their results; for *redemption is not a passive or mechanical process.* This is the vital distinction between forgiveness and redemption. If we tell a dearly loved child not to play with fire and it disobeys and is badly burned, even burns down the house, we may forgive the disobedience and even shower upon it more sympathy and love because of its suffering, but the child must still reap the results of the disobedience until the burned tissue is redeemed by the regenerating action of the life-force. The redemption does not take place simply because the child is sorry, repents and is forgiven, but because of a positive and reconstructive use of the life-force in the body.

Just so is it in our spiritual life. When we sincerely repent we are forgiven for our disobedience to the Divine Law, but we must still suffer until our use of the inflowing Christ-force (Divine Life) counteracts and regenerates the results of our disobedience. Nowhere in the *Bible* are we taught that the Christ can prevent the scar or the loss of the burned house. Because of the Christ-force invoked through prayer and aspiration the pain may be eased and the burn healed more quickly, but it cannot prevent the scar nor the ruin of the home. They belong to the outer and material expression of life and must necessarily follow physical laws. All such things are taken care of by the action of the Law of Karma.

Today the redemption of the great mass of mankind is being slowly worked out a little at a time, and with much inevitable suffering, through the Law of Karma. Through past ages even the more advanced have spent incarnation after incarnation adjusting the Karma generated by their ignorance of the workings of the Law and their willfulness and self-indulgence. And why? In spite of the Law being set forth in all ages in all the great scriptures of the world, we have found it hard to learn except through actually experiencing the results. But he who learns to recognize his shortcomings *and corrects them* at once or redeems as he goes, needs no Karma to teach him. Hence, no karmic debt can accumulate for him which, being so long deferred and so separated from its causes that he cannot see the connection, often seems unjust.

In former ages it was difficult for us to accept our burdens and sufferings without rebellion, because the workings of the Law were not explained so we could understand them, and we were asked to take it all on faith that somehow it was just. But in these days of scientific discovery of the modus operandi of the Law in Nature we see that all things are accomplished as a result of the specific action of some law or laws. We can now understand not only *why* the scriptural teachings are universally true—even though misinterpreted—but *how* the results are obtained.

We now see that redemption is not merely a religious conception, but is *an actual scientific process*: the result of the radio-activity of the Christ-force within us; a new inner radiation of the Christ-love. But this process must be voluntarily set into operation by us if we would advance more rapidly than the slow tide of age-old evolution. To light our home we must make use of the electric current by voluntarily turning the switch. The power is waiting, the wiring has been built in by the builder, yet both are useless to us without our co-operation. So, while we say we light the house, it is really the power of the current from the central station which we utilize which lights it. We merely use it by correlating with it. But if we refuse consciously to turn the switch and insist on using only a tallow candle, we must expect only candle light, altho all the current of the power-house is available for our use once we comply with its laws.

While we must turn on the Christ-light and be our own redeemers, nevertheless we can only do so by utilizing the

Cosmic Christ-power whose avenues of manifestation are built into the house (body) in which we dwell on Earth, and which is within us waiting to be utilized. The power has always been there, but we must learn to turn it on and utilize it. Therefore, just as the electric power-house bears the strain and burden of the load we place upon it by our use of the current, so hath the Christ-power literally "borne our griefs, and carried our sorrows . . . . was wounded for our transgressions, he was bruised for our iniquities; the chastisement of our peace was upon him; and with his stripes are we healed."[4]

Yet we must not look upon the Christ-force as a mere mechanically generated impersonal power like the electric current. It is the outshining of the radiant currents of Divine Life and Love of the celestial Divine Being, the Ever-living One, the mighty I Am Presence, within whose Divine Aura we live and move and have our being, and who gives freely of His Divine Life that we may have life more abundantly.

This understanding of the Christ within and its manifestation within us removes the objection of those whose sense of justice is violated by the doctrine of an innocent man suffering centuries before their birth for their mistakes and misdeeds, and who refuse to accept such a vicarious redemption. It is therefore not Jesus the Avatar who takes our sins upon Himself—altho of course He does suffer because of the inharmonies we have set up—but the Christ-principle within Him and us. For this is the Christ within "Who his own self bare our sins in his own body . . . . that we (the personality) being dead to sins (*i.e.*, being redeemed), should live unto righteousness: by whose stripes we are healed. For ye (the personalities) were as sheep going astray; but are now returned unto the shepherd and bishop of your souls."[5]

---

[4] *Isaiah*, LIII, 4–5
[5] *1 Peter*, II, 24–5

Let us then seek to correlate ever more and more fully with this redeeming Christ-light as it shines through even the tiniest crevices of the little door of the sacred shrine of our hearts where our Real Self stands and knocks, patiently waiting for us to open that door that He may enter into our consciousness and life and sup with us. Let us stop making excuses for our failures or even asking for mere forgiveness. Let us draw closer and closer to the little door of the heart and ask that the divine illumination of the Christ-light may grow brighter and brighter and reveal to us our own shortcomings and wherein we fail to work with the Law, that we may correct and redeem them.

Let all who truly desire to worship the Christ and who seek for true redemption establish a definite practice of making daily visits, in prayer and meditation, to this sacred shrine of the heart where the angel of our Divine Selfhood stands waiting to open the door of what has so long been the tomb of our materialistic consciousness, and let that Self come forth, freed from the grave clothes of our materialistic conceptions, out into the glorious day of spiritual realization. For the Christ is crucified and hangs suffering upon the cross of man's materialized conceptions until a majority of Christendom has so enlarged its comprehension that it recognizes that it must be the Christ-light radiating within their own Hearts which alone can accomplish the miracle of redemption.

Chapter XVII

RELIANCE

"Thou shalt not be afraid for the terror by night; nor for the arrow that flieth by day; nor for the pestilence that walketh in darkness; nor for the destruction that wasteth at noonday. A thousand shall fall at thy side, and ten thousand at thy right hand; but it shall not come nigh thee. "*Psalms*, XCL, 5-7.

Amid the turmoil and unrest of present-day conditions, in which all the inhabitants of the Earth are finding old ideas, social conditions, forms of government and conceptions of life turned topsy-turvy, as though in a seething caldron of some witch's brew, there must be something fundamental to which we can turn for assurance and comfort while we wait in patience for the ultimate adjustment. Such a fundamental basic principle, which is both the cause of the unrest and its ultimate cure, we therefore lay before you that its meaning may sink deep into your consciousness and give you the courage to face conditions quietly and act understandingly during this period of darkness and unrest ere the New Day fully dawns. For the world is not falling back into Chaos, but is in the transitional process of taking a most important and vital step on its path toward a perfected Cosmos. This change is now transpiring before our eyes, and every awakened Soul has his or her part and lot in its manifestation.

All who are spiritually awakened have grasped the idea, as a fundamental truth, that there is a Divine Self within us, a spiritual super-consciousness—our individual Ray of the Christ-consciousness—which is inspiring our ideals, guiding our actions and gradually purifying and perfecting even the atoms of our physical body, making it a glorious Temple within and pleasing if not beautiful without, a fit dwelling place for the Christ-consciousness. From the experiences which the awakening of this understanding has brought, we have learned fearlessly to face our old life, knowing full well that the Sun of Righteousness as it rises will surely drink up the mists which have hidden the Spiritual Sun from us. Hence we can await in confident patience while the dense mists of misunderstanding and the dank vapors of selfishness that unfortunately befog the minds of mankind as a whole are being lifted and absorbed until all finally see the Sun itself.

The world is simply passing over, on a larger and grosser scale, the same experiences which each of us who have reached a certain degree of spiritual enlightenment have passed over in miniature. In the individual the desires and appetites of the lower self have each clamoured for self-determination, self-expression and independence. And before the Soul has attained peace and harmony each has had to have its hearing and be taught that, while each is right and proper in its own place and for its own purpose, all must learn to fulfil their own missions in such a way as to cooperate in harmony with the others, all working together under the guidance of the Higher Self for the good of the body as a whole. During this process everything that will not work harmoniously, everything that rebels, that refuses to cooperate in a constructive way, every evil tendency, thought and desire, had to be gathered together and cast into the burning for transmutation. This burning may be disappointment, discouragement, sickness, bereavement, poverty or other Soul-trying conditions, but after their transmutation each shall yield its grain of gold.

While this was going on we might seem to be preparing only a witch's brew into which we have cast all the loathsome things hidden so long in the background and darkness of our life; all those things so wonderfully symbolized by the witches of Shakespeare's *Macbeth*:[1]

"In the poison'd entrails throw—
Toad, that under coldest stone, . . .
Swelter'd venom sleeping got, . . .
Fillet of a fenny snake,
In the cauldron boil and bake:
Eye of newt, and toe of frog,
Wool of bat, and tongue of dog,
Adder's fork, and blind-worm's sting,
Lizard's leg, owlet's wing,
For a charm of powerful trouble,
Like a hell-broth boil and bubble."

If these lower tendencies are not controlled and guided, but are left to the manipulation of "the witches three," they gather together and brew and breed and bring forth greater and greater selfishness and evil, just as the witches of Macbeth sought from the brew of everything loathsome to bring forth a powerful spell of black magic potency.

How much better, through reliance upon the fire of Divine Love, to brew a healing broth of divine realization that will purge us of all inharmony and evil! For under this pot we have lit not the fires of hatred, envy and lust for power, seeking thus to gain either advantage or control over others, but the fire of Divine Love, that all that these things signify in our own nature may be transmuted, that out of even this seeming hell-broth there may be decocted the pure Elixir of Divine Love and Wisdom.

Having to some extent undertaken this task of purification and transmutation in our own life we are now called upon to stand by and watch the bubbling of the brew which "the Sisters three" are today mixing in the pot of the world at large: for only we who have gathered in the "upper

---
[1] Act IV, Scene 1.

chamber" of the Christ-consciousness, can see that the glory of the Sun of Righteousness is already illumining our minds, melting the hardness of our hearts, opening our inner eyes and shedding its streams of healing blessing upon whomsoever cometh in His name. Only thus can we face these dread Sisters undismayed—who in this sense are what the world calls the three Fates who weave into the warp of Destiny the woof of man's own creations—because we have proved to ourselves, through the positive experience of realization, that underneath all the outward confusion there are reaching out the "Everlasting Arms" of Divine Love.

We know that the angelic forces of light and truth are only waiting to cast into the caldron—when it has reached the point of boiling where the mass is ready for transmutation—the Philosopher's Stone which will transmute the entire mass into the pure gold of truth and justice, peace, harmony and righteousness. Therefore, "Let not your heart be troubled, neither let it be afraid." Take fast hold of the hand of the Father whose child thou art and realize that not one sparrow shall fall to the ground without His knowing.

From out the great Womb of Time there come forth at definite periods certain cosmic forces which, if there be those who can recognize them, correlate with them and manifest them in their own personal lives, can be used to bring about a great advance for all humanity. They can thus help to purify and counteract the selfish and inharmonious forces created by humanity which tend to prevent their manifestation. But if these cosmic forces are poured forth and there are no enlightened minds, loving hearts and willing hands ready to receive them they do not accomplish their mission, hence are indrawn into their cosmic centers there to await the next turn of the Wheel of Time. Such an outpouring is taking place in the world today. How shall we make ourselves ready to receive and utilize it?

The troublous times through which we are now passing

in these overlapping "last days" of the old and new cycles were clearly referred to by Jesus[2] who, as the Avatar for the Piscean Age, the Alpha and Omega, left both a description of the conditions and directions for meeting them. He also left with us the Comforter[3] or the Divine Mother-principle, with the assurance that this wonderful love and comfort would abide with us "even unto the end," and that during all the dark days so graphically foretold it would bring all things to our remembrance whatsoever He had told us. And today we can feel that Comforter hovering over the world's chaos, drawing Her children to Her with invisible cords of love. And through the lips of many Messengers the words of comfort and the promises of safety that Jesus left with us are being called to our attention and their memory poured out like refreshing dew.

How clearly we can trace present events—even prohibition—in the prophecy given in the first and second chapters of *Joel*! And those are chapters that all should study in these days. But fail not to note and understand that through all the dire calamities that are there foretold to come at the end of the Age, there runs the most comforting promises of protection and deliverance for all who "harken unto the voice of the Lord" or who love the Lord or who call upon Him for protection. If we realize that the word "Lord" as used in the *Bible* means the great and divine Law of Good or God's plan to bring to ultimate perfection all humanity, we will understand that to "harken to the voice of the Lord" means carefully to note and work with the Lord or the Law of Good, realizing that all the underlying forces of evolution are working toward ultimate good; that to love the Law is to live in a constant realization of and obedience to the Christ-consciousness, both within yourself and in the world, and to rest in the assurance of the divine indwelling mighty I Am Presence, and fear naught.

---

[2] *St. Matthew*, XXIV.
[3] See Lesson, *The Comforter*, Curtiss.

To "call upon the name of the Lord" means to ask continually for the Great Law to work through and guide you into that which is best for you, even in the little things of everyday life. In short, it means that during these trying times especially, it will be only through understanding, obedience, love and devotion that we will come safely through. No amount of mere calling "Lord! Lord!" or talking about our religious principles can help us. Mere lip service will not avail; for that sort of outer religion and worship in the world is already tottering on its throne and will ultimately be cast down. The great Law of Protecting Love (the Lord of Life and Love) is manifesting more strongly and expressing more definitely; is gathering the children of the Father together from the uttermost parts of the Earth into the upper chamber of the higher consciousness and personal realization of the Christ within, even as a hen gathereth her chickens under her wings when danger impends.

How then can we have all the wonderful promises fulfilled for us and make the Great Love our shield and buckler? How shall we be sure that we are not merely crying vainly outside the gates, "Lord, Lord, have we not prophesied in thy name? and in thy name have cast out devils? and in thy name done many wonderful works?" only to be turned away with the words, "I never knew you."[4] The answer is to recognize and correlate with the Christ within and *absolutely rely upon* Him *in all things*.

To all you who feel within the urgent desire for a higher life, a greater consciousness of the Christ within; whose hearts are torn by the widespread inharmony and suffering you see around you today and who desire to help better the conditions of humanity, there comes as a guerdon of your Soul's travail the assurance that within you is born the Christ-consciousness which is capable not only of guiding and protecting you, but of developing within you just those powers and forces which are necessary to bring to you

---

[4] *St. Matthew*, VII, 22-3.

everything needed for your betterment, your evolution, your ascension, that you may fulfill your part in the perfection of humanity as a whole.

A guerdon[5] in one sense is a reward, but in another sense it is a necessary and inevitable result of sincere and persistent effort. The degree to which this guerdon is actually yours is determined by the efforts you make toward realization; the constant and persistent repetitions you make to your rational mind until it responds and realizes the seriousness of your convictions—and from there is reflected and acted upon by your sub-conscious mind—of the reality of the I Am-consciousness within you and of its power to manifest in your outer life and carry you safely through the turmoil of present-day conditions, if you will only act upon this knowledge and permit it to manifest

Some day into each heart this realization will suddenly flash into flame. Some incident in our life may awaken it. Perhaps we may come dose to the gates of death and a glimpse of the glory will shine through and leave its indelible imprint upon our consciousness. Perhaps some great and terrible sorrow may come upon us; we may lose some dear one; may suddenly have all our friends fail us or our worldly possessions swept away. Then there will flash into our consciousness the thought that all such manifestations belong to the outer and transient phases of life and that the only things really worth working for are the immortal realities of the Inner life.

Then we will no longer think in a vague way that we have within us this Christ-light and life and love, but will say to ourselves: "Not only have I the Christ within me, but it is illumining my intellect, warming my heart, vivifying my whole being and radiating in streams of living power and irresistible constructive force. And I must not allow the mask of my personality to hide or impede it, but must make it express my Real Self, the Christ within." We should re-

---

[5] See "The Soul's Guerdon," *The Message of Aquaria*, Curtiss, 460.

peat this again and again until we have gained something of a realization of its truth, for it is far more than a matter of mere affirmation; it must be a realization or be made real to us.

While the power of the Christ is within us, it is not ours consciously to use until we have *realized it* and endeavoured to *give it expression* in guiding our daily life. For no matter how much we talk about it, nor how much we try to explain it, until through travail of Soul it is born in our consciousness and *begins to bring forth* in our life it is not consciously ours. But once the birth has taken place, once the realization has been attained, we have touched a live wire, we are standing on the third rail tapping a power which, if we permit it to manifest, will bring to us whatsoever is needed—protection, peace, poise and plenty, plenty of mercies and joys.

The protection will be against all that would interfere with our real life; the peace of duty well done; the poise of perfect balance of idealism and common-sense, the poise that has not only said, "Not my will, but thine be done," but that has realized that the Will of the Father is the ultimate perfection of all His children. The plenty will be that abundance of blessings promised to all who have gained the true understanding of and obedience to the Great Law, hence no longer need the lessons of limitation. As long as we need them, limitations are a blessing, for only through the lessons thus learned will we empty the earthly vessels of our understanding and perverse personal will that the golden vessels of our purified understanding may be filled with the abundance of blessings.

Therefore, *have faith in* and *rely upon* the power of the Christ within to both protect us and to guide our daily life. If we listen continually for this guidance and obey we will make ourself a center of peace, poise and power in our environment, no matter what the outer conditions. Then we need fear naught, for "it shall not come nigh thee."

Chapter XVIII

THE GREAT WORK

"Would to God. . . . all men might become adepts in our Art—for then gold, the great idol of mankind, would lose its value, and we would prize it only for its scientific teaching."—*Eirenaeus Philalethes*.

"It thou return to the Almighty, thou shalt be built up, thou shalt put away iniquity far from thy tabernacles. Then shalt thou lay up gold as dust, and the gold of Ophir as the stones of the brooks." *Job*, XXIII, 23-4.

During the Middle Ages, the science and learning of the day was in the hands of a few advanced Souls called mystics and alchemists, who, with inquiring minds, delved into the secrets of Nature, and became enthusiastic advocates of what they called the "Great Work." This was commonly understood to be the transmutation of the commonest and basest of metals into gold. Although there are many records which claim the alchemists actually produced gold, there is not one of them who did not die poor; yet we are told that they were the happiest of men. This was because they looked upon alchemy not as a mere means of making gold out of base metals, but as a means of demonstrating the Great Work.

How was this accomplished?[1] And how was it that not one, but many, gave up family, home, friends, and all that man usually holds dear, and lived in poverty, even burning their scanty furniture at times to feed the fires under their retorts, and yet that they should think so little of the gold they produced and of wealth, that they died poor?

While it has been the modern fashion among a certain

---

[1] See also "Man and the Elementals," Chapter XXI, herein.

class of narrow-minded scientists to ridicule the whole idea of
alchemy, and look upon such men as Hermes Trismagistus, the
father of Alchemy, Albertus Magnus, Thomas Aquinas, Nicholas
Flamel, von Humboldt, Cagliostro, Thomas Vaughn, and many
others, as either self-deluded fools or unscrupulous impostors,
nevertheless, the leaders among scientific men today are already
acknowledging the possibility of the alchemists' claims, especially
since the transmutation of radium into helium by Sir William
Ramsay in 1903.

All occult students, however, who are willing to look into the
past with unprejudiced eyes, and see behind the many veils which
successive epochs have thrown over the esoteric truths taught
by the Initiates, recognize that in alchemy, as in astrology and
the great scriptures of the world, we have to do with a mass
of symbols, myths, and allegories, all in their last analysis,
illustrating the one Great Work, *i.e.*, the transmuting power of the
One Divine Life penetrating matter, and through the slow process
of evolution, transmuting the base into the refined, the human
into the Divine, bringing all forms to their ultimate perfection,
or transmuting all into spiritual "gold."

For the individual man, this gold is the spiritual oneness with
his Father-in-heaven, and for the Race and for the planet, the
Golden Age or the ultimate fulfilment of their evolution. For the
Great Work pertains not only to the transmutation of metals, but
also to man and the planet itself, with all its flora, fauna, and
myriad inhabitants. In short, alchemy seeks to explain through
symbols and to demonstrate through results, the theory of the One
Life, and how man can consciously work on with it to perfect
both himself and the lower kingdoms, far in advance of the slow
processes of unaided Nature and attain his ascension.

The Great Work was and is but the recognition by certain
advanced Souls that man is indeed a microcosm, and
hence, like the macrocosm, must have within him the trans-

muting power of the One life. Therefore, if he can learn so to control this Power that he can direct it by his purified Will, he can take his place as God's ambassador on Earth, and become a conscious helper with God in the transmutation and redemption of humanity and the lower kingdoms. For just as the Elohim said: "Let us make man in our image, after our likeness," and impressed upon the human kingdom the type of that to which it should evolve and manifest, so must man consciously impress and uplift the kingdoms below him, as he has already unconsciously impressed upon them his mistakes and inharmonies in the past, and thus ultimately become their conscious guide and mental sponsor. This is the great underlying truth beneath every alchemical experiment

Just as the great alchemists gave up all that man holds dear in physical life, and passed through the most rigid testings and trials that they might strengthen their wills and accomplish the Great Work, so must we be willing to give up our minds and hearts and lives to the Great Work of transmuting the base in us into the Divine. Through their disciplined will and through meditation, the consciousness of the alchemists became not only imbued with the power of the One Life, but through the shutting off of all else, became one with it, and enabled them to prove their premise, *i.e.*, that there is but one Divine Essence or God, and that man is indeed made in His image, and hence can have dominion over, and even accelerate the evolution of, the lower kingdoms and the so-called inanimate substances in the Earth, as well as within himself. Thus can he overcome the retardation which his disobedience and selfishness has placed upon them. For to transmute baser elements into gold is not to perform a miracle, but merely to accelerate the evolution through which they would have passed in the process of time without man's help. This physical transmutation was indeed a mighty demonstration of man's power, through his purified will, to touch the border of Omnipotence, or the hem of the garment of the Christ, and achieve his ascension.

One of the by-products of the Great Work was the Elixir of Life, and the history of the Middle Ages teems with marvellous stories of the efficacy of this wonderful Elixir; of its possessors' living far beyond the allotted three score years and ten, and finally leaving this Earth more as a conqueror might retire from active work to take up private life, than because either death or decay had laid hold upon them. As we learn to correlate with the One Life of the Christ, to that extent does it become our Elixir which shall purify and transmute the atoms of our flesh and enable us to retain it as long as we need to manifest on Earth.

The world collectively has advanced rapidly in intellectual development since the days of the alchemists, and in its intellectual pride, it seeks to sweep aside with the staff of ridicule all the marvels of the ancients and accuse anybody who has the temerity to avow his belief in transcendental principles, of being "superstitious" and "gullible." The true occult scientist, however, knows that all evolution advances in cyclic waves with an upward and onward spiral movement. That which has been shall be. And today the most advanced scientists are reaching a point where they can grasp the possibilities, of transmutation, and recognize the occult law that that which man has accomplished in the lower arc of the cycle and in the lowest and densest physical matter, he must and shall accomplish at every step on the Path and in all states of matter, even to the very top of the spiral.[2] Some day man must reach perfection and stand at the apex and have dominion over the Earth and all its kingdoms. But in reaching that point, before he can unfold new faculties within him, he must unfold and use those he already has, just as a tree cannot unfold its two higher possibilities of flower and fruit, until it has perfected its growth in root, trunk, branch and leaf.

As the alchemist dominated the baser metals, and by the

---

[2] See "The Spiral of Life," *The Message of Aquaria*, Curtiss, 196.

power of his will transmuted them into gold, so must we, by the power of our will, conquer the baser aspects of the personal self, illumine and spiritualize our present senses and powers before we can expect to conquer the higher and more ethereal forces and make them obey our spiritualized will. The alchemist was able to do this because he recognized his oneness with God and Nature, and then believed it so thoroughly and determinedly that he proved it, and by his will was able to give to certain common and familiar substances marvelous manifestations of the life-force.

The Law of Reincarnation applies to the rebirth of ideas, forces, and life-waves as truly as to Souls. And the world today is entering, as an infant, upon a period of rebirth of those old alchemistic days, but in a higher realm. Today we hear much of using the power of will to bring us gold, or, as the more common expression is, prosperity, health, and freedom. But, like the many who sought to participate in the results of the alchemists' labours, many seekers today fail to attain their ideals because they do not realize that it is often by the things we give up and the sacrifices we make for an ideal that the force is generated which makes that ideal take root and grow. Nothing can manifest the One Life unless it is a growing thing, for the One Life either brings about growth and evolution, progressing successively through body, mind, and Soul, or disintegration and dissolution. This is equally true of ideas and of faculties, in short, of everything. A thing must grow if it is to manifest the One Life, and the faster it grows the more Life it manifests, and the more Life it manifests, the more vital it is. Hence, if we would have an idea or ideal grow within us, we must cultivate it and water it with much loving thought; for if it stops growing it is at once attacked by lower parasitic forces which will ultimately destroy it.

Many students recognize the possibility of spiritual gold, and become very enthusiastic and desirous of accomplishing the Great Work at once. They eagerly read the teachings and books on philosophy, and attend meetings and courses of lectures, but when they are asked to place their lives in the retort, gather the fuel for the fires, and give up their pet pleasures, their money, or even their worries, to tend the fires, they quickly abandon all real effort and say that spiritual gold is but an alchemist's dream; and their ideal becomes overlaid with frivolous ideas which, like parasites, find in it fertile soil, and by their growth, sap its vitality and disintegrate it. In fact, they are like the stony ground of the parable. When the seed fell on it, it quickly sprang up, but having no depth of soil, it as quickly withered. Therefore, unless we are ready to toil and make sacrifices similar to those of the alchemists, we cannot expect to demonstrate the practical results of transmutation and ascension. In the Great Work, the mind has a large and important part to play; for thought is the Mercury of the alchemists, the messenger between Earth and heaven. The mind is dual, consisting of a higher and lower *manas*; but even its lower aspect, the human intellect, has an important work to do if we would make Mercury our messenger to lift us up to God-consciousness. But the intellectual faculties must be taught to obey our will, and must then be put to work; for, between the Higher Self and the lower personality which we would transmute into spiritual gold, there is a great gulf fixed, and ere we can reach the farther shore, we must build a bridge. This bridge is called the *antaskarana*, which it is the work of the lower mind to build, through a comprehension of the laws of divine manifestation and a realization of its unity with the One life. Hence, even though the task may seem as hard as transmuting the base metals, we must begin at once and set the mind to work under the guidance of our will, for the bridge must have its lower piers and abutments laid in the personal self. Then, like all bridges, it can build out and out until the chasm is finally spanned and the bridge firmly fixed to the spiritual shore.

To start this bridge, we must determine that henceforth we will think of ourself as a Spiritual Being; that like the alchemist of old, we will make our life circle round one idea, the idea that everything we find in our lower personal self we will transmute into spiritual gold. We must not strive to kill-out anything we may find in the lower personality, but simply throw it into the crucible and let the fires of Divine Love and Wisdom transmute it. Perhaps our conditions in life may seem as dead and hard as a stone, but even then be not dismayed, for the Philosopher's Stone, which was the chief object of the Great Work, at a certain stage seemed black and dead and lifeless. But the wise alchemist, instead of becoming discouraged at this stage, knew that its very blackness was a promise of final success. Remember that just as the alchemists gave up all that life held dear, not merely for a vague ideal, as so many think, but that they might make a practical demonstration of the power of will to correlate with and utilize the One Life manifesting in all things, so must we today refuse to follow the beaten path of a mere theory, but transmute the personality and demonstrate the Great Work in our lives.

Philosophers had, for ages, been teaching the theory of transmutation, but the actual demonstration of the Great Work had to wait until there arose some who were brave enough and determined enough to prove it. We too can demonstrate the Great Work if we follow the same law of absolute faith, trust, purity, and humility. But we too must study the laws of transmutation, and then resolutely strive to put them into practice. We must prove on the mental, psychic and spiritual planes, as well as on the physical, that things we have heard with our ears, seen with our eyes, and believed in our hearts are not mere theories, but are truths capable of actual demonstration. For we must transmute intellectuality into the Pearl of Great Price, Divine Wisdom; but to do so, we must be willing to sell all that we have of personality, and follow the Christ. We must transmute every wave of psychic force that sweeps over us, into the pure gold of spiritual perception, and every glimpse or ideal of spiritual consciousness into a realization of oneness with the I Am Presence within.

If the alchemists could overcome the resistance inherent in matter, and triumph on the physical plane, we should be able to triumph on all planes, for we have the strength of their past experiences, since every victory won for the Race is the heritage of the Race. We may not have the technical knowledge of how to transmute metals into gold, but we have their reservoir of will-power laid up for us to draw upon, and we know that it will accomplish similar results if applied with equal persistence and determination. The Great Work, however, cannot be accomplished by one whose mind vacillates from one phase of teaching to another. We must be steadfast to the teachings or method of transmutation we have chosen. Those who today are awake to their possibilities must be the pioneers who shall lead their more fearful and timid brethren across the Threshold into the super-human state and worlds.

Modern chemistry is largely founded upon the laws which alchemists demonstrated, yet because it refuses to reckon with the One Life as a vital and living principle and has left out of consideration the fact that man and Nature are one and that through the power of an illumined will, he can so correlate his consciousness with the One Life that it becomes a quickening Spirit capable of accomplishing all things, just as modern chemistry is unable to accomplish physical transmutation, it fails to find the cause back of chemical affinity.

This is the secret. This is why only those who recognize their Art as a divine gift can succeed. In the words of an ancient alchemist, "In the first place, let every devoted and God-fearing chemist and student of this Art consider that this arcanum should be regarded not only as a truly great, but a most holy Art. Therefore, if any man may desire to reach this great and unspeakable Mystery, he must remember that it is obtained not by the might of man, but by the grace of God."[3] Students were also admonished to lift up their hearts to God, and great stress was laid upon purity and sincerity of heart, and a conscience free from all ambition, hypocrisy, and vice. They were counseled to overcome all faults, especially those of pride, arrogance, boldness, luxury, and all iniquities; for it was held that certain failure would result if the Great Work were attempted without this purification. While this Order does not believe in the necessity for strenuous fasts, long prayers repeated by rote, or other ceremonial observances, to bring about in the student the right state of mind and attitude of Soul, still definite efforts should be made to strengthen the will and make the end for which he is striving more real and vital, altho the danger of training the mind to depend upon ceremonials and *things to do* is apt to offset the good derived from them.

We are living in an advanced age, and the One Life is manifesting through more ethereal channels; hence less physical methods of strengthening the will should be employed. The most helpful practice to strengthen our will and hold fast to our determination really to make a practical demonstration of the transmutation of our baser nature into spiritual gold, is to meditate upon Divine Love. We should make this our *Elixir Vitae*, and teach ourselves, by constant practice, to think of ourselves, not as erring physical beings, the helpless victims of all the vicissitudes of life or what we call our Karma, but as immortal Spirits, one with God and Nature, the middle link, as it were.

We should think of ourselves as a part of a great electrical system drawing energy from one mighty Dynamo. By turning a little switch—the mind, under the influence of the will—we can connect ourselves direct to the main line of force. Then by turning various other switches we can control the current received and make it flow wherever we

---

[3] Quoted by Redgrove in *Alchemy*, 4.

will, and accomplish that which we will to accomplish. But this can be attained only by continued effort and a determined holding to the one idea.

Many talk glibly of "ruling their stars" and drawing everything they wish to them, but until we become spiritual alchemists we do not realize that there is but one thing we really want, *i.e.*, to accomplish the Great Work and make the ascension. Only too often by our very affirmations and willpower we draw to us things which entail much suffering and require the working out of bitter Karma ere we learn their lesson and find out that they were not what we really wanted. Hence we should meditate upon the realization of the Great Work and then never cease our determined efforts until it is attained.

We must realize firstly, that there is but one divine Cosmic Christ-force manifesting through the One Life in all forms, and that this One Life is the Soul of the World, the Christ made flesh and dwelling among us. Paracelsus, in his *Book of Revelation of Hermes*, speaks of this Soul of the World as follows: 'This is the spirit of Truth, which the world cannot comprehend without the interposition of the Holy Ghost, or without the instruction of those who know it. The same is a mysterious nature, wondrous strength, boundless power. . . . By Avicenna, this Spirit is named the Soul of the World. For, as the Soul moves all the limbs of the Body, so also does the Spirit move all bodies. And as the Soul is in all the limbs of the Body, so also is this Spirit in all elementary, created things. It is sought by many and found by few."

Secondly, we must believe in this power of the Christ to accomplish the transmutation of everything in our nature into pure gold. Thirdly, we must definitely determine that since our spiritual evolution is the end and aim of our existence, that we will set about it at once and make its accomplishment the first and only real aim of all our efforts. Fourthly, we must so order our lives that all we do and all that we think shall work toward the great end which we have set ourselves to attain, *i.e.*, an unquestionable demonstration of the Great Work. The demonstration may not be recognized by the world at large any more than was the practical demonstration of transmutation by the alchemist of old; yet each one who has made the demonstration within will be the happiest of mortals, no matter what ridicule he has had to meet or what hardships he has had to endure, for he will have the spiritual gold to prove his success.

Above all, let us remember that it is only by the fires of Divine Love and Wisdom, fed by an indomitable will, that the black and base metals of the personal self can be transmuted, first, into the *white sulphur* or purified earth, then into the orange of purified life and illumined mind, and finally into the rosy glow of the perfect Rose, the symbol of Divine Love and Wisdom made manifest and taking form on Earth. In other words, the disciple must permit the Flame of the Christ-love to permeate every atom of his being and make every fault and shortcoming not something to be killed out, but to be transmuted into a necessary part of his character, and take form around the Christ-center as a petal in the Rose of his Individuality. But these fires must burn pure and steady and continually or the Philosopher's Stone will lose its virtue. If love be tainted with passion, it becomes, not a purifying, but a consuming fire. If the fire be permitted to cover itself with the deadening ashes of selfishness, indolence, pride, or self-righteousness, or any other cinder of personality, it will die out and die Great Work will fail, and our ascension will have to wait until a future incarnation.

Chapter XIX

KING DESIRE

"And they had a king over them, which is the angel of the bottomless pit, whose name in the Hebrew tongue is Abaddon, but in the Greek tongue hath his name Apollyon." Revelation, IX, 11.

The Absolute, the One Eternal Truth, that which was and is and ever shall be, expresses itself upon this plane of differentiation through its three great attributes, the Divine Trinity of the Godhead. This Trinity may be roughly defined as Divine Love, Divine Wisdom, expressing through intuition, and Divine Will, through which the fruition of the Trinity is focussed and made manifest on all planes. These divine attributes are the three Kings which should rule the world and to which all must ultimately bow.

Back of the well-known allegory of the three Kings or Wise Men, who sought the cradle of the Christ and laid their gifts at His feet, stands this same great truth. This truth was so precious to the sages of old that during the dark ages of persecution they embodied it, together with the fundamental truths of occultism, in what appeared to be a mere game of cards, the *Tarot*. And the same truths still appear in the modern playing-cards where the three Kings have prominence.

The first King, Divine Love, is represented by the King of Hearts. The figure of the heart is a conventionalised representation of the *caduceus*, or the evolution and ultimate blending of the two serpents—the positive and negative aspects of the creative force—through Divine Love.

The second King, Divine Wisdom, is symbolized by the King of Diamonds, the shape of the diamond being an exoteric and conventionalised representation of the interlaced triangles, or Seal of Solomon, a glyph which indicates the riches of Divine Wisdom.

The third Attribute, Divine Will, through which Love and Wisdom are brought to fruition, is symbolized by the King of Clubs, representing the Father or masculine Principle. The conventional form of the trefoil symbolizes the Trinity, for this King must synthesize the power of all three to bring to fruition Love and Wisdom, its lowest aspect being that which is brought forth by toil and labour upon the earth-plane.

These three Divine Rulers should reign supreme through their perfect reflection in matter and should have their thrones in man. In other words, man must ultimately come under the sway of and swear allegiance to these three Kings who worship forever at the feet of the Christ. These Kings rule in man as human Love, Intuition and Will, but Will, through man's disobedience to the Divine Law and through his misuse of his free-will, has become a usurping King who sets up the kingdom of his lower manifestation in man as personal, material desire. Desire as a principle, the desire to manifest and to attain the highest expression of each manifested form, is one of the basic motive forces back of all manifestation, but the selfish desires of the personality and the desires of the flesh so predominate over the higher and unselfish desires in most people that it is these lower material desires of the flesh that so often rule as King Desire.

The King of Spades, whose emblem is a heart reversed, symbolizes Divine Love (King of Hearts) which is so often degraded into King Desire. The stem of the spade shows that it sprang from the earth, and its color indicates that it is Divine Love perverted. This King only too often rules through the perversion of the Divine Trinity in man by enticing man to give his allegiance to its lowest aspect, sexual desire, when not illumined by pure love. Only as the downward pointing spade of sex desire is reversed from animal lust to pure heart love, can it attain its highest ends; for only then can King Desire become the servant of the King of Hearts or Divine Love. The spade indicates man's power to dig in the mire earth and undermine the foundation of the Temple of the Christ. The fullness of the reign of the Three Divine Kings on Earth is hampered because of the misconception of their powers and the limitations placed upon their manifestations by man — the opposition of matter to spirit — and through the opposition of King Desire whom man has enthroned.

King Desire synthesizes the lower aspects of the three Kings and through them rules the world. From the King of Love he steals the golden sceptre and transforms it into a rod of iron — animal lust — with which to thrust into the mire the highest ideals of mankind, crush tender, loving hearts and blast human lives. From the King of Wisdom he steals and destroys the sceptre of intuition and in its place rules through the powers of intellect, through mere reason, plausible sophistries and what passes in the world for logic. The King of Divine Will he dethrones and drags at the wheels of his chariot which is driven by his henchmen Greed, Avarice and Lust. Hence the King of Spades or King Desire is called the King of This World. He is also known as the Adversary, Apollyn, Abaddon, etc.

These four Kings manifest on Earth in duality through their feminine aspects, the four Queens, and thus bring forth their various potencies and powers, which are symbolized by the numerals of their progeny, the spot or pip cards.

It is the vassals of the King and Queen of Desire who people the lower planes of life with all the manifestations which we call evil, and it is these Rulers and their kingdom which man must transmute, lift up and transform ere the

Divine Kings—Will, Love, and Wisdom—can manifest their higher attributes.

There is a tendency in these days to ignore and deny the reality of the King of Evil, to call him but a chimera of mortal mind, a figment of man's imagination. Yet while denying him, man still bows before him and pays him tribute. The great task of man's spiritual evolution is to transmute and lift up this power so the kingdom of his Soul shall be ruled by Divine Will instead of by King Desire. Man can never transmute and lift up a thing whose existence he denies. He must recognize and conquer rather than ignore and kill out this King Desire. Transmutation is a definite process in which the substance to be transmuted must be recognized, placed in a crucible and the fires lit which shall purify and uplift it. It is a constructive process in which that which is impure is purified and used as the basis of a new product. Mere denial or negation is futile. It is but a pushing away of the problem and can never help the Soul take one step in the transmutation of the human into the Divine, which results in Mastery.

Among advanced students there should be no misunderstanding as to who this King Desire is or how he dominates all flesh, for he and his Queen bring forth all the misery, disease and death that can be traced to the perversion and degradation of sexual desire in its various manifestations. It is not that sexual desire is impure or evil in itself, for *it is essential* in its proper place and for its proper purpose. It is only its degradation to minister to animal lust and perversion that turns it to evil ends. For man must grasp the mighty truth that nothing that God has given can be evil, but when properly used under His guidance is a blessing and for man's highest good. When used as a gift of God for a God-given purpose it can bring forth only good. Whatsoever God has created and given to His children has been given because it holds within it a mighty blessing which should and ultimately will be understood by His children, even though many incarnations and much suffering is required if they refuse to learn by precept and demand experience.

Every evolving Soul has felt the yoke of this King and must know something of the results which allegiance to him inevitably entails, such as sickness, premature old age, and senility. Yet how powerful is his sway! How faithful are his votaries! How tight is his yoke upon the necks of his slaves! With what thongs does he bind his victims to the wheel of the Law that descends into the mire of earthly suffering!

This Order stands pre-eminently for the upliftment and purification of the ideas of humanity with regard to the creative power, through a clearer understanding of its laws; for the transmutation of sexual desire into an avenue for the manifestation of Divine Love. Therefore to understand the workings of this Divine Creative Force upon the higher planes, we have but to tear aside the outer coverings of its manifestations on the physical plane to grasp the deep spiritual realities back of them. Each must learn to seek back of this force the manifestation of the synthesized power of the Godhead expressed as Divine Love.

But this King Desire is not to be killed out, for killing is not mastery, but just as he has usurped the throne of Divine Will so must he be dethroned and take his rightful place as the obedient servant of the three Divine Kings, for Desire is the stepping-stone to Deity when we throw off its yoke from our necks and place it beneath our feet, *i.e.*, master it through understanding (feet). As long as mankind is the slave of King Desire, the Christ, the creative potency of the three Divine Kings, is crowned with thorns and crucified. The mystic Christ who is crucified is the Great Creative Principle which must be brought forth immaculately through Love, Wisdom and Will.

Therefore search your own heart diligently and see if

while you are striving to climb the Mount of Attainment to serve the trinity of Divine Kings, you are not secretly paying homage to King Desire and permitting his polluting influence to cling to your garments as you seek to enter the holy Temple. For many who think they have killed it out have only suppressed it, only shut it up in a dark closet of concealment into which they enter from time to time and feed it with their thoughts and sustain its power. For desire when ruling as King is the enemy who sows thorns and thistles in your garden while you sleep.

As a candidate for spiritual attainment you are professing the name of the Christ. You are donning the pure white garments provided by the Master of the Feast and are seeking to partake of the Marriage Supper with the Christ. Can you not see that if you hold allegiance ever so slightly to the world's king your marriage garment is false? You are like one who is not a virgin coming to the marriage feast under false pretences. Your allegiance to the Christ must be undivided and you must come with singleness of purpose, just as a bride must give undivided allegiance to the bridegroom in purity and love.

It is not, however, those pure and perfect Souls who are born upon the mountain-top or who have never bowed the knee to King Desire who behold the transfiguration, but those who have passed the weary way through the Valley of the Shadow of Death where King Desire reigns; they who have laboriously climbed step by step to the mountain-top; who have slipped and fallen again and again, yet who have determinately and persistently turned their faces upward. But if such do fail at times, much is forgiven them since their aims were high and their efforts sincere. Only greater strength was lacking. Even though the phantom of Desire is dogging their footsteps as they climb, striving to turn them aside from following Divine Will, still they cry: "Get thee behind me Satan, Saturn thou tester of my Soul. Power is given to thee only to try me, and I will not yield."

Only such shall one day reach the Mount of Initiation and there behold that this evil thing that has dogged their steps, pulled them down and sapped their life has now become transfigured into Lucifer,[1] Star of the Morning. And through the dark folds of the outer garment which they have grown to fear shall shine the glorious light of the Shekina. The Light of the Christ-force lifted up shall break from out the darkness and they shall know that they have conquered through Love; that indeed the King of Evil has been conquered and has sworn allegiance to the Kings of Light, Love and Immortality.

Fear not to face the tempter. Climb the mountain, no matter how dark the way, no matter how fierce the storms of desire may beat, no matter how the call of the world, the flesh and the devil may sound in your ears. Press on, no matter how impossible it seems to climb, no matter if there come days when you say, "What is the use of striving? What is the harm in living free and enjoying life? There is no end to evolution and some day, after I have fully gratified the desires of the flesh, the desire of wealth, for love and admiration, when I personally have found them all but Dead Sea-fruit, then it will be time enough to seek for higher things." But, alas, as long as you seek wealth, happiness, companionship or love in the realms of King Desire you are seeking among the ashes of the dead for coals to light your torch of life. Leave it all behind you and climb to the mountain-top and light your torch at the Sun of Righteousness. There only will you find what you seek. Only in the bright rays of that Sun is desire transmuted into Divine Will.

Every one upon the Path who stops to play by the roadside or dance for a few idle hours in a wayside inn of the mind or senses becomes a tempter for his comrades. Enough if you would eat of the Dead Sea-fruit. Tempt not your brother or sister. Discourage not those who are

---

[1] See chapters on Lucifer in *The Message of Aquaria*, Curtiss

bravely climbing. Besmirch not the garments of those already dressed for the Feast. Let all unite in mind and heart and Soul to throw off the yoke of the King of This World. Let us refuse to eat of his black bread which brings naught but disaster, sickness and death. Drink not from his iron cup filled not with the blood—the spiritual life-force—of the Christ but with the tears of bitterness and agony shed by those whose hearts are crushed, whose homes are wasted and whose lives are desolate, blasted by the worship of King Desire.

Make desire subservient to the will of your Father-in-Heaven. Thus shall you transmute the forces of evil brought forth through desire into the powers of the Three Kings, Love, Wisdom and Will. Then shall they reign in you and make you an active factor in the redemption of the Race, a co-worker with God or Good.

CHAPTER XX

THE MYSTERY OF THE ELEMENTS

HYMN TO THE ELEMENTS

Earth, my Mother, bid me learn,
Truth in darkness to discern.
Like thy forces, silently,
Work in true humility.

Stream of Life unceasing flow,
Wellspring of the Christ bestow.
Fill me till I thirst no more,
Bear me to Thine eternal shore.

Air that blows from heaven's dome,
Waft me to my Father's home.
Whisper softly words of Love,
To all mankind from God above.

Holy Fire from on high,
Enter in and purify.
Burn the dross and cleanse from sin,
Make me pure and true within.

Harriette Augusta Curtiss

In a certain mystic ceremony a pertinent and everlasting truth is revealed to the Neophyte in the formula, "Let the earth and the water, the air and the fire be thy servants to draw thee closer to the Heart of Love." Yet how few, even among those who have studied long and laboriously within the circle of accepted ones, have really drawn close to that Heart! How few have even a conception of how the elements can be made their servants, theirs to command; obedient, trustworthy, capable! Remembering that the Lords of Karma are the presiding Spirits of the elements, and that the elements should help man in his great climb upward and onward, think what it means to have those Great Beings as your servants! Yet this is a covenant made with every accepted Neophyte. And it will be fulfilled if he is sincere and faithful.

How shall we have these servants work? Shall we, of our own free-will, determine and predict? Shall we will to be pushed on by the good of the gods, or must we eternally suffer ere we learn? Is it not possible for us to enter into an appreciation of our great privileges and possibilities and at once claim our heritage as "Sons of God"? If we have heard those mystic words pronounced, or if we have invoked the forces of the elements in the Silence, they will come to us with the power and divine potency of the great Hierarchies of Heaven. But if such an invocation falls on deaf ears; if the forces come to one who, having invoked them in a moment of ecstasy or unthinkingly, forthwith passes on and forgets them, they will come again, but as an earthquake, as a flood, as a whirlwind or as a consuming fire. Thus it is ever with servants who are permitted to become masters; servants whom, in our indifference and lethargy, we have permitted to don the purple, mount the throne and hold the sceptre over us.

It is our privilege to make the elements our servants to draw us closer to the Heart of Love. How can we rule these servants? The law is simple, plain and effectual, if we but grasp it. Since the inner essence is the product of Divine Life and Divine Love, he who works through the Law of Love will find the elements his servants. In speaking of the elements, we do not refer to the outer and gross physical elements, although even they must ultimately obey the inner urge when it is controlled by those who understand and exercise their power over the inner essence, but we refer to the Spirit of the elements, or the conscious intelligences in Nature which manifest through the elements.

The things which we perceive with our physical senses are not the realities, are not the things themselves. They are not the things either to strive for or to avoid. They are but limited and imperfect materializations of certain aspects of the inner ideal or pattern of that which they strive to manifest in the material world. They are merely signposts set up for those who are spiritually unawakened to indicate that back of the physical manifestation there is a great Reality, just as we might set up a stake to indicate that beneath the outward and commonplace appearance of the earth there existed a deposit of gold. Let us, then, take account of our powers and possibilities. Let us seek the inner mystery, the power back of the elements. For once understand that the Lords of Karma are the governing Spirits of the Elements, and we will realize that it is not the physical elements which bring to us our ills or blessings; that bring the just compensation for that which we have sown and the just retribution for that which we have slighted or neglected, but it is a mysterious force connected with them and ruled over by the great Lords of Karma, which never fails to bring about the ultimate adjustment.

Let us begin with a study of the element earth and its mystic possibilities. Many indeed realize the power of Earth conditions to push them on, to bring them suffering to be endured, lessons to be learned and experiences to be garnered, but this is only one phase of Earth. The Earth is a material aspect of the Great Mother, in the darkness and depths of whose bosom the germs of all things are nestling; those hidden things that we must ultimately grasp and understand and use as stepping stones to ever greater attainments. She is the mother of our physical expression. But only as it is nourished by the Waters of Life from the spiritual aspect of the Divine Mother can it aid us in bringing forth spiritual fruits in us.

And in our lives it is the power of this same Mother-force, this darkness that is pregnant with the powers of all the other elements, that brings forth in the Soul and manifests in the character the germs that are hidden in the dark corners of our nature where we scarce dare look; germs of good and germs of evil; the germs of our possibilities. This is the mystic power in man which corresponds to the element earth, the power of the Mother to bring forth the unmanifested.

Each Soul has within him these mystic depths into which the Light from the Higher Self must penetrate that this earth element may become his servant to bring forth at his command. Learn then to correlate with our possibilities. And as we let the Divine Love enter in and bring forth the hidden germs, if we find weeds springing up in our garden with the flowers, pull them up at once lest their rank growth choke out the blossoms we would bring forth.

To apply this practically, at every contact we make with the physical earth, let our minds go forth in an understanding appreciation of what the earth is; that of itself it is but a barren desert until moistened by water, warmed by fire (the Sun) and breathed upon by air, but that when all four elements are combined in harmonious proportions it will bring forth all things.

Then let us realize that we also have the earth element within us and that it must be moistened by the waters of Divine Love and be purified and redeemed; for we have helped to make it what it now is.

We should remember how the Earth was made, *i.e.*, by the gathering together of the failures and leftovers of the past,[1] transmuted by the mighty forces of evolution. Realize that just as there is hidden within the bosom of the Earth vast undeveloped powers and possibilities, so are there in our element of earth if we will open our hearts to them and correlate with the Divine Mother and bring them forth.

The element of water symbolizes the outpouring of Divine Love, the "showers of blessing," the "dew of Herman" and the "Water of Life" so often referred to in certain hymns. For as water comes from heaven to refresh the thirsty

---

[1] See *The Voice of Isis*, Curtiss, 181.

Earth, and sinking into its bosom softens the hard shell of the seeds until by its alchemical action it bursts them asunder, so must Divine Love descend from Heaven above. It must be the outpouring of our Divine Nature and must sink into the deep places in our lives and burst the outer husks of the germs of our godlike possibilities which the Great Mother has been hiding in the darkness of her bosom. For only Divine Love can soften the hard conditions in our natures and lives and bring forth to perfection the sprouts of the Christ-life within.

Therefore, to make the element of water our servant, meditate upon the reality of the Divine Love that is poured out like water, expecting no return. Drink the physical water often during the day, and every time a sip is taken think of it as not only enabling the blood to dissolve and wash out all the impurities from our bodies, but think of its inner mystic potency as dissolving and washing away all selfishness, unkind thoughts and all impurities in our natures. Determine that we *will* correlate with the power of the Divine Mother and wash from our lives everything that is retarding the putting forth of our spiritual life, no matter how hard and dark may be the conditions we find either in ourselves or in our environment.

The element air represents the Breath of the Spirit which must move on the face of the waters of our lives. For while Love, even in its physical aspect, is an aspect of the Water of Life, softening, cleansing and purifying, still, only as the Breath of the Spirit moves upon it and blows from it the mists of selfishness, self-seeking and animal desire—the determination to be loved rather than to love—can the Waters of Life (Love) become the universal solvent or Alkahest. Only when the Spirit moves upon the face of the waters are we ready to say, "Let there be light," and have the fire—in its highest aspect of Light—enter into our hearts and lives.

Every school of occultism recognizes the importance of

the breath, but it must be the real spiritual breath and not merely the physical that is inhaled, for no amount of mere physical breathing exercises can awaken our spiritual faculties. Only a realization of the mystic power of the air we have herein set forth can make the breath our servant to unfold within us the mystic life.[2] In correlating with the inner mystery of the air and making it our servant, strict attention should be given to keeping the physical breath pure and sweet and in not allowing it to become polluted with the effluvia and impurities which should be carried off greatly diluted or through other channels. Nor must the breath be polluted by using it to utter unkind or impure words.

We should breathe deeply when out of doors, and as we breathe in the air make it our servant to carry to every tissue and cell in our bodies the spiritual as well as the physical oxygen.

A good rhythmic exercise, in this connection, to take while walking outdoors is to breathe deeply while you take four brisk steps, saying to yourself the following words, one for each step: "I breathe in life." Retain the air in the lungs while you take the next four steps as you repeat: "God is in me." Breathe out during the next four steps, repeating: "I breathe out love." Hold the lungs empty during the next four steps while you say: "I thank my God." Then begin the cycle over again. This may be repeated for several minutes until you feel fully charged, not only with the fresh air, but with the consciousness of God's life filling and overflowing through you to all you contact. In fact, recognize that back of the physical manifestation the air is truly the Breath of the Spirit.

Of all elements, fire, or the Flame, is the king, or, we might say, the upper servant who controls and rules the others. There is an old adage that children should not play with fire. And if this be true upon the physical plane with the outermost garment of this sacred element, how much

---

[2] See *The Mystic Life*, Curtiss.

more true is it when we enter the aura of the Divine Flame itself and catch a mental glimpse, if not a realization, of its surpassing radiance! For within each heart, and in the midst of every life, there is a reflection of the Flame which burns eternally upon the altar of the Most High, the great All-seeing Eye, whose fiery glance penetrates to the inmost secrets of the heart.

Hence they are no vain words that are used when we invoke the elements. We cannot worship this Divine Flame if we have not erected an altar of truth and purity in our hearts and lives, for it is like a physical fire. Unless the chimney is unobstructed, and we are careful to see that the fire is kindled upon the hearthstone, the fire will become destructive, our home will be burned and our most cherished possessions consumed. This law is so well known and fire is held in such respect that on the physical plane no one presumes to take liberties with it, for while well regulated it is a good servant, it is a terrible taskmaster. Hence it takes little thought to understand that if fire can be so disastrous on Earth, yet so useful, comforting and cheerful when properly used, so on the higher planes its proper use can be proportionately helpful and its misuse proportionately disastrous.

To correlate with the Divine Flame realize that it is the Radiance of Divinity shining in our hearts, the Jewel in the Lotus, or the glow of the Spiritual Life-force surging through our hearts; for during life a golden Soul-glow, composed of myriads of dancing points of light, is focused in the heart and shines in the blood. But when the Soul withdraws from the body no trace of this fire or light can be found and the body becomes cold and lifeless.

The forces of the elements should not be invoked carelessly. One of the saddest things in life is to see students uttering the most sacred words and vows with little understanding of the forces they are invoking. Yet, beloved, no Master, Being or God on any plane can give us that understanding unless the Flame of Divine Potency has entered into our hearts and lit the fires upon our altars. Perhaps we come to worship at this holy shrine with an intellectual receptivity for Divine Truth, perhaps eager to know and understand, but with little realization of the underlying mystery of its potency, hence the world finds little difference in our lives.

On the other hand there comes into our lives many great and unexpected trials. To one comes sickness, and the very foundations of his life seem dissolved. To another comes the stress of poverty, the loss of friends or physical disaster, until he may think that there is some personal force working against him and he blames the "evil powers" or the "black brotherhood." But understanding the Law it is plain to see that this is not the explanation. It is simply that he has invoked the Living Fire, has invoked the Divine Elements and has asked that the Flame be his servant—the Flame which on the spiritual plane is the great Eye of the Eternal searching the Soul, and on the psychic plane is a consuming fire, and on the physical plane disintegration of old conditions, on all planes working as his servant to purify and spiritualise his life. Therefore, unless we have made preparation for the Flame by erecting an altar within our hearts and placing upon it the things we desire consumed, we must expect disaster. If we wish to bake bread and light our fire upon the floor instead of beneath the oven, ought we to be surprised if the house burned down and the bread refused to bake and came forth from the burning but a charred and blackened lump of dough?

We hear many talk of the great sacrifices they are willing to lay upon the altar: but have they fully considered what fuel is needed to consume them? For, know well, that when the Divine Flame touches our lives it becomes a consuming fire unless we have prepared for it. And unless we have laid the fuel so that it may burn steadily and in the right place to consume our sacrifices, our whole life is sub-

ject to conflagration. This generally begins with the physical
body and physical conditions, especially when we invoke the
Eternal Flame to consume all traces of evil and impurity. By every
such invocation we place a match to the tinder, and unless we
have supplied the fuel of love, obedience, humility and childlike
confidence, we may expect the Flame to sweep over us and
consume many things to which we have clung in the past. But,
beloved, it is not always necessary or desirable that our lives
should be made desolate or that we should pass through such fiery
trials to purify ourselves, to test our sincerity and faith or to push
us onward toward our goal. Such conflagrations are the natural
phenomena of our invocations, as natural as the conflagration
that would follow if we lit a fire on the floor instead of on the
hearthstone.

How then are we to invoke the Flame in our lives? Are we to
stand aloof because it is too dangerous? If we say, "I will stay out
in the cold for fear of the fire," we will find the cold is death. *First
banish fear*. Then boldly enter the sanctuary of our hearts and face
the Flame upon the altar. When we have done this, like the three
prophets of old when cast into the fiery furnace, we will find the
Christ walking with us. To invoke this Flame in safety repeat the
following *Prayer for Light* on awakening in the morning and ere
you drop asleep at night, and many times during the day.

O Christ! Light Thou within my heart
The Flame of Divine Love and Wisdom,
That I may dwell forever in the radiance of Thy countenance
And rest in the Light of Thy smile.

Visualize the descent of this Light as the beam of a great
searchlight pouring down upon you from above. See it
shine round about you in a great circle of Light, the "Ring
Pass Not" within which no inharmonious thing can pene-

trate without being consumed by that Divine Fire. Then see it illumine your mind, expand your consciousness and deepen your understanding of life. Then see that Light illumine your heart with its golden glow, sending an actual glow of warmth throughout your physical body, purifying, transmuting and spiritualizing the very atoms of your flesh by its spiritual radio-activity. Then think of the smile which the Divine One turns on all those who tune in to His consciousness through the aspirations of their hearts. And rest in the joy of that smile.

Pray that the Light of the Divine, the Flame of Divine Potency, be lighted in your heart, and as you go out into the world, strive to become a Light-bearer. How often have you talked of your desire to be Light-bearers! Yet you have but lighted a lantern and walked along in the darkness holding it in front of you for the world to see. Have you ever walked in the darkness with the light of a lantern shining directly into your eyes without stumbling? Yet you go along blindly, thinking how the world sees your lantern and is following you. But there is a more excellent way. Make your personality the lantern and let your whole being become so transparent that the radiance of the creativeness of the Christ shall illumine you and shine forth. Then you will no longer be holding up a lantern for the world to see, nor will the light you are trying to show forth blind your eyes and cause you to stumble. Then there will be no more effort, no holding up of a lantern and weeping bitterly because the world gives no heed. "Let your light so shine before men that they may see your good works, and glorify your Father which is in heaven."

Just go about your Father's business, each day accomplishing the tasks that are yours. Make your dwelling place within the radiance of the countenance of the Christ, each day doing the little things, bright eyed, clear visioned and *with a cheerful countenance*, seeing the stones and ruts in your path, but able to see how to step over or around them because the Light within your heart has become the Light of your world, combining Love and Wisdom. Let the Light of the Christ, the Flame of Divine Ecstasy in your heart show forth its radiance in your life, then rest. Rest, knowing that even if you sleep the smile of the Christ is over you, guarding and protecting you, even as a smiling mother watches by the cradle of her babe.

Fire is a power which comes to Earth through the Sun, but in you it is the Sun of Righteousness, the Christ-force, which must be sent forth with such power that it shall descend into the depths of your earth-conditions and carrying with it the forces of the water and the air, bring forth your divine possibilities. Fire was given to man alone of all the creatures, and there is not a beast of the jungle which cannot be subdued if you wave a firebrand in its face. This is also true of the Beast which rules the jungle of earth-conditions today. It cannot stand if you wave the Flame of the Christ-light in its face. If each of you earnest students will remember that this Flame is a power given you as a servant with which to conquer and accomplish, and if you will unite in its use, you can free yourself from the hampering physical conditions with which the Beast is fighting your development and success.

Every time you meditate, enter the Silence or turn your thoughts to this Order, wave in the face of the Beast the Flame of Divine Love and Wisdom and say: "We shall be free! We shall be free! All hampering physical conditions shall disappear, that both I and the Order may be free to accomplish more perfectly our great mission for humanity."[3] This is an exercise in practical occultism of great importance.

Do not expect the Masters to furnish material conditions for the spread of the work. They will not; for it is within *your* power to create them. The elements are your servants to bring forth the crops of increase, the rain of plenty, the

---

[3] *Prayers of the O. C. M.*, Curtiss, 14.

air of rejuvenation and the Flame of Divine Love and Wisdom. Therefore *Dare* to claim your heritage as Sons of God. *Do* your duty as creators. And *Keep Silent* as you protect the Flame from the winds of adversity.

Many of you have made great progress since you entered the radiance of this Order. You have made progress because you have turned your eyes toward the Light within, have forgotten your personalities, cast aside your lantern and lit the Flame in your hearts, and like little children are nestling in the smile of the Christ. This lesson is given you as a staff in your hands, showing you how to accomplish. Remember that the gift of the Holy Ghost is the power to light the Flame in your heart, to rest in the smile of the Christ. Let each one make the above *Prayer for Light* his own. Repeat it day by day and hour by hour. For you cannot repeat it regularly without its mystic meaning entering into your consciousness and its radiance illuminating the dark places of your own life, and that of the Order.

Chapter XXI

MAN AND THE ELEMENTALS

Part I. Earth and Water

"The Elementals are the various orders of entitized nature forces which, obeying the will of the Creative Hierarchies, bring into material manifestation the details of the Grand Plan of the Universe. In other words, they are the means by which the Divine Life-essence expresses the ideals in the Divine Mind through form. . . . These rudimentary elemental lives are the very essence of the physical substances themselves, and their life manifestations give to the various forms of matter their characteristic properties." *Realms of the Living Dead*, Curtiss, 158-159.

"Man is composed-of all the Great Elements—Fire, Air, Water, Earth and Ether—the Elementals which respectively belong to these Elements feel attracted to man by reason of their co-essence." *The Secret Doctrine*, Blavatsky, II, 313.

Since man is a Cosmos in miniature, an epitome of the universe, his body must contain the essence of all the elements of the Cosmos. And since the injunction "Man, know thyself," is written over the portal of the First Gate on the Path of Attainment, and since we must have some comprehension of its significance ere we can intelligently follow that Path, in this chapter let us consider how we should strive to know ourselves in relation to the elemental lives which go to make up our bodies and which play such an important part in our lives, that we may learn to work in harmony with and rule them. These elemental lives differ in each human being, thus making each person a separate and distinct expression of God and His forces and substance which each one manifests in varying degrees.

The statement that man's body is made "out of the dust

of the ground" means that the same elemental forces which both fashion and compose the Earth also fashion and indwell in his body. These elemental lives are far more than insensate mechanical and chemical "forces of Nature" as science calls them. They are sentient atomic or electronic lives; as sentient, if not more so, as the myriad living animal-culae revealed by the microscope in a drop of water. "The Elementals, the Nature-forces, are the acting, though invisible or rather imperceptible, secondary causes, and in themselves the effects of primary causes, behind the veil of all terrestrial phenomena."[1]

Again, we are told, "Nature-Spirits or Elementals of countless kinds and varieties; from the formless and unsubstantial—the ideal Thoughts of their creators—down to the atomic, though to human perception, invisible organisms . . . . are considered as the 'spirits of atoms,' for they are the first removed (backward) from the physical atom—sentient if not intelligent creatures. They are all subject to Karma, and have to work it out through every cycle."[2] "In general they are divided into four great kingdoms, each under the direction of a great Master belonging to one of the creative Hierarchies (the Sixth). These four kingdoms are Earth, whose elementals are called Gnomes; Water, whose elementals are called Undines; Air, whose elementals are called Sylphs; and Fire, whose elementals are called Salamanders. Each of these four divisions is broken up into many races and tribes, each with its own characteristics."[3]

Among the old Alchemists the necessity of recognizing the various tribes of these living elemental lives and of working in harmony with them was well known and was given due importance in the accomplishment of their Great Work. And only as these living forces were first invoked and then

---

[1] *The Secret Doctrine*, Blavatsky, I, 170.

[2] *Ibid*, Vol. I, 241.

[3] *Realms of the Living Dead*, Curtiss, 158. Also look up "Elementals" in the index of "The Curtis Books." See also "The Great Work." Chapter XVIII herein.

made the servants of the alchemist and obedient to his will, could he perform the great transmutation of base metals of his lower physical nature into the pure gold of his Divine Indweller. This is the true symbolic meaning of the victory of Spirit over matter, the spiritual over the animal man. The time is drawing near when there will be great changes in the Earth and its forces, and as these Nature Spirits or elementals will also be involved, it is wise for us to know how to recognize, correlate with and control them. Such recognition gives them great joy, and they are easily controlled through kindness and love.

In certain mystic ceremonies the earth elementals were invoked and controlled under the symbol of Salt.[4] Salt symbolizes and is the vehicle for the forces of purgation, purification and preservation, and without it neither the life of man or beast can be sustained, the only animals which do not crave and eat salt directly being the flesh-eaters of various kinds which obtain sufficient quantities in their food. In reality salt represents a radiant aspect of the Divine Life-force which is necessary for the life of the planet, as well as the proper development and maintenance of man's physical body, being necessary to maintain the fluidity of his blood, etc. Since the Earth was prepared for the manifestation of man, it lacks nothing that is necessary for his support, growth and perfection. All these substances are built into the Earth by the earth elementals, but man must learn to correlate with the elementals and thus more consciously and harmoniously appropriate and assimilate the essence of their forces.

Jesus says of those who manifest the Christ-force, "Ye are the salt of the earth: but if the salt have lost his savor, wherewith shall it be salted?" One interpretation of this saying is that just as salt sustains life in the earth—the earth being barren where salt is absent as surely as where it is in excess—so must the true follower of the Christ mani-

---

[4] See "The Symbol of the Salt" in *The Voice of Isis*, Curtiss, 386.

fest the ever-renewing Spiritual life-force in himself and in
the religion which he professes—yet not over-salt them with
fanaticism—or both his life and his religion will lose their savor
or that inner spiritual force which characterizes them and makes
them vital. For if kindness and brotherly love fail in us then our
mystical salt has lost its savor.

Like the Arabs, who sacredly consider as a brother one with
whom they have eaten salt, we should use the salt of purity,
spiritual oneness and the unity of thought to bind us to our fellow
men. In other words, we should so salt our lives that they become
vehicles through which the Christ-force can draw all we contact
closer to the Heart of Divine Love. For just as the physical heart
requires a definite percentage of salt in the blood to keep it so
liquefied and fluid that the heart can properly pump it to every
tissue in the body, so the Heart of Divine Love, which is the
Spiritual Heart from which all love flows and to which it must
return, requires the presence of all who recognize the significance
of the salt and who determine to be "the salt of the earth" and
not lose their savour, ere that current of Divine Love can freely
circulate and vitalize the body of humanity.

The earth elementals are, therefore, living forces of which salt
is but one symbol, namely, the forces of purgation, purification
and preservation, which lend their forces to the earth, and the
earth in return gives back to them the essences on which they
live. We must realize that the earth is not mere lifeless material,
but is charged with various kinds of radiant energies, forces
and lives, all of which are built into our bodies. And since
man is made in the image of God he must ultimately become
the Lord of Creation. But to evolve to that ultimate attainment
he must recognize, correlate with and control the hierarchies
of lesser lives in his body over which he is to rule, and make
them obedient to his spiritualized will; for like all servants they
will neither obey nor work efficiently for an ignorant master.
Man is destined to become one of the Creative Hierarchies, and

even now he creates both good and evil through thought, altho now more or less unconsciously.

"The Celestial Hierarchy (Sixth) of the present Manvantara will find itself transferred, in the next Circle of Life, into higher superior Worlds, and will make room for a new Hierarchy, composed of the Elect ones of our mankind."[5] It is this Sixth Celestial Hierarchy which is now ruling in the physical realms and from which man derives all but his highest and his lowest principles, his Spirit and body.

The earth elementals build into man's body the many tissue or cell salts, a proper proportion of each being necessary to bodily health and vigour, and these salts are the mineralized aspects of corresponding spiritual forces which work through them to purify, refine and spiritualise our flesh. If we realize that these spiritual forces are universal they can be utilized to help draw us closer to the Heart of the Universe. And we will then understand something of our relation with and what we owe to the earth elementals, for the salts are informed and manipulated by them. This understanding should awaken in us both love and gratitude for the unrecognized help they continually give us, and through this love and understanding we can correlate with and rule them more easily and completely than if we attempt it through will alone.

As we rule these forces within us in perfect harmony we help to harmonize and uplift the whole Earth; for the influence of our harmonized life radiates from us infinitely in all directions and in all realms. When we learn to rule one element in ourselves that element becomes our servant wherever it may be found. Hence, as we really know and rule ourselves we also rule the Earth. When we reach this stage of self-mastery we will recognize that because our body is made of the same substance as the Earth or is "of the earth, earthy," the currents of Earth magnetism and life-

---

[5] *The Secret Doctrine*, Blavatsky, I, 242.

force are flowing through us and charging us with physical vitality or one aspect of the One Life which animates all things, and without that physical magnetism and vitality we are physically depleted, mentally negative, psychically open to invasion by discarnate intelligences, and spiritually more or less deficient.

The above is to be distinguished from those spiritual night-periods of the Soul when nothing of Earth attracts us; when we seem to be like a dying flower, no longer able to drink in earthly joys, and everything seems dark and cheerless. These are night- or winter-periods of the Soul. But if the roots of our spiritual realization are planted deep in the soil of truth and are watered with Divine Love, a new day-period or spiritual springtime is as sure to follow as in Nature and bring forth the blossoms of new spiritual unfoldment.

After we have reached a certain stage on the Path to Mastery we cannot advance further until we recognize the relation of our physical body to the earth elementals and our duty to them and to the Earth itself, namely, to radiate to and permeate them with the higher mental and spiritual forces which as Sons of God we should be expressing for the help, uplift and advancement of everything we contact.

Therefore, every time we come in close contact with the earth, whether lying, sitting or walking upon it, we should quietly meditate and enter into close communion with it, realizing that the earth is that aspect of the Divine Mother in the darkness of whose bosom the seeds of all life are germinated, and in our lives represents the inner Temple of Silence, pregnant with the forces of all the elements, in which the germs of all our godlike possibilities are nourished until they come forth in our lives as blossoms and fruits of the Spirit.

But without water the Earth is barren. And as we see in the description of Eden[6] —symbolizing the perfected Earth,

---

[6] See *The Truth About Evolution and the Bible*, Curtiss, Chapter IX.

also man's perfected and spiritualized body—given in the *Bible*,
the Lord (Law) never intended the Earth to be barren, for He made
four great rivers to water the whole land. And this element is also
made up of myriad lives. Man uses water to quench his thirst,
refresh him when weary, to cleanse and purify, to generate power,
etc. Water symbolizes the love aspect of the Divine Mother, as
earth does the nourishing aspect; that which beautifies the Earth
and in man brings forth his spiritual qualities.

When man became fully materialized and he took the law into
his own hands and refused to let Divine Love flow through his
heart and manifest in his life unimpeded, the waters of the Earth
grew less and less until vast deserts appeared, just as similar
deserts appear in our lives for the same reason. The myriad tribes
of the water elementals were grieved at being denied their former
field of manifestation and became more or less antagonistic to
man, for their chief instinct is to moisten the earth and help it
to bring forth, also to purify and bless man. Hence they fight
against the personal will of man and against the inharmonies and
impurities with which he has cursed the Earth and so diverted
them from their mission. Therefore, only as man correlates with
and properly utilizes both Divine Love and its physical symbol,
water, can he make the Undines his glad helpers and willing
servants. Until he does this the water will flow from his eyes as the
bitter tears of sorrow, suffering and repentance, and no permanent
happiness will be his. Hence we are told that, "Before the eyes
can see (spiritual realities) they must be incapable of tears," or
the life must be so purified that tears of sorrow and suffering will
no longer manifest.

In the beginning "there went up a mist from the earth,
and watered the whole face of the ground," but after man
had cursed the Earth, many parts of the land had to sink
beneath the water to be purified[7] so the waters were diverted

---

[7] See "An Undine's Prophecy" in *Realms of the Living Dead*, Curtiss, 174.

from their former relations to the land. And since that time the proper re-distribution of the waters necessary to make "the desert blossom as the rose" has been left to man and so again became subject to his perversion and pollution. And how often have we seen man use all his powers of brain and brawn to impound the waters and compel them to obey his will! When such works are conceived in the spirit of true helpfulness and co-operation for the benefit of both man and Nature, and constructed in fairness and honesty, what a blessing they bring to the land and to those who till and live upon it! They thus help to redeem the curse. Yet when such works are conceived in selfishness and with the idea of exploiting those who need the water, or when the construction is dominated by greed, graft and profiteering how often do such structures fail or the dams burst and cause devastating floods which spread ruin and death over the land! And since all helped to create the Race Karma, many seemingly innocent ones must suffer.

The great flood which is mentioned in the allegory of Noah resulted from similar causes of inharmony and impurity set up by the peoples of the early Races, and similar results will always follow similar causes, varying only in manner and degree. Noah, "a man after God's own heart," was commanded to build an ark which would ride the turbulent waters in safety. Into it he took his family and all the beasts, birds and reptiles that he could influence and guide, and all were saved to re-stock the Earth. Noah, or that which he symbolizes, still lives today, and each one who can hear the command of the Lord (Law) and is willing to obey, must build and perfect his ark (body) so that the forces of all the lower kingdoms (elementals) may enter in and ride out the storms of life in safety.

All such disasters could be avoided if man planned and worked in the true spirit of co-operation with Nature and with his fellow men, recognizing that the elementals, born from the essence of Divine Love, can be controlled only by the law of harmony and love; for they obey only one who builds his ark and fills it with the radiance of the Christ and rests calmly in the arms of Divine Love. When a majority of mankind grasps this fundamental idea of consciously working with the living forces of Nature then, and then only, will the desert places of life blossom as the rose and the four great mystical rivers which flow throughout Eden[8] become the foundation for a new "mist" which shall water the whole Earth, not a physical mist, but the soft radiance of Divine Love filling the hearts of men and resulting on Earth as a perfect distribution of land and water, because of man's correlation and co-operation with the elementals.

To help accomplish this, every time we see water let us think of the great power of Divine Love to bring forth in us our highest ideals. Every time we drink let us sip slowly, realizing that every sip of water adds just that much fluid to our blood, thinning it and enabling it the better to carry refreshment and nourishment to all our tissues and to dissolve and wash from them all impurities and worn out atoms, and eliminate from our bodies all impediments to the flow of the higher forces.

Then let us realize that we, like the elements, have a mighty work to do in the expressing of the Grand Plan of Manifestation, which work we can accomplish only as we work in harmony with the Law. While our personality may seem to be but an obscure tiny life, one tiny drop of water in the sea of humanity, *yet it can be an avenue* through which the mighty stream of Divine Love can flow more fully over the desert of physical existence to make it blossom as the rose. For some day all the desert places must be reclaimed by the waters of the four great mystical rivers. And altho we may be but tiny drops we can bring cheer, refreshment and help to all we contact. And as we grow

---

[8]   For details see *The Truth About Evolution and the Bible*, Curtiss, 97-101.

and flow and refresh and comfort, to that extent we help the great streams of Divine Life and Love to redeem the waste places of physical existence as irrigation does the desert.

(To be continued)

CHAPTER **XXII**

MAN AND THE ELEMENTALS

PART II. THE AIR[1]

"Fire, Air, Water, Earth, were but the visible garb, the symbols of the informing, invisible Souls or Spirits. . . . In their turn, the phenomenal subdivisions of the nomenal Elements were informed by the Elementals, the Nature-Spirits of lower grades. . . . The intimate connection of these Elementals, guided by the unerring hand of the Rulers, with the elements of pure Matter—their correlation we might call it—results in our terrestrial phenomena, such as light, heat, electricity, etc." *The Secret Doctrine*, Blavatsky, I, 498, 17.

While the elementals which form the foundation of the manifested universe fall into four distinct groups, Fire, Air, Water, Earth, nevertheless each of these groups has its seven subdivisions, and performs seven distinct functions. As given by *The Secret Doctrine*, these functions are cohesion, fluxation, coagulation, accumulation, station and division. Hence in each element there are certain tribes which are specialized to perform each of these functions. For instance, among the Gnomes cohesion has to do with the aggregation of atoms into the various rocks and minerals; among the Undines putting various substances into solution and thus sorting them out from their former condition and massing them together; among the Sylphs this is performed by evaporation, which leaves behind a solid residue; among the Salamanders cohesion is accomplished through melting into a homogeneous mass; and so on through all the seven functions. In this way the Earth, which was once a seething

---

[1] See *Realms of the Living Dead*, Curtiss, 157-177, also the references to Elementals in the other Curtiss Books.

chaotic mass, is differentiated into its various aspects which underlie the beauty and symmetry of Nature as we see it today. Fire and Air are considered as manifestors of the Father-force of the Godhead or the Progenitor, while Water and Earth represent the Divine Mother-force or the Bringer-forth.

As in Nature, so in man; for in man's body all the constituent elements of Nature can be found, with their fundamental properties. "For instance, if man has a preponderance of the earthly, gnomic Element, the Gnomes will lead him towards the assimilation of metals . . . . and so on."[2] Hence, only as man recognizes that the elementals are the forces chosen to bring about a perfect blending of the four fundamental elements, and through his higher intelligence correlates, co-operates with and guides them, through his ideals and principles of life, can perfect health, beauty and the true Image of God be expressed through his physical organism. For the Divine Ray from the Omnipotent Godhead which constitutes man's Divine or Higher Self, in order to manifest on Earth must be clothed in a body made up of the four elemental kingdoms, after the manner of the Earth itself, but with the vital difference that man is far more than his body. The body is of the Earth earthy, but the mind is a reflection from the Divine Mind in the Mental World, with its seven realms, whose substance is pure thought, while the Spirit of man is a direct emanation from God Himself.

Because man thus contains the forces of all the four elemental kingdoms, it is possible for him to rule the elementals, first in his own body and then in the Universe. For once his consciousness has been illumined by the Spiritual Light of his Higher Self all the elemental forces automatically obey him.

We can work toward this point of attainment by an understanding of our relation to the forces of Nature, by a

---

[2] *The Secret Doctrine*, Blavatsky, I, 313.

deliberate choice and guidance of our thoughts, and especially through an inner determined seeking to know both the elemental characteristics which predominate in us and the ideals which our Higher Self is striving to manifest through us and the lessons it is therefore necessary for us to learn that we tread the path of our choice, make the attainment and accomplish the object for which we incarnated. Thus shall we be able to take our true place and accomplish our part in the Grand Plan of the Universe.

Altho in the earlier stages of our spiritual unfoldment the elementals have much to do in shaping our personal characteristics and affecting our emotions as we contact their realms, once we have made the union with our Higher Self the elementals no longer have any dominion or influence over us, but become our obedient servants and willing helpers.

In this brief outline of the elementals we have purposely begun the study with the Earth elementals and proceeded upward in the scale of vibration, altho Fire and Air are the first to manifest in the formation of the globe. We have done this in the hope that the subject would be more easily grasped if presented in this way, altho to thoroughly understand it, all that we have written on the subject, together with other supplementary reading, should be studied.

Each of the seven divisions of the Air elementals or Sylphs is composed of countless tribes, each with its special work to do. Every type of Air, from the soft summer zephyr of land or sea to the devastating hurricanes, is sincerely seeking to accomplish its appointed work. And as we enter into the Aquarian Age, in which the Air will play an increasingly important part, we will be brought into closer touch with the Sylphs. We have already begun to conquer the Air and make it our servant, but we are apt to find it a very capricious, disobedient and dangerous servant until we truly learn how to take our place as God's representative and rule all the elemental forces both within and without. We will therefore try to explain certain fundamental principles which should enable those who are working with or in this element to understand it more fully.

We must understand first that the Sylphs, while naturally tender, gentle, pliable and rhythmic, are nevertheless powerful, inexorable and extremely vindictive when antagonized or when their laws are violated. Hence they should be treated much as we would treat a temperamental friend who is known to have similar characteristics. The Sylphs are more antagonistic toward man than the Gnomes or Undines, because man has made them so. Not only does man rend their element with the raucous and inharmonious noises of modern industrial and commercial enterprises—to say nothing of desecrating their domain with the shattering roar of cannon, the bursting of shells and bombs, and also by the fierce warfare in the air—but they are not accustomed to have man— whom they look upon as only in the infancy of his development and a much later inhabitant of the planet than themselves, and heretofore confined to its surface—presume to enter and traverse their domain.

The Sylphs are antagonistic also because man's presumptuous interference—through wrong breathing, impure thinking, vile or inharmonious speech, as well as the smells of his impure emanations and effluvia—has brought great inharmony and destruction into their domain. It is well to remember therefore that whatever taints the Air or the breath and makes it impure will bring corresponding suffering to myriads of these elemental lives; for as part of their work is to help purify that which is vile— especially that which give off bad smells—like brave warriors in countless myriads they must expend their very life-force in an effort to overcome the evil and purify the air. And, what is worse, in their efforts they may spread disease, poisonous gases, noxious smells and impure air through the various currents of air, storms, etc.

Often those who are sensitive—especially to the Sylphs— or more or less psychic, suddenly smell a most obnoxious odor, altho there is nothing present physically which could produce it. This was most marked during the late World War, for it is an odor of death and decay which ascends into the higher air currents and by them is distributed around the world. In these higher currents the Sylphs purify it of all but its heavier residue which gradually sinks again to earth, but so diluted that it is practically but an astral smell and hence is recognized only by the sensitive. In the same way the odors and perfumes of trees, flowers and plants are distributed throughout the atmosphere and are absorbed by all forms of life with constructive and helpful results.

This is one reason why astral perfumes are often smelled by sensitives, altho such perfumes often indicate the presence of some spiritual Being whose emanations naturally have "the odour of sanctity." This is one of the reasons why we advise against the use of artificial perfumes.[3] Evil astral odours can be dissipated and purified by prayer, song and melodious sounds. The use of properly selected incense is also helpful.

Aviators especially should remember not only to keep the body in such perfect condition as to elimination of all wastes so that the breath is kept pure, but should also keep the thoughts pure, the emotions controlled and the temper serene, especially never to use profane or vile language, especially while flying, even under extreme provocation. Instead, they should learn to commune with the Sylphs in a friendly way both mentally and audibly when alone, either by talking to them or by singing some rhythmic melody, much as the cowboys chant by the hour to quiet their herds when restless because of an approaching storm, and as sailors are said to "whistle for a breeze." Since, "Esoteric Science teaches that every sound in the visible world awakens its corresponding sound in the invisible realms, and arouses to action some force or other on the occult side of Nature,"[4]

---

[3] *The Key of Destiny*, Curtiss, 162.
[4] *The Secret Doctrine*, Blavatsky, III, 451.

the above is by no means as fanciful as it may sound to one who knows nothing of Nature's unseen forces and whose opinion is therefore of little value. Its truth can easily be proved by putting it into practice.

It would also be well for aviators to realize that they are entering a domain which corresponds in many ways to thought or mental air whose currents, guided by living conscious entities, enter the brain of Nature to make it—when not perverted by man—a mirror or materialization of the Grand Plan in the Divine Mind. The Air corresponds to thought for one reason in that it must ever be in motion. Altho energizing every function of Nature—for all things breathe or utilize oxygen in some form, save certain anaerobic bacteria which utilize other gases—yet it cannot be confined for long and still retain its life-giving powers. It must ever be in circulation, now penetrating the earth to give life to the smallest seed, again reaching up to heaven and drawing renewed life from the Sun, now entering the lungs and being carried throughout the body of the tiniest of creatures and of man, now circling through the Universe and bringing back mysterious forces from unknown spheres. It is Air, in its higher aspects as ether, electricity and even Akasha, that implants the mystic germ or vortex of life-force—the Christ-force—in all things.

Just as we breathe in the Air and through its control bring about a perfect transmutation of our food into tissue, energy, etc., so must we do with our minds; for thought is mental Air, and in our higher bodies we must control and direct it into proper channels or they will be poisoned. If we breathe impure Air our physical body is poisoned and our mind beclouded. Similarly, if we allow impure thought currents to flow through our minds our mental body will be poisoned and our mind perverted.

All elementals respond to certain rhythms, each class and tribe having its characteristic vibrations, both constructive and destructive. Because of this fact, through experience the very few persons who can contact the elementals consciously can tell not only which class of elementals is present, but also when one tribe goes and another takes its place, and even a particular tribal ruler can thus be recognized.[5] Such elemental rhythms are often reproduced in the body of the sensitive. They also appear in certain types of poetry such as the so-called "bucolic" type. But the Sylphs are especially responsive to sound, particularly of the voice and all wind instruments which produce Nature notes.

Among the earliest representations of the Lord Krishna one is as the Beloved, the Flute-player, whose breath is the Divine and whose Flute is the Heart of Man. And among the natives of India, especially among the hill-tribes of Sikkim, Nepaul, Bhutan and Kashmir, the reed flute has been used with marvelous effect from the time "when God first taught man to make paths in the jungles," not only to express the longings and emotions of the player, but also to propitiate or harmonize the various Nature elementals and to protect the player and his people. "The hill-flute sounds in the still evening air from distant mountain-sides with an indescribable wild-bird note, plaintive, questioning and, to western ears, completely unresolved, which expresses perfectly whatever of elemental sadness is in the forest."[6] Among the Lepchas of Sikkim there are three types of flute, the lingbufeniam, the lingbunemia and the tolling. "The oldest is the lingbufeniam, which is, in fact the original form of the hill-flute . . . . It is handed down from father to son as a treasured family possession and is naturally regarded as the special instrument of the patriarch of the family. . . . It has the property of being able to protect him on a journey in wild, unknown parts of the forest, where nature-spirits have full sway. . . . Different melodies are used for hills, lakes and rivers."[6] It is well known to those versed in mystic lore that the

---

[5] See *Realms of the Living Dead*, Curtiss, Chapter XIV.
[6] *Echoes of Himalayan Flutes*, Brown.

vibrations of certain kinds of music—particularly that produced by the voice and by wind instruments—can not only charm serpents, quiet both animals and man, but can also dispel storms, dissipate and prevent diseases—especially those borne by the Air—and prevent others from precipitating out of the astral. In fact, there is in this country today a steadily growing musical therapy being developed for the scientific treatment of disease by music.

From the above we can see that it was not entirely the ignorant superstition of the Middle Ages which caused processions of trained monks to pass through districts which were stricken with plague and other virulent epidemics, chanting certain specially selected airs, and while burying the dead. Altho living in its very midst they did not contract the disease. This was, firstly, because of the tranquillity of their minds, owing to their harmony and faith, which dispelled that fear which paralyses all the forces of man's natural immunity which normally protects him from all disease, and secondly, because the vibration of the music—also the symbols carried—not only directly killed the disease germs through destructive vibration, but incited to action certain warrior tribes of elementals which responded to their rhythm and helped to destroy the disease. In fact, in *The Secret Doctrine*[7] Madame Blavatsky tells us that she was "saved thrice from death" through the occult use of sound.

In certain temples in India a special class of priests are trained to chant occult mantra in certain melodies to the accompaniment of the vina, which have marvelous healing and other magical properties owing to the elemental forces—largely the Sylphs— which they invoke. Such melodies are considered as sacred, and their use is confined to a hereditary cast which is trained to understand the forces thus invoked and how to direct them, as it is considered dangerous for those who are not so trained to use them. In

[7] *Vol.* I, 606.

this there is much of truth, for having been brought up and trained from childhood in this mystic science, their spiritual and psychic development enables them to correlate with and direct the elementals in the accomplishment of their marvelous results.

The above gives us a glimpse of one aspect of the scientific processes back of the forces at work when music is used in religious services. It is also one of the reasons why music is used at all the healing services of this Order, especially the service used each day at noon when the great currents of spiritual force are broadcast to all humanity in all parts of the world. They are also especially focused on those who have asked for the help of the Order and who are mentally and spiritually tuning in to its radiance.

On the contrary, broken or syncopated rhythms, such as the so-called jazz, are almost maddening to the elementals—particularly to the Sylphs and Gnomes—who quite naturally retaliate on man by reproducing in him corresponding vibrations which incite him to a wild desire for further excitement and to a recklessness which may be carried to the extreme of committing crime almost unthinkingly and before he is really aware of what the consequence will be. Such crimes must be classed with those of "irresistible impulse" due to obsession by disembodied criminals,[8] altho in the former case it is due to obsession by elemental forces of the disharmony generated by man himself. In Nature inharmonious sounds and syncopated rhythms add their destructive forces to other forms of inharmony and evil created by man, which ultimately find expression in all kinds of storms, pestilences and even earthquakes,[9] for of all the elementals the Gnomes and Sylphs are most readily incited to destructive action by broken rhythmic cadences and inharmonious sounds.

The Sylphs should be man's greatest helpers, or let us

---

[8] See *Realms of the Living Dead*, Curtiss, 112.
[9] See *The Voice of Isis*, Curtiss, 172.

say upper servants, for one feature of their work is to help implant in man's consciousness the great truth that he can breathe in higher and finer ethers and spiritual and occult forces for the purification and uplifting of both body and mind. Hence these tiny elemental lives are forever seeking to fan into Flame in his heart and life that Spark of Divine Fire which must unite him to the higher worlds. Yet both Sylphs and Salamanders are called the "devourers," because they ultimately devour or destroy all that hinders the completion of evolution and the perfect unfolding and expression of the Divine in man. In some of man's misguided philosophy fire and violent winds are related to hell, for hell is pictured as a place of eternal flames and violent winds, of weeping and wailing and gnashing of teeth, yet the Sylphs and the Salamanders are the most spiritually helpful of all the elementals.

(To be concluded)

Chapter XXIII

MAN AND THE ELEMENTALS

Part III. The Fire

"Fire is the most perfect and unadulterated reflection, in Heaven as on Earth, of the One Flame. It is Life and Death, the origin and end of every material thing. It is Divine Substance." *Secret Doctrine,* Blavatsky, III, 146.

"Tradition shows the celestial Yogis offering themselves as voluntary victims in order to redeem humanity. . . . This voluntary sacrifice of the Fiery Angels, whose nature was Knowledge and Love, has been construed by the exoteric theologies into a statement that shows 'the Rebel Angels hurled down from Heaven into the darkness of Hell.' " *The Secret Doctrine*, Blavatsky, II, 257.

> "Teach us thy magic O Day Star of Light,
> That the seeds we have laid in the bosom of Earth,
> Tho watered by tears through the pitiless night,
> Shall, out of the sorrow, the cold and the gloom,
> At Thy shining forth burst into mystical bloom."
>
> *Harriette Augusta Curtiss.*

Although in the previous Chapters we have tried to give an outline of the Nature Elementals, the subject is so vast and intricate that we feel we have lifted but a corner of the veil. And now that we come to the Fire Elementals we are confronted with a task that seems almost hopeless in the space at our disposal; for before us we see veil after veil to be drawn aside ere more than an elementary comprehension of this great mystery can be revealed. Indeed we might say that here we find not only seven veils to be lifted, as with the other elementals, but seventy times seven.

Fire is not an Earth element at all. That which is known on Earth as Fire is but the lowest and outermost covering of the highest element, that which brought forth the manifested universe. And it is this lowest and grossest aspect which is manipulated by what are commonly called the Fire Elementals, altho' its higher forms have corresponding higher forms of elementals through which to work. It is not surprising then that the very heart of all great religions springs from the thought of Fire in one form or another, from the worship of the Sun as its source and the adoration of the perpetual Flame upon the altars of the Ancients to the Christian statement that "Our God is a consuming fire." And even today in the highest form of Fire, namely Divine Radiance which is Divine Life or Spiritual Fire, it still finds its place in our worship and is represented in many symbolic forms. The gift of Fire, as represented in the myth of Prometheus and the sufferings he endured as a result of bringing Fire to man, is the crux of all the various myths of the sacred Sun Gods.

The use of Fire, even in its lowest form, marks the line of differentiation between the lower animals and man; for all animals fear Fire, man alone controlling it as a servant, yet even then with fear and awe of its avenging power. "Fire is not an Element but a divine thing. The physical Flame is the objective vehicle of the highest Spirit."[1]

The elementals which work in and manipulate the physical Flame have very little consciousness on Earth, for their work is to reflect the consciousness and manifest certain forces of the higher realms. Hence they are the most difficult of all the elementals for man to contact. They accomplish their work by contacting and working through all the other elementals, all of which are their obedient servants when not interfered with by man. Therefore, for man to make the elementals his servants he must follow the advice given in the previous chapters, *i.e.*, from those of the Earth he must learn *humility* and *silence*, that stillness which permits the Fire from the Sun to be so tempered in the bosom of the Earth that it brings forth her fruits. From the water he must

---

[1] *The Secret Doctrine*, Blavatsky, III, 589

learn *unity*, *helpfulness* and *love*, ever striving to forget self that he may the more completely co-operate in God's Grand Plan of the Universe. From the air he must learn to *soar ever upward* nearer and nearer to Divinity. And through all of these he must sense the Divine Fire. Then indeed will the Fire fulfill its true destiny and express its inner life-essence to draw us closer to the Heart of Love.

In the text heading this chapter the mystical sacrifice of the so-called "Fiery Angels" does not really refer to angels at all, but to a class of superhuman Beings who correlated with the Spiritual Flame during eons of lives on other planetary chains and systems, yet who voluntarily incarnated upon this infant planet as Light Bringers to help on man's evolution. And there are many such now in incarnation, with varying degrees of realization and manifestation of their mission. But besides these comparatively few very advanced Souls, at the birth of each new planet there are hosts of Souls who are so affinitized to the conditions that planet will embody that they become children of the new planet because in past lives of more ethereal states of existence on other planets or systems they practically created the conditions which demanded a planet where greater density of body and other conditions could manifest. Hence, such a planet was created out of the leftovers of past systems by thoughts and desires so dense that no semi-material planet could express them. Hence the Earth was created not as a place of trial and cruel discipline where man was to be forced into submission through suffering, but in obedience to the Great Law "As a man thinketh in his heart so is he." Yet even here every help was given and every provision made for his advance Godward.

And when, through his experiences here, man is ready to say, "Thy will, not mine, be done," this planet will shine as a Day Star of living Fire surpassing all that have gone before. Just as the most precious jewels are formed in the dark, hard conditions of the Earth, created by the fierce flames that burn in her bosom, so will the divine Lord of Life, when He cometh to make up His jewels, find many in the darkest conditions where the fires of suffering have purified and made them fit for His crown.

The Fire elementals are tiny lives and centers of consciousness which exist in different degrees on all planes and interpenetrate all kingdoms. Since Fire is life, there being no life without some form of Fire—according to science absolute zero being the negation of both life and matter—we are told that God, the Source of all Life, is a consuming Fire. And since there can be no planet or realm where God is not, the Psalmist was quite correct when he said: "If I ascend up into heaven, thou art there: if I make my bed in hell, behold, thou art there. If I take the wings of the morning, and dwell in the uttermost parts of the sea; even there shall thy hand lead me, and thy right hand shall hold me."[2] Heaven is the state or condition in which the flames burn pure and bring healing in their wings, while hell has ever been expressed by the Sages as the state or condition in which the lower aspects of Fire, as a consuming Flame, destroy the evil and make way for a higher aspect of Divine Life. It is here on this Earth that the Fire elementals work and where the so-called fires of hell manifest in their outer aspect. Hence on the Earth-plane and in the lower astral realms is the only hell, except as man creates a lower hell by his belief in it and constant thought of it.

The lower Fire elementals are the emanations sent down by the "Gods of the Elementals" to manipulate and manifest the lowest aspect of the Flame in the chaotic conditions of the fiery stage of the planet in which they clothe themselves to do the bidding of the "Lords of the Flame." On Earth they take form and can be seen, by those whose inner sight is developed to their level, as the Salamanders who flit in the flames. Altho they possess but slight intelligence on the physical plane—by some they are said to have none—

---

[2] *Psalms*, CXXXIX, 8–10

nevertheless, because they interpenetrate everything, being the
spark of life in all, they contact all the different kinds and grades
of beings in all realms and so become aware of at least the general
vibration or trend of thought of man. They are related to the sense
of sight much as the air elementals are to sound. Just as through
sight our feelings can be aroused or we can sense the "feel" of
an object whether hard or soft, etc., and as through the sight of
moving lips the deaf can understand the meaning of sound, and
by the sight of food the salivary glands begin to secrete and we
arouse the sense of taste, in a similar way the fire elementals
vaguely sense the thoughts of man.

Through a peculiar form of transmutation the lower aspect of
Fire becomes the life-germ or fiery lives which dwell in every
atom of our physical body and give it the warmth of life. When
these fiery lives leave the body it grows cold in death, for the
Flame of Life has been withdrawn. While normally the fiery
lives bring warmth, health and happiness, they can also manifest
destructively in the burning fever of dread diseases of the physical
body, while in the mental world they burn as anger, passion and
unbalanced love, all of which burn up the heart. In the mental
world the Flame can also burn as altruism, philanthropy and love.
On the astral or desire plane it can burn destructively as intensified
earthly passions which seek to obsess and find expression through
weak or negative mortals, or, on the other hand, it can burn
constructively as ardour for helpful service to humanity.

At the present tune, the transmuting aspect of the Divine Flame
is burning throughout the world as a mighty destructive agent,
fanned by the inharmony and evil of "man's inhumanity to man"
and the great lack of the constructive forces of peace, harmony,
brotherliness and co-operation. In this connection there was recently
given to the Founders of the Order a prophecy from the King of the
underground kingdom of Agharte and called the King of the World,

and as it has to do with the spread of the transmuting Flame we will include it in this lesson.

PROPHECY FROM THE KING OF THE WORLD

"I see a great and devastating Flame sweeping the world from East to West; a Flame of fire; a Flame of sword and famine, of anger and murder and bitterness and death.

"I see the peoples of the Earth, each one with its hand lifted against its brother; each country seeking for its own; men dying, dying and cursing God with every dying breath and sowing the seed of new and more frightful Flames.

"I see descending from on high the mighty Angel with the Flaming Sword, for only fire can purify hate.

"I see this Flame of Purification sweeping the Earth from East to West, from the rising of the Sun to the going down of the Sun.

"Five countries are left; the rest sink beneath the seas.

"I see a great mountain lifted up in the midst of the countries which are left, and from its top there radiates the Light of the Spiritual Sun. And I see the remnants of mankind bathed in its Radiance.

"Five countries! Five lands like the fingers on a man's hand! Four shall be great and one small, but out of the smallest there grows the greatest Light; there comes redemption; there comes that which alone can make this world to be reborn, once more human, like a babe laid in a manger, cradled in its mother's arms.

"Think not that any country in this broad world can escape. The Flame sweeps onward and over. Only those who have the Flame of the Living Christ in their hearts shall survive.

"I speak, for this is my world. Into my hands it has been given. I stretch out my hand[3] and each finger represents

---

[3] This vision is fully explained in *Coming World Changes*, Curtiss, Chapter IV.

a point of force, a place where the great living Power of the Sun has breathed in it the life (Fire) which is immortal.

"Where are my children? They are dying. They are being murdered and starved. They are being scattered like sheep on the cold bare mountain tops, homeless, friendless. For a time I bow to the inevitable. I wait. I wait that a Greater than I may read to you the riddle of this Dark Star."

As we have explained elsewhere,[4] each planet of this system has a Divine Ruler who is the manipulator of that aspect of the Divine Flame which animates the planet. Mark well that such Planetary Spirits or Rulers are not to be confused with the various astrological rulers or Regents. Each of these Planetary Rulers is one of the seven-fold aspects of the one Godhead, one of the seven Elohim or Angels of the Presence mentioned so frequently in the *Bible*. They are differentiated aspects of the one God just as the seven color-rays are differentiated aspects of the one white Light, each color being the ruler over the special functions it is to manifest. The Divine White Light is the Flame which manifested the Earth. The Earth is the youngest of the planets and the latest habitation given to humanity to show their ability to meet tests which they have never met before.

Out of the bowels of each Planetary Spirit comes forth the substance with which to clothe the Souls specially chosen through karmic law to be those whom we call the "children" of that particular planet. There are many millions of Souls who thus belong to this planet, who are real Earth-children, whose Progenitor dwells within the most mysterious part of the planet and is the guardian of the great mystery of all mysteries. We call this Planetary Spirit their Progenitor because it is through His force that they are assimilated into the very essence of the planet and by Him breathed forth imbued with the characteristics of this planet. These are the Souls previously mentioned who so longed for a planet of dense material conditions and bodies of like material.

---

[4] Especially *The Key to the Universe*, Curtiss, 220-9.

They correspond with those today who are never satisfied except with those things which they can see, handle, dissect and analyze with their physical senses.

"In view of the above we can now understand why the destructive aspect of the Flame of Purification is spreading from the East to the West and will ultimately sweep all nations, each suffering according to the amount of inharmony, unbrotherliness, antagonism and evil there is to be consumed. We can correlate with the Flame and make the fire elementals our servants only as we strive to become one with the Divine Fire of the Living Christ and willingly allow it to burn from us all inharmony and impurity, all that holds back the manifestation of our Real or Divine Self."

"Once we have grasped the idea that the Flame consumes only that which is evil or which must be transmuted to make room for the Divine Life and Joy of those who fearlessly face self and bravely strive to conquer all that is not in harmony with the Law, then, like Shadrach, Meshach and Abednego, even though we seem bound hand and foot and thrown into the midst of the fiery furnace—the flames of purgation now sweeping the earth—when the morning of the New Day dawns we will be found walking free in the midst of the Flame because the Lord Christ walks with us.[5]

The above prophecy presents the picture as it stands today on the Screen of Time, but we are told that for the Elects' sake these days shall be shortened. Therefore those who elect to help shorten these days should send out their aspiration, love and compassion in constant prayer. If our *Prayer for World Harmony* is used,[6] pause after each sentence and meditate upon it, visualizing its radiance going out to all mankind, consuming the evil and stimulating all good. For it is only through softening the hearts of mankind, through the spread of the warmth of Divine Love and the power of the Living Christ, that the evil can be overcome and these days be shortened.

---

[5] *Coming World Changes*, Curtiss, 62.
[6] See *Appendix*.

Chapter XXIV

THE REALM OF BE-NESS

"The Visible that was, and the Invisible that is, rested in Eternal Non-Being. . . . This Infinite and Eternal Cause—is the Rootless Root of 'all that was, is or ever shall be.'. . . It is 'Be-ness' rather than Being." *The Secret Doctrine*, Blavatsky, I, 56, 42

"And be shewed me a pure river of water of life, clear as crystal, proceeding out of the throne of God and of the Lamb." *Revelation*, XXII, 1.

In this age of transition many of the things once considered not only important to salvation, but absolutely necessary to the living of a so-called spiritual life, have been pushed aside. Many, nevertheless, who truly desire to do right and who, like the Wise Men of old, are as eager to find and follow the Light of the Christ Star, search the heavens in vain. No such glory shines out. No angelic voices resound through the blackness of the night. In vain they wait for a phenomenal proof that all these wonders, once accepted without question, could possibly be true. Many are asking sadly and sorrowfully: "Has the Star of Bethlehem sunk forever into the dense darkness of this frivolous age?" Others, with a shrug of superiority, are saying: "We are past the days when childish stories and fables can be accepted as truth. Unless we can be shown something real and substantially true in religion we must make our own religion; since we are no longer children we must not be content with fable and tradition, but through understanding must formulate a wise and helpful concept of the truth."

As the festival of the birth of the Lord Christ approaches, let us try so to understand it that we can wisely explain it to all these hopeless yet heart-hungry unbelievers. As this wonderful Aquarian Age is slowly overshadowing the former Piscean Age many, many are beginning to understand mystical truths which they formerly saw only vaguely shining out of the darkness caused by the overlapping of the two Ages. Formerly we saw "as through a glass, darkly," but as the New Age emerges from the shadow of the old we will "see face to face."

This is the season in which to study and meditate upon the mystical truths of the wonderful *Bible* story; to "feed on them in our hearts with joy and thanksgiving," and do our best to live them in our lives; for only through our heart's realization can we wisely interpret them. The fact is that our beloved Christmas story is indeed mysteriously true. The watching shepherds, sitting humbly on the ground, symbolize those who, even though they do not know intellectually, yet believe, because they realize that this wonderful story is to be mystically understood. The flocks they are watching are the flocks of their own thoughts. The wolves they are guarding against are the prowling evil thoughts and desires of their own animal nature and the similar thought-currents of the community. Because of their loving trust in the Christ-power they are willing to sit patiently and humbly upon the ground, but high up on the Mount of Attainment where the night winds sing loving lullabies to their hearts and quiet their grazing sheep.

To all such who are sincerely trying to do their best the heavens open and bands of angels appear, singing, singing, forever singing. Through all the ages of oppression; through all the years of sorrow, of poverty, of human misunderstanding, ever have the heavens of spiritual realization opened and the never-ending song has been heard: "Glory to God in the highest and on Earth peace, good will toward men." But, alas, as yet, of those who know the truth in their innermost hearts but few dare to proclaim it abroad lest they be ridiculed. For as yet the Wise Men have only begun to plan their journey to find the cradled Babe who shall surely bring peace on Earth. But the Wise Men of this Age must be scientifically sure; must journey over steep and barren mountains and desolate deserts, and explore many deceptive, misleading trails, ere they can find the Child. For today, although the Child is lying in the manger of the heart of every one born into the world, for many it is still wrapped in swaddling clothes of misunderstanding and misconception.

Today, alas, the so-called Wise Men are searching the heavens, are exploring the atom and studying the relativity of matter, space and time in their search for Truth. Yet ultimately, as the Aquarian Age unfolds and emerges from the shadow of the Piscean Age of ignorance of the masses, these Wise Men will surely find the Christ-child and truly worship at His feet. For they will find Him manifesting where'er they sincerely look: in the mystery cradle of the atom, in relativity and in the marvels of the inter-planetary spaces. When thus found they will bring their gifts of wisdom and will bow down reverently in true worship before Him.

It must be these Wise Men who will help to teach humanity to stop their childish quibbling over the literal meaning of the words of the allegorical stories of the *Bible* which were believed by the unthinking multitudes as physical facts, instead of spiritual truths to be spiritually discerned. Thus will those Wise Men who have given their lives to discover, classify and find a use for the minute hidden little things, of which the great things are built, help to open wide the door of understanding for the masses in the New Age, even though they do so unthinkingly, looking only for a sure physical footing on which their science can be based. It will be such sincere and honest seekers for the ultimate truth who will find His cradle in the atom, who will "strive to teach humanity how to use its intellectual and magnetic powers to redeem both its bodily inharmonies (diseases) and also to redeem the Karma of its mistakes, thus helping to place its feet one step higher on the upward Path of Attainment." [1]

In the search for truth science is approaching a realization of the mystical statement that: "The Visible that was, and the Invisible that is, rested in Eternal Non-Being—the One Being." [2] While this was applied to the pralaya or period of rest between two World Periods, yet during our evolution we too must pass, in a lesser degree, through all the phases of evolution that the Cosmos has passed, and also through a similar pralaya.

In humanity, yea in every human being, as in the Cosmos, periods of activity, illumination and understanding are destined to follow periods of quiescence, intellectual darkness, stupidity and spiritual sleep. Let us call such periods Be-ness and Non-Being. By Be-ness let us understand that, no matter how deep is our sleep of ignorance, still all the vital facts and possibilities we are capable of ultimately building in or attaining to are sleeping within the mystery chamber of our hearts, waiting to be brought forth by our own awakening powers.

Radium has always been hidden in the Earth, yet as far as man was concerned it was as though it were in the realm of Non-Being. Only when man had advanced to the point where he woke up to its presence and its powers, could he bring them into Be-ness and make them serve him. So it is with the God-powers of life and health. While we are children in spiritual understanding we cry to our Father-God: "Give me life and health! Give me understanding!" But when we grow up in consciousness, as many are now doing, we begin to study the deeper mysteries of Be-ness for ourselves, and begin to learn how to grasp and manifest them. They are for us what "Non-Being" is to the planet, "The visible that was" or our Spiritual attainments gained in past lives, while "The invisible that is" is that which we

---

[1] *The Message of Aquaria*, Curtiss, 388.
[2] *The Stanzas of Dzan*, I, 7.

are destined to unfold. But until we have awakened spiritually to the New Age, as far as we can realize, both are resting today in Non-Being. Yet as the mysterious call of the New Age pulses through us we must turn Non-Being into Be-ness.

What does this mean? We know that all the possibilities of our unfolding powers lie concealed in Be-ness; that is, for us nothing can come to pass that does not already exist now, altho it may be asleep in Non-Being yet it is capable of being brought into manifestation as Be-ness. And we will reincarnate again and again until we have brought out of Non-Being into Be-ness and manifested, all the possibilities of the Christ-child now wrapped in swaddling clothes within us. This Be-ness is God-consciousness, which does not manifest the same for every one, yet each one has a phase of it to manifest, without which God cannot be fully manifested on Earth as He is in heaven. This is one meaning of the Word that was made flesh and dwelt among us. The word that must be spoken in the heart of each one of us today at the dawning of this New Age is, firstly, the *recognition of* our latent God-Powers. Secondly, it is the *setting of these powers to work*, first within our own hearts, then in our lives, then in society, that all shall begin to recognize the God-ordained Path of Attainment, and feel the desire to walk in it. In every human being, as in every age of Brahma, there is a "Conscious Spiritual Quality. In the manifested worlds, it is, . . . like the film from a Divine Breath to the gaze of the entranced seer."[3]

One of the greatest desires of humanity has always been to find a sure and absolutely definite way to heal all the sickness of body and mind to which human flesh is heir; for sickness so dulls and depletes man's powers that it must be overcome if man is to manifest his powers of Be-ness. Almost every school of spiritual teaching claims to have found the true way to health. Still mankind sickens and dies, and

---

[3] *The Secret Doctrine*, Blavatsky, I, 309

the cry of suffering humanity still fills the air. Yet we know it would be quite impossible for the universal belief in spiritual healing to have ever sprung into being, let alone persist age after age, unless it was a divine truth. But, alas, how many who thought they had found such a sure path have long since passed from so-called life! Where are the former great healers? Where are the healed?

Although spiritual healing is a divine everlasting truth, yet we read of it as a surety only in the last chapter of the *Bible*. "And he shewed me a pure river of water of life, clear as crystal, proceeding out of the throne of God and of the Lamb."[4] To find the Water of Life and use it to heal all diseases we must find the "Throne of God." This cannot mean to wait until we are in heaven, for we never can be sick in what we understand as heaven. Our healing must be *now, here in this physical world*. And until we find this true spiritual healing we will continue to suffer from sickness and death; yet every ill is but a text-book out of which we are meant to learn a great lesson. Therefore, let us positively declare that there is a Path, a method of spiritual healing, even though for most of us it is at present still sleeping in the Realm of Non-Being. Yet if it Be, we can and must find this Path as we find God within our hearts. This Path leads directly into the world of Eternal Life. The door to the Path is not necessarily the door of death. In one sense it is death, yet a death only of those things which we no longer need. Sorrow may endure for a night and sickness may grip hard and try to overwhelm us ere it lets go, but if we turn upon it the River of Life, ultimately it will cleanse us of all inharmonies and disease, all fear of death, and fill us with Life Eternal. Eternal Life does not always have to abide in the heaven-world afar from attainment by humanity, but can be brought down to Earth and override disease if we seek the right Path and have faith and believe.

As the New Age passes out of the shadow of the old, let

---

[4] *Revelation*, XXII.

us all look up into the clouds of glory that announce its coming. There will we see a vision of the River of Life proceeding out of the Throne of God, the center of divine Be-ness. Each one must realize that all things that *Be* are meant to be deciphered and realized by every one who is enough in earnest to seek in the right Path for the answer. This Path leads within. It is hidden deep in the cave of lost understanding and we must determine that we *will* find it once more, and find it now. For as our consciousness expands with the downpouring of the Christ-light and love, as His Chariot of Fire draws near the Earth, all those who are gazing steadfastly up into heaven, will have their mystic inner vision expanded. They will then understand that there is within them a Realm of Be-ness, in the midst of which is the Throne of God, and there all things given them by their Father, ere He sent them forth into this far country to perfect their education, are safely stored away.

Many are beginning to dream vital dreams about the God-powers that are awaiting only for their realization to be manifested and used. To accomplish this we must awaken from our lethal sleep of forgetfulness and ascend the Path to the realms of Be-ness and bring these powers into manifestation. Let us seek until we find the life and health where the Father has placed it, namely, in the Realm of Be-ness within our hearts. This is no more difficult than to seek for an understanding of health and disease through years of medical research and the study of the physical body only. Even if the physical scientist fails to recognize the Real or Spiritual Self who is the arbiter, guide and protector of the physical body, we should keep that Self, our mighty I Am Presence, ever in mind as it dwells in our Realm of Be-ness, resting before the Throne of God, whence flows the River of Eternal Life.

Let each of us solemnly and determinedly say, again and again, until it resounds through every fiber of our earth-dulled consciousness: "I will arise and go unto my Father where I shall feast in joy and peace and health at His table in His house, which is my true home. There He will give me of His wondrous healing power and lead me into His Realm of Divine Be-ness whence flows the River of Eternal Life."

CHAPTER **XXV**

SATURN AND CYCLIC LAW

"Saturn—one of the Sons of Light manifesting as stern justice.
. . . It is his part in the Divine Plan to further the redemption of man
by helping him to eat of the fruits of his own sowing and experience
the bitter results that he may be ready the sooner to turn from them
and learn to seek the fruits of the Tree of life. . . . Yet he leads them in
love, for it requires Divine Love for one of the Sons of God to accept a
task involving so much misunderstanding, ignominy and contumely as
the guidance of evil to its own destruction." *The Message of Aquaria*,
Curtiss, 320.

Cyclic law rules the world. Everywhere we see alternating
periods of outbreathing and inbreathing, of involution and
evolution, of expression and withdrawal, or day and night periods,
periods of activity and rest. There are cycles within cycles. Just as
the cycle of the year has within it the lesser cycles of the seasons,
the months, weeks and days, so the cosmic Cycle of Manifestation
has within it planetary cycles, racial cycles and individual cycles,
yet it is but the outgoing phase or current of Divine Will which
sweeps the whole divine Plan of the Universe into manifestation.

While the Law of Manifestation is one law for all things,
nevertheless it is modified and adapted to each and every form of
life in all God's universe. And as Nature is but a reflected expression
of a part of the Divine Plan, naturally many aspects of the one Law
are found in the so-called laws of Nature. There is a law of the
seasons, the tides, the crops, etc. Each growing thing, each form
of life, has its own law which is adapted to its own cycle of life,
a law through the fulfillment of which alone it can reach the per-

fect expression of that detail in the mighty pattern of the Divine
Plan which is its destiny to manifest. So is it with man. There is
the law of the functioning of the various tissues and organs of
his body—each with its own aspect of law—whose harmonious
expression we call health. There is the law of mind, with its varied
currents of thought and its various reaction, emotions, etc. And
there is the law of the spiritual life, of spiritual growth, with its
stages of unfoldment and its steps upon the Path of Attainment.

The *Bible* tells us that, "Till heaven and earth pass, one jot or
one tittle shall in no wise pass from the law, till all be fulfilled."
Not one law in the universe, from that of the stars in their courses,
down to that of the tiniest blade of grass: from man down to the
microscopic amoeba, can pass away until its manifestation has
been fulfilled. Man was sent to this planet to learn these laws, to
co-operate with them harmoniously and ultimately so to master
them that he can rule them and fulfil his destiny as the Lord of
Creation. He was cast out of the Garden of Eden[1] that he might
learn, not merely the ultimate, but also the "jot and tittle" of their
manifestation through experience, since he refused to follow the
divine guidance of the Lord God (Law of God) and learn in any
other way.

It is much like a young man studying some handicraft or
profession: it is not enough to know the general principles, the
ultimates, he must understand their application to the details of
their manifestation. So must we learn and obey the laws of the
spiritual life, the laws of Nature, the laws of the mind, and the laws
of the body, and work harmoniously with them all if we expect
to reap health, success, happiness, serenity of mind and spiritual
unfoldment as the result of our striving. If we learn this voluntarily
through observation, study and intuition, we will save ourselves
the pain and suffering that come through the experiments which
make up experience. We can either work with the law and hasten

---

[1] See *The Truth About Evolution and the Bible*, Curtiss.

its fulfillment in ourselves and in the universe or we can work against it and retard its fulfillment and bring upon ourselves the results of such retardation. God does not tell us the details of just what to do or what not to do, but He does give us His guidance, but we must learn to listen for and follow it. Through incarnation after incarnation, age after age, as we learn in one way or another how to cooperate with the Law, all opposition or hindrance to its perfect working will disappear and we will attain perfect peace, poise and happiness and radiate them to everything we contact.

One of the hardest phases of cyclic law to learn is that which pertains to the closing of old cycles and the beginning of new. This aspect is that of reaping and testing. In the cycle of the seasons this is the period of fall and winter when the season's crops are garnered and their quality tested; when the soft growth of the summer is tested and condensed into solid wood by the icy grip of winter. In the cycle of the day this is the night-period when the food we have eaten is built into growth and repair; when the activities of the day are consolidated into the lessons of experience. In the cycle of our spiritual ongoing it is the phase of testing which the Law brings about through the events of life whenever we reach the end of certain cycles of unfoldment. In the cycle of humanity and the planet it is the cataclysmic changes which must be faced and passed at the close of each of the twelve divisions or Ages (2160 years) of the Solar Year (25,920 years) as our solar system enters a new sign in the greater zodiac, just now the new sign Aquarius.

At the close of each cycle it is an aspect of Saturn, the Judge and Tester, which manifests and rules and which must be met and conquered or His decrees worked out. Among the seasons this testing manifests as Winter, during which Saturn is represented as reaching out with cold and icy fingers in an effort to snatch from Nature its life-force.

In the cycle of the day this is the night-period, when we are faced with the results of the day's activities and our consciousness is withdrawn from the physical plane as the sap of the trees is withdrawn into their roots in winter.

In the cycle of our spiritual unfoldment also Saturn manifests as the Judge and the Reaper. He is pictured as a skeleton waiting to cut down the crops that man has sown, the tares with the wheat: cutting down all false growths and preparing them for the fires of purification. It is He who makes us recognize and acknowledge the tares: the tares of selfishness, unbrotherliness, of impurity, cruelty, etc. For we could never learn how to reach up to Godhood without this facing of our faults. There He stands, gaunt and inflexible, the implacable Judge, barring our entrance to the next higher spiral of our Path[2] until we have passed the first great test of the Candidate — that of fear — and have dared to face Him and prove that we have gained the necessary strength of character which makes us fit to pass on. In the cycle of humanity He also manifests as the Judge and Reaper, forcing nations to face themselves and reap the results of their national and racial activities and creations. For the planet He is the great Adversary whose rock-like calm and inertia must be broken up ere the Earth can be prepared for a new springtime of planetary manifestation. Only those who know what Saturn is can understand.

For the past two thousand years humanity has been passing through the mighty day and night periods called the Piscean Age, during which marvelous discoveries have been made and wonderful achievements attained by humanity in outer and material affairs. But the Sun of that day has long since set, and the dread darkness of a spiritual night has descended upon and covered the minds of men with a pall of materialism, blotting out the bright shining of the Sun of Spiritual Enlightenment and even obscuring the Moon of Intuition. In earlier days, when mankind were

---

[2] See "A Message from Saturn," in *Realms of the Living Dead*, Curtiss, 273.

like ignorant children, this was a time of dread and horror; for they believed in the power of the inhabitants of the darkness and in the terrors of the invisible world. But those days have passed and we have in a measure grown up. Men's minds have definitely set about investigating that which was formerly called superstition. Today science leaves no problem, no matter how fearsome, uninvestigated that its falsities may be exposed and its dangers rendered innocuous or at least guarded against.

Today, as the new Age of Aquarius dawns, humanity is passing through the darkest hour which precedes the coming day and is feeling the bitter chill of the newly awakened dawn-wind; that hour when the Moon has set and the light of the stars, which were so brilliant through the night, fades out as they seem, one by one, to be withdrawn behind a dark curtain, as though they had said: "Our vigil is over. Our task is done. Goodnight." Then comes the darkest hour, when all Nature is still with an ominous calm, as though afraid of breaking the dread silence. This is Saturn's hour, and this is the period when humanity must face Saturn, at this particular time not merely as the Judge and Reaper of the closing cycle, but also as the Ruler of the first decan[3] (700 years) or the Aquarian Age. It is therefore the duty of those who would be wise to understand something of this dread Tester and Judge so that as the New Day dawns we shall see Him as He really is and He shall become the Initiator of those who dare to face and conquer Him.

Altho we must experience the power of this grim specter whether we wish it or not, like many things which seem fearsome while in the distance or in the darkness of ignorance, understanding robs them of their terror. Since fearless investigation is a fundamental law of scientific research, and since as mystics we are both fearless and as devoted to the enlightenment and uplift of humanity as is science, let us investigate this subject where physical science leaves off,

---

[3] See *The Message of Aquaria*, Curtiss, 27.

i.e., in the higher super-physical and metaphysical realms.

We are told that there is nothing that is hidden that shall not be revealed, and surely this includes the many mysteries of life and consciousness which are beyond purely materialistic analysis. Hence those who wish to sit at the footstool of the Masters should so purify their hearts and illumine their minds that they can enter into those inner conditions, which though hidden are destined to be revealed, and grasp something of the unseen causes back of the outer manifestations; causes that are beyond the ken of the materialistic mind, no matter how scientific.

Saturn has been vilified by mythologists and astrologers for ages and His influence has been blamed for a large proportion of the ills that afflict mankind, yet were it not for the testings of Saturn, the supposed opponent and adversary of man and the so-called antitype of God, it would be impossible for man to condense his forces and consolidate his gains into the inherent strength of character necessary for his upward climb. Therefore, it is necessary that we meet Saturn at every turn in the upward circling of our Spiral of Life. As we have said elsewhere, Saturn is the first "to go forth into manifestation from the bosom of the Infinite, that He might establish the boundaries of the circle within which the universe was to manifest and to create the stability upon which subsequent manifestations might rest. . . . Hence Saturn is called both the Initiator and the Tester who determines the degree of stability of our foundation before each advance is attempted. His force will necessarily be the last to return, because the laws of stability must be maintained until the Dot . . . . has fulfilled its cycle of manifestation."[4] Saturn is therefore the "Alpha and Omega, the beginning and the ending, saith the Lord, which is, and which was, and which is to come."[5] He is, therefore, an aspect of the Cosmic Christos or the night-side of the Sun

---

[4] *The Key to the Universe*, Curtiss, 165
[5] *Revelation*, I, 8.

of Righteousness, the terror-aspect of the Christ as the Judge. "For we must all appear before the judgment seat of Christ; that every one may receive the things done in his body, according to that he hath done, whether it be good or bad. Knowing therefore the terror of the Lord, we persuade men."[6] "And he commanded us to preach unto the people, and to testify that it is he which was ordained of God to be the Judge of the quick and the dead."[7]

Since man dislikes to face himself and accept the results of his own creation, it is difficult for him to realize that his tests come in love, even to his being removed from incarnation lest he continue his evil ways and accumulate such a mass of destructive forces that they would overwhelm him and retard his ongoing for many incarnations, or lest he venture on into conditions where his lack of strength and spiritual unfoldment would foredoom him to disastrous failure. Therefore, man fails to recognize the loving Christ when covered with the black and purple garments of fear and misconception with which man has clothed Him.

Since the Christ abides in us and we in Him, unless we respond to that Indwelling and strive to give positive and constructive expression to it we tend to build up a negative expression — through our own evil thoughts, words and deeds — in the image of man which hides the loving Christ from us. Instead of looking within and recognizing Him in our hearts we turn our backs upon Him and look outward and see the projection of our own creations, and like the woman at the tomb cry out: "They have taken away the Lord out of the sepulcher, and we know not where they have laid him." But the dark tomb of man's own fashioning, altho sealed with the stone of his stupidity and misunderstanding, could not confine Him, and He cannot be found there, for He is risen and stands before us, no longer in the aspect of loving tenderness which we have flouted and

---

[6] *II Corinthians*, V, 10, 11.
[7] *Acts*, X, 42

refused to accept, but now as the Judge, the embodiment of stern Justice.

And, alas, few there be who can recognize Him thus as He stands in the Path of man's further advance and cries: "Unless you face me and wrestle with me, O man, and tear from me this mask and these dark garments of human frailty with which you have clothed me, you cannot pass on." The Earth trembles at His words and the destructive manifestations of Earth-forces — storms, floods, droughts, famines, cataclysms, etc., — sweep away those who fear to face and recognize Him or those whose Karma requires their withdrawal from Earth life. Only those who have recognized Him in the inner sanctuary of their own hearts; who have striven to do His will and express His force in their lives, can recognize that this dread Judge is really the Lord Christ dressed in the shabby garments of illusion which man has placed upon Him.

It is man's selfishness and self-sufficiency which refuses to recognize or believe in the reality of the Christ within and thus delivers Him to be crucified by the rabble of his lower vibrations, desires and perverted life-forces. Then man wraps his conception of the Christ in the grave clothes of his own fashioning and tries to shut it away in a tomb of darkness and closes the door of his mind to it. But we know that it will come forth again in power and great glory to judge the quick and the dead.

While the *Bible* story is more symbolic than historical, nevertheless *it is an actual and universal fact* at a certain stage in the unfoldment of the Christ-consciousness in every Soul. Therefore, ere the Soul can reach Mastery, each must face the ultimate of what the death and burial of the Christ means in their lives and in the life of mankind. We must see Him as He would have been had He lain in the grave through all these ages. We must see Him as a gaunt skeleton and must wrestle with Him in this guise until the true inner ideal of the Christ is uncovered and recognized within:

until the wonderful love of the Christ, so long buried under misconception, comes forth: until we recognize that the specter of Saturn is but a dark garment of illusion created by man himself as a screen to hide his own vileness from the All-seeing Eye, a lay figure on which he thinks to hang the responsibility for his shortcomings. We must be ready to recognize Him as Saturn, the Judge of our frailty, the Tester of our strength and the Initiator of our Souls. Then we will know Him as He really is.

The great unfoldment destined for mankind during the Aquarian Age will include a fuller, truer and clearer understanding of what Divine Love is and how it manifests. All the many materialistic, limited and false conceptions with which man has clothed the Christ must be torn from Him that He may be recognized in all His aspects and manifestations and live in the consciousness, hearts and lives of humanity. Only as He rules as Saturn, and humanity faces Him, overcomes its false conceptions of Him, wrestles with Him, passes His testings and gains His power, can He reign as the Messenger of Peace during the New Age.

Chapter XXVI

GOD, MAN AND THE PLANET

"O Lord, how manifold are thy works! in wisdom thou hast made them all; the earth is full of thy riches." *Psalms*, CIV, 24.

"As for me, I will behold thy face in righteousness; I shall be satisfied, when I awake, with thy likeness." *Psalms*, XVII, 15.

Many thoughtful students today are pondering over and seriously questioning why it was necessary for man to incarnate on this planet Earth and be clothed with a dense physical body, when he had already evolved many faculties and functions on other planets far less dense and hampering and in spheres far more ethereal and spiritual, wherein he had built up from their substance a pure and highly spiritualised body. To have to incarnate in a dense material and animal body largely dominated by the all-powerful sex instinct, with which he had no previous experience on other planets, at first glance seems unfair. It seems like setting before an innocent, spiritually-minded and trusting child a great temptation of which it had no previous warning, and then seemingly punishing it for failing to understand and master its problem when such failure would seem inevitable.

We are told that only here, on this most dense yet marvelously constructed planet, where the two creative aspects of the Soul—masculine and feminine—were for the first time to function in separate bodies, could he learn to perform the most marvelous miracle and meet his final test as to his ability to use his Godlike power of creation on all planes and in all states of matter, namely, his ability to mould matter to the pattern of the ideal or Spiritual Man and to dominate and utilize to their highest ends the animal instincts. Only thus could he accomplish his mission in matter and demonstrate to all the other kingdoms over which he must ultimately rule that he was, in very truth, created in the image and likeness of his Father, with all the God-powers inherent within him and capable of unfoldment and manifestation.

Only on this dense planet, ruled by the law of duality, was it said: "Then shall your eyes be opened, and ye shall be as gods, knowing good and evil." But to manifest "as gods, knowing good and evil" on such a planet, man had to evolve out of the self-same substance as the planet a body through which his unfolding God-powers could manifest, despite the limitations of material conditions. It was much as though a scientist had conceived of marvellous properties or powers which he believed were present in a certain region, yet to demonstrate them he would need an experiment station or laboratory set down in the midst of that region and equipped with specially designed instruments with which, after much experimentation, he could ultimately demonstrate to the world that such powers were not imaginary or mere theory, but were capable of demonstration under suitable conditions. And it was for such a marvellous test and demonstration that man descended from the more ethereal spheres to this dense material plane. Yet in very truth the planet is but little more dense than man himself, for it also has its ethereal counterparts[1] and its latent powers which will be unfolded in due season.

While we can only speculate more or less imperfectly as to just why the formation of man and his subsequent victory over matter was a necessity in the Divine Plan, we can give much light upon the various phases through which he has passed and still has to pass once his Cycle of Necessity was begun.

---

[1]　See diagram in *Realms of the Living Dead*, Curtiss, 42.

The Eternal Being, the Lord God or the everlasting Divine
Law back of all manifestation in all worlds and on all planes,
usually personified in man's thought as a Great Being, a great
King above all kings, pervades all space and all states of substance
and consciousness. And since science has proved that "thoughts
are things," definitely formed, tangible and demonstrable things,
the formulated Divine Ideation of such Beings as can see the
end from the beginning is of such tremendous dynamic creative
power as to go on and on creating various expressions of itself
down through all the worlds of manifestation until it is ultimately
embodied in the dense matter of this planet. Hence man, made
in the image of God, is an out-breathing or projected thought-
wave of God, which once sent forth must clothe itself with the
substances of all planets and worlds into which it is projected.

Since man was breathed forth to accomplish certain definite
ends in the Divine Plan without which it would be imperfect,
he must learn the lessons of all planets, spheres and planes of
manifestation through which he passes. Hence he must experience
the conditions to be found on other planets and planes of being
and ultimately learn the much more difficult lessons made
necessary by the density and inertia of the material conditions of
this Earth-plane. Upon reaching this dense plane of manifestation
he does not incarnate in entire ignorance of its conditions, for
they have been foreshadowed as he passed this way before while
clothed in an ethereal body composed of the substance of the
super-physical planes of this Earth-chain,[2] but he is here now
in this dense material body to take his final degree. But he still
has many Godlike lessons which he must go on learning here
on Earth, altho like the infant in its mother's womb, he already
embodies the main traits which he must express. Many of these
are like swaddling clothes which must be undone and cast aside
as he advances in unfoldment.

---

[2] See *The Voice of Isis*, Curtiss, Chapter XV.

Man now finds himself no longer clothed in an ethereal body and responding to the vibrations of Divine Guidance, but clothed in a body of flesh, with a childlike consciousness and childlike reactions to animal instincts and the outer world, hence is easily led astray by the serpent's guile—the temptations of the senses—for his garment of flesh is as blinding to his spiritual sight as is the dust of the earth to his physical eyes. Having brought about inharmonious conditions by his disobedience, he is blinded and afraid, and this fear has led to many of his subsequent mistakes and failures whose results he, naturally, has to reap in sorrow and suffering and in the sweat of his brow.

He is now no longer a super-conscious mind manifesting through a harmoniously attuned super-physical body in perfect peace and harmony, but finds himself now utilizing only a reflection of that super-conscious mind in a dense body of flesh. But the super-conscious mind is a manifestation of the mind of God and overshadowed and guided by His consciousness, the radiophone through which He broadcasts His thoughts to the human mind. In other words, man should be, and ultimately must evolve to be, a *consciously responsive* instrument to work out and manifest in matter the thoughts projected from the mind of God for the fulfilment of the Divine Plan. Hence, we are truly made in His image and after His likeness, even though now outwardly clothed in the dust of the ground, or the accumulated materialized substances of the planetary conditions through which we have already passed and upon which we have placed our stamp while passing through their more ethereal aspects in the higher planes.

As a miner must delve deep into the earth and little by little dig up the "pay dirt" or ore and wash and pan it ere he can separate and acquire the pure gold for his use, so must we delve deep down into the depths of our innermost selves ere we can attain the gold of spiritual consciousness and the full use of our God-powers. And, paradoxical as it may seem, the deeper we dig the higher we climb. And no matter how deep we dig or how high we climb, we can never get away from God; for our bodies are within the aura of His substance and our minds are within His mentality, and His radiant life-force penetrates the very cells of our bodies, for us to appropriate.

No one can think the same thought over and over continuously in exactly the same manner, for the thought we meditate upon follows the motion of the spheres, and we thus see it from all aspects. And only when we have thus meditated upon all its aspects or experienced all its phases do we truly comprehend it. This law accounts both for the endless diversity of human beings and the endless vagaries of the human mind; for each of us is but one aspect of one of the many thoughts of God, and it takes all mankind to make up the whole. Each thought may be likened to a branch or a rootlet of the Tree of Life that is planted in our midst: in the very soil of our body. It will lead us upward into the freedom and light of God-consciousness or it will wander downward seeking out something good, some needed lesson, in the debris and muck of life. For there are not only many branches to our Tree of Life, but many rootlets tapping many and diverse substances. Therefore, we cannot expect all men to be exactly alike or to express a given thought in the same way. Only as we look upon the various personalities as different branching twigs or rootlets of the one Divine Tree, each gathering for the benefit of all some necessary force or experience from various conditions, can we see humanity as a whole express in its entirety the thought of God.

From another aspect let us think of God as the mighty central Sun-behind-the-Sun sending out living sparks of Divine Fire. Each such spark gradually gathers together and illumines the substance of the realm or region through which it passes, impregnating it with its life-force until it unfolds its fiery heart and is clothed upon by matter as a human being. All these Divine Sparks naturally are a part of the substance of God and are the instruments for His manifestation and the accomplishment of His will. Therefore, in his inmost being or Real Self, man is one with God, while in his outer being or personality he is an instrument of God, with marvelous possibilities and great responsibilities. The trouble arises because, as these sparks were thrown out or emanated from the Spiritual Sun and entered the world of form they were surrounded with more and more dense coats of matter until they became so encased and absorbed in it that they forgot whence they had come and what ultimate mission they were sent forth to accomplish.[3] Since the planet is the materialization of a thought of God it naturally reflects all the beauty, diversity and usefulness needed to aid and perfect the evolution of man, the Divine Spark. But this perfect Earth has had imposed upon it the imperfections and limitations due to the density of man's understanding. For as man evolves within and through his dense coverings, by and through the free-will use of his divine creativeness he generates an atmosphere of his own formation, containing all that he desires or thinks he needs, and this finally impregnates the Earth and finds expression upon and through it. Thus man creates his own limitations and reaps the results of his own thoughts, acts and creations instead of responding harmoniously and co-operatively to those of God in Nature around him. Hence, today we find man and woman no longer living in a perfect Garden of Eden, but thrust out into an imperfect world of matter through their disobedience and misuse of the serpent-power within them, and hiding from God when He calls in the cool of the day: "Adam, where art thou?" meaning what point in evolution have you reached? When they do come face to face with God they realize that they have done little to clothe themselves with the Divine Ideal of the true Inner-Man and so are naked before God and ashamed; for even as fig leaves

---

[3] See lesson *The Object of Physical Existence*, Curtiss.

are an unnatural and inadequate clothing for man, so the flimsy creations of desire, vanity, pride and self-esteem are inadequate garments wherewith to clothe the Divine Man within.

After the middle of the Third Great Race[4] we find man no longer a more or less ethereal being, conscious of the divine world about him and the nearness of Divine Guidance, but clothed in a dense physical body, no longer Godlike to look upon, but fashioned to express the animal traits and habits which he had fostered and perfected. Yet his God-given power to create through thought was never completely taken from him. It still colours all he does, yet through that God-like power of creative thought must he climb upward once more to a realization of his God-consciousness; for God-consciousness is man's heritage: And even though shut out of Eden, all who listen with the inner ear can still hear the Voice crying: "Adam, where art thou?"

Not only did God make this Earth a garden full of beauty, but filled with all things needed by man for his growth and happiness and unfoldment. Even when man and woman shut themselves out of Eden and went forth to till the earth that it might bring forth just what they desired or thought they wanted, even then did the all-knowing and all-loving Father-Mother provide for them, in the herbs of the field and in the minerals and forces of the earth, a balm for every wound, an antidote for every poison and a cure for every ill that man was destined to bring upon himself in his God-foreseen pilgrimage through ages of darkness after he had turned his back upon the Tree of Life in the midst of the Garden.[5] For it was through his misuse of his God-given powers and materials that man created for all humanity the seeds of inharmony and disease, all that kills joy and happiness, so that each joy has its sting, and happiness endures for but a day.

Even at the present day when man has begun to recognize

---

[4] See *The Voice of Isis*, Curtiss, 233, 284
[5] For details see *The Truth About Evolution and the Bible*, Curtiss.

that he is responsible for all things harmful to himself, the lower kingdoms and the planet itself, and the things which shorten and lessen the efficiency of his own life, there are some schools of thought which deny the helpful gifts of God and both ignore and scornfully refuse to use the healing potencies given to man as a surcease for his ills and suffering. This is a picture of man as he is today and an explanation of why he is as he is. But it also points out the only means for the redemption of both man and the planet.

(To be concluded)

Chapter XXVII

GOD, MAN AND THE PLANET

Part II. The Book of Remembrance

"Then they that feared (revered) the Lord spake often one to another; and the Lord harkened, and heard it, and a Book of Remembrance was written for them that feared the Lord, and that thought upon his name." *Malachi*, III, 16-17.

Just as the subconscious mind of man is that aspect of his mind which controls all the automatic activities of his bodily functions[1] —circulation, respiration, digestion, elimination, repair, etc., just so—for comparison's sake only—may we look upon that aspect of the mind of God which controls all the activities of Nature and the lower kingdoms, and which inspires and seeks to guide the outer activities of the body of humanity, as the subconscious mind of God. And just as the subconscious mind of man functions through the solar plexus of his body, so the subconscious mind of God functions through the solar plexus of our solar system, namely the Sun; in this case not the Spiritual Sun, but the physical luminary which gives life, light, health, vigour and the joy of expression to all forms of life in this solar system, enabling them to unfold and manifest their inner pattern and possibilities.

While this subconscious mind of God reaches and governs the physical manifestations of Nature and man through the radiations of the physical Sun, the Divine or Spiritual Mind of God reaches and uplifts humanity through the radiations of the Spiritual Sun manifesting through the heart as the Cosmic Christ, the only begotten Son of the divine Father-

---

[1] See *The Voice of Isis*, Curtiss, 90.

Mother. Therefore, all the functions of Nature and all the functions of man's body and mind are but various aspects of the manifestation of the Divine Mind, and are all animated by His divine radio-activity, the outshining of His life, light and consciousness. For, just as the physical Sun is the shining radiance of the physical manifestation of the Christos, set in the midst of our planetary system to warm and vitalize into manifestation and redeem from the deadness and inertia of non-manifestation the germs of all forms of physical life upon and within this system, so is the shining radiance of our individual Christos—our mighty I Am Presence—the spiritual life and light which is set in the midst of us—"that light which lighteth every man that cometh into the world"—to warm and vitalize into manifestation and redeem from the deadness and inertia of non-manifestation the germs of all spiritual life latent in all humanity.

As the physical Sun lights all the Earth periodically, producing day in one hemisphere while it is night in the other, so does the Spiritual Sun have its cyclic day-and-night periods for each heart and for humanity as a whole. For we have need of the night as well as the day: periods of rest, quiet and darkness during which we can think over and assimilate the lessons of the day-period and build them into spiritual growth and character. It is only in the heaven of Spiritual Consciousness that there is no night; for day and night are alike when we abide in the eternal radiance of the Christ-consciousness.

The Spiritual Sun floods each heart and illumines each Soul during its spiritual day-period: then it seemingly passes away for a time, and for us it is then night. Yet in this night there are great lessons to be learned and blessings to be understood; for just as it is with the lower consciousness, so is it with the higher. During the night, when the physical brain is inactive, the Higher Mind can rule and impress the lessons of the day deep down through the soil of ignorance of the lower mind so that ultimately they will put forth sprouts in the outer consciousness. And even if the waking consciousness does bury them deep beneath its materialistic activities and conceptions, yet in time they grow and come forth as new ideas and conceptions, the ripened fruit of experience. Hence, we must determinedly learn that during the night, while the physical brain is resting and recuperating, the Spiritual Mind is pouring in the wisdom which sometime we must realize, learn and manifest. Therefore, let us determine to learn it now, for "now is the accepted time; now is the day of salvation."

Each Soul has a life task or destiny which it must accomplish. Therefore, instead of frittering away our time and opportunities in the vanities of material enjoyments or in ignorant murmuring against the Great Law, let us set to work to learn our personal lessons in this outer life, that we may the sooner pass on to higher things and learn more pleasing lessons. God waits patiently and utilizes all the forces of the universe to push us onward and upward as fast as our stage of unfoldment and strength will permit. Yet we often whimper if the Sun fails to shine in our lives for an hour or two, forgetting that we would seldom even try to learn the more difficult lessons if we were bathed continuously in sunshine and prosperity.

Some students are over-enthusiastic for a time—their day-period—but later on, as the Sun sets in their hearts and minds, they seem to lose interest and so give all their attention to outer things. They are like a plant which droops in too strong a sunlight or too long a day, hence must have shade and a nighttime of rest to build in that which the day has brought forth. These are not to be condemned or blamed, but must be allowed to sleep for a while under the sheltering wings of the Divine Mother until their next day-period dawns, bringing them greater interest, courage and power to conquer. We know that a new day must inevitably dawn and the Spiritual Sun again shine in their hearts, and that they will take other steps onward and upward until finally they shall awake in His image—the Image of God[2] impressed upon them in the beginning—and they shall be satisfied.

The sunlight is the physical redeemer of the Earth, for without it nothing could grow and manifest; nor without it could the dead forms and offscourings be fermented and transmuted into helpful substances for future use. The noxious weeds and seemingly vile substances in Nature, while possessing the essence of the one Divine Life, are nevertheless manifesting it through perverted and obnoxious forms created by man through his thoughts, his misuse of the creative force,[3] etc., whether through ignorance or vileness. Hence the redemption and upliftment of the lower forms of life and the very Earth itself must come through the purification and upliftment of man's mind and creative forces.

In a similar manner the radiance of the Christos is the redeemer and saviour of mankind, for without it the seeds of his spiritual life could not grow and manifest, nor could the noxious weeds of his perverted forces, his selfishness, inharmony, lusts and the offscourings of his mind, be transmuted into good, even though this requires the experiences of fermentation and transmutation. Therefore, the redemption of man and the upliftment of his lower forms of manifestation must come through the upliftment of his mind to a realization of and correlation with the radiance of the Christos or Christ-consciousness.

Man, with his inherent ability to reach up and respond to the Christ-consciousness and thus attain the sublime heights of Divine Wisdom, has, nevertheless, evolved for himself a lower mind for use in the material conditions of the physical world, altho in essence it is but reflection of his Higher or Spiritual Mind, much as the Sun is reflected in the waters of a lake or pool. An ignorant child might mis-

---

[2]　See *The Truth About Evolution and the Bible*, Curtiss, Chapter XIX.
[3]　See *The Voice of Isis, Curtiss*, 219.

take such a reflection for the Sun itself, altho the reflection would be distorted by the ripples of every passing breeze. Just so undeveloped man, being but an ignorant child in spiritual things, thinks his lower or rational mind is his real mind, all the mind there is, altho in truth it is but the reflection of his Spiritual Mind distorted by the ripples of every desire of the flesh, every ambition of the personality or every passing breeze of doctrine or theory.

All these ripples and distortions have gradually lessened man's power to reflect his Spiritual Mind clearly, and hence have decreased his power of conscious, constructive spiritual creation through thought. In the early stages, as his thoughts were largely confined to things of the outer world, they responded but faintly to the redeeming and transmuting power of the Spiritual Mind and so grew perverted and evil and had a greater influence over him than had the good. He thus grew to believe in evil and that it had more power than good. And through this wrong thinking he found it easy to pervert his thought power so as to create inharmonious and destructive thoughts and acts which resulted in inharmony, trouble, sickness, blights, pests and even storms,[4] so that the beautiful Earth, God-given for man's happy use and peaceful progress, became a place of inharmony, mighty struggle, suffering and sorrow. And because of all this that man has created and brought upon himself, he came to believe that the loving and omnipresent radiance of God—the Christos—was a Being either so far off as to be uninterested in him or was an avenging Nemesis to be appeased, watching to punish him for the slightest infraction of seemingly arbitrary laws, or else was a helpless if not imaginary power subservient to the powers of evil.

Life was never meant to be a bitter struggle with evil; for evil is but the offscourings of man which he has unconsciously spread like manure over the fields of life because he could not trust God and believe that these fields could

---

[4] See *The Voice of Isis*, Curtiss, 172.

bring forth if fertilized only by the gentle rain, the pure air, the warmth and magnetism of the Sun and the radio-active substances which God had implanted in the Earth when He spake the word, not only to man, but also to the newly created Earth: "Be fruitful, and multiply, and replenish the earth." Yet since man has spread over all the fields of the Earth the effluvia of his evil creations, he must learn to transmute it and extract from it every vibration of perverted life-force, with the vileness of which his ignorance and disobedience has saturated the Earth. Thus must he become the redeemer of his own creations.

The beautiful book of Nature, written by the finger of God, has been thumbed over for ages by ignorant and untrained interpreters who refused to listen either to the Voice of God or of Nature and whose materialistic interpretations have made that great Book seem obscure and hard to decipher. Thus has man obscured the Light and crucified the very Power which alone can be his salvation. For the Christ has been crucified by man's misconception and materialization and still hangs upon the cross of matter where the Law of life Eternal is crossed by man's desire, his ignorance and his disobedience, his self-made suffering and death. And "Since by man came death into the world, by man must also come the resurrection from the dead."

The Christ must hang upon this very real man-made cross until the Christ-consciousness in man has been freed from the bonds of materialistic conception and through illumination and manifestation he begins the redemption of the personality, and through man the redemption of the very ground itself which was accursed by man through his disobedience to Divine Law. But the all-loving Father-Mother, full of compassion and patience, still points out the way so clearly proclaimed by Their only begotten Son, the Cosmic Christ, whose voice still sounds through the ages: "I am the way, the truth and the life: no man cometh unto the Father, but by me . . . . Behold, I stand at the door and knock; if any man hear my voice, and open the door, I will come in to him, and will sup with him, and he with me."

If the physical Sun can bring up out of the mire of Earth all kinds of beautiful flowers, healing herbs and foods for man's physical well-being, how much greater is the power of the Spiritual Sun to bring up out of the mire of man's lower self, out of his bitter experiences, his evil creations, sin, sickness and death, the beautiful flowers of spiritual unfoldment which were implanted by God as seeds in man in the beginning ere he became embodied on this planet!

Since Nature is a manifestation of God, it must inevitably contain, not only an expression of the one Divine Life, but also an expression of the one Divine Consciousness; for all manifestation is fed and sustained by the Divine Life-force manifested through the ever-living Christos or Cosmic Christ. For it is this Cosmic Christ-force that is the animating spark of life in every form of life, from the tiniest electron to the mightiest planet. It is the radio-activity of radium, bombarding all things within its range with its emanations. It is the light of the sunbeam sent forth to illumine, warm and redeem the Earth. It is the power which enables the tiny rootlet to pierce the dark earth and extract from its environment the exact nourishment needed for its particular form of life. It is the incessant urge which enables the tender sprout to push up through the soil and overcome all obstacles to its reaching out into the sunlight. It finds its expression in the perfume of the flower: in the refreshing qualities of the fruit: in the nourishment of the food. It is heard in the sounds of Nature: in the happy laughter of children, and finds its highest expression to man in the Still Small Voice which seeks to guide him to the harmonious and happy fulfilment of his destiny.

The voice of Nature, altho an octave higher than the outer ear of untrained man can hear, is nevertheless forever singing the Psalm of Life, and can be heard, or at least felt or sensed, by all who listen with an inner self-attunement to Nature's harmonies, for it speaks in a subtile way to all. And even if this speech is a language they cannot interpret in words, still, be they attuned ever so slightly they can feel the life-thrill of oneness and can understand.

The subtile vibrations of life all manifest some form of sound, either audible or inaudible to man. The Psalm of Life is made up of chords composed of the notes of all living things, from angelic Beings, Devas, elementals and mortals down to the tiny blades of grass, and the almost invisible insects, and the electrons circling around their nucleus, the proton. All have their part and sing it in rhythmic perfection and exquisite harmony when not perverted by man.

Each creature and growing thing sings its part in the Anthem of Creation and thereby explains its reason for being, its lesson and its ultimate destiny. Blessed are the ears that can hear, the hearts that can understand and the minds that to some extent can interpret it. As Nature sings this endless alleluia chorus the Psalm of Life rises like a mighty paean of praise to God in notes so high and clear, yet with a bass of suffering endured, sins overcome and mighty lessons learned without self pity or doubt, that only man's absorption in material vibrations and concerns prevents his hearing it. It is this bass which completes the harmony of the spheres, for it tells of the greatest wisdom, the greatest patience and love of God manward.

The Book of Remembrance, written by the hand of God, is revealed to man by his every effort to overcome his faults and failings, to unfold his higher possibilities and attain perfection. "Be ye therefore perfect, even as your Father which is in heaven is perfect" is the wonderful injunction given for man's encouragement and a wonderful ideal for his attainment, but we must understand how it can be accomplished. We cannot become perfect in a day, nor in a year, nor in one life, but the process can be greatly hastened, mistakes avoided and their suffering prevented by consciously correlating with the Christ-force and with its help striving to manifest our highest ideals.

Do not think that we must be punished in order to become perfect, for the God of Love and Wisdom demands no such process. Even unenlightened humanity is finding out that the more it punishes without enlightenment, the more resistance is aroused, the less progress is made and the worse conditions become. The Divine Law as Karma and Reincarnation constantly works for the perfection of man and the Earth by bringing man face to face with conditions which gradually teach him the lessons of his former mistakes and failures, the only punishment being the reaping of what he has sown until he learns not to set up the causes which necessitate such reapings. Through all this God helps us even more lovingly because of our suffering, as we pass through our self-made Karma and press on toward perfection. For God is always love, ever near us, comforting, aiding and encouraging us by the out-pouring of that love, even in our darkest hours.

Let us all take courage then. Let us strive individually, and also hold together and work with our comrades of like mind and ideals that we may the more efficiently help the weak, enlighten the ignorant, uplift the fallen and encourage all who will to push ever onward to victory, the glorious attainment of that perfection which is our ultimate destiny.

Greater is he who overcometh than he who was never tempted. When tempted beyond our strength or our faith to believe let us say to ourselves: "God is in me and I am in Him. By the power of Godhood that is within me I must conquer sometime, why not now? If a tiny seed can take root in the mire of Earth and by the persistent urge of its ideal can reach the sunlight and bring forth the image God has implanted within it; if it can transmute the vilest mire of Earth into power to grow into a mighty tree, in spite of storms and bitter cold and burning heat, in spite of insects and blights and pests, so can I, a tiny Spark of God-consciousness, take root in the densest Earth conditions and among the offscourings of man's iniquity and utilize as fertilizer all apparent evil and, through the power of the Christ within me, lift it up into a true expression of that image and likeness of God which is my mighty I Am Presence, my Real Self."

As this is accomplished more and more, man will take his destined place in evolution, namely, the ruler of his destiny and the helper and benefactor of all the lesser expressions of life on Earth and the perfector of the Earth and all that therein is until he makes his conscious ascension into the higher worlds through the gate of translation, like Elijah, instead of through the gate of death.

God's Book of Remembrance keeps record, not of our failings and mistakes, but of every aspiration and effort we have made to realize and manifest the image of God within.

Listen with understanding, O man, while the angels sing together their mighty anthem: "Glory to God in the highest, and on earth peace, good will toward men." But let us remember that this can come to man only as he attunes his mind to and correlates with it and gives it expression on Earth.

CHAPTER XXVIII

THE THIRD EYE

"The Third Eye was once a physiological organ, and later on, owing to the gradual disappearance of spirituality and increase of materiality, the spiritual nature being extinguished by the physical, it became an atrophied organ .... the Inner Vision had to be awakened and acquired by artificial stimuli; the process of which was known to the old Sages. ... It is the chief organ of spirituality in the human brain." *The Secret Doctrine*, Blavatsky, II, 309, 308;III, 506.

"The light of the body is the eye; if therefore thine eye be single thy whole body shall be full of light" *St. Matthew*, VI, 22.

Our cosmic philosophy teaches that during the Third Great Race (Lemurian) the Third Eye or *pineal gland*, now atrophied and hidden away in the center of the brain, was a normally functioning organ connected with the creative thought-power of *Kriya-shakti*. But since the middle of the third sub-race of the Atlanteans, when the consolidation and full materialization of the body was completed, it was not only hidden from sight, but its higher functions were gradually lost and its organ atrophied. Creation through the pineal gland took place before the separation of the sexes, hence long before creation through physical generation. The creative functions of the pineal gland at that time were largely connected with the creation of spiritual ideation and other special conditions needed by the more spiritual and super-physical races, for at that time both aspects of the Soul (masculine and feminine) were manifesting in the one super-physical body. Both were absolutely one and required the same love and care, and both were learning the same lessons of life's beginning together as spiritual twin Souls.

These spiritual powers and ideals had to be developed and

function in man's spiritual nature and consciousness so that, later on, after his physical body and its functions had become materialized, he would still possess his spiritual powers even though he was no longer outwardly conscious of them. It is because of their presence in the inner man, even though latent to his outer consciousness, that they are capable of being awakened, through appropriate means, and act as the *Antaskarana* or bridge over the great abyss or chasm which yawns between the consciousness of the outer animal man and his inner, true or Divine Self, the Image of God within. For it is the presence of this Divine Self within man which constitutes the mighty and essential difference between the highest animals and man.

During the first three Races man was in conscious touch with the forces of Nature and its various forms of life and consciousness, and with the higher, angelic and super-physical Beings who were his teachers. This conscious touch with the invisible worlds was lost because of the materialization of the former semi-astral body and the loss of function of the pineal gland. In the early childhood of physical man he was taught the fundamental virtues as a child is taught, namely, to love God; to recognize in his brother man the same God-like powers that he felt within himself; to realize the absolute oneness of the two opposite poles of his nature, masculine and feminine; the relation of the Inner Self to the outer world; the object of incarnation in the flesh, etc. But after the symbolic Eve was taken from Adam's side[1] during the "deep sleep" or *pralaya* between the Third and Fourth Races, mankind had to learn new and greater lessons, for the current of unfoldment or evolution sweeps us ever onward and upward with only temporary retardations to learn minor lessons.

While at the end of each *magnum annus* or solar year of about 26,000 years the Earth seems to return to its former

---

[1] For details see *The Truth About Evolution and the Bible*, Curtiss, Chapter VIII.

position in the heavens, it is only approximately so; for the Earth is like a rolling wheel, turning over and over, yet always advancing into new regions in space and into new conditions. Nothing can be gained by going backward. Even the lapse of old age into so-called "second childhood" cannot take place unless the Real Self or Soul has passed on into the higher worlds, leaving only the human personality behind to go over and over the more deeply impressed incidents of early life, and little physical happenings whose memory adheres to the meshes of the animal consciousness after the Soul has withdrawn.

Thus would it inevitably be if the Race tried to go back to the conditions of its childhood as a Race and attempt to manifest the male and female again in an androgynous body, in which the two reproduced by fission—as the amoeba does today, the two dividing into four once every forty hours—as in the pre-physical days. Once the separation of the sexes had been accomplished and the preparation made for the crowning achievement of physical embodiment, *i.e.*, the manifestation of unity in duality or the one spiritual Being in separated aspects, there can be no going back, any more than a child can return to its mother's womb, or a flower into the seed from which it sprang. Once the auric egg, in which both were germinating, had been planted in matter and had hatched and brought forth the man and the woman, they must go on and on up the spiral journey of the celestial Soul's pilgrimage through matter until, through the union of the two who are one, there is manifested the Christ-power which shall rule all things and make of this planet the glowing star in the East for a new system which is its destiny to become.

In the childhood of the Race the God of Love and Wisdom taught mankind how to build for themselves a physical body, an ark into which was gathered every type and manifestation of life in the animal and lower kingdoms. After they became separated the Soul found itself endowed with two ways of looking at life and its problems, two windows through which it could view the panorama of life in both directions. And, if willing to remember their earlier lessons and obey the laws then taught them, they could still find the Lord God walking in the Garden of their dually manifested Spiritual Self.

In endeavoring to set forth the principles of this mighty subject during the less enlightened ages, many blinds necessarily had to be used; for until the brain of man had passed through the stage of mechanical expression, as exemplified in the present mechanical age, it was not sufficiently unburdened of its urge to material expression to be ready to listen and respond to the stage of spiritual expression of the inner Spiritual Man, who alone is taught of God face to face. Hence the truth of this subject could be taught only to the Elect, those whose spiritual unfoldment was such that they could grasp and understand without misconceiving and materializing it. To all others it had to be expressed in parables. Only to those Elect did Jesus say: "Unto you it is given to know the mystery of the kingdom of God: but unto them that are without, all these things are done in parables: that seeing they may see, and not perceive; and hearing they may hear, and not understand."[2]

In spite of the fact that the spiritual mysteries are always veiled from the spiritually unprepared, many are going about the world today offering to teach all who can pay the steep price, not only all the mysteries, but—for a still higher price—all the major and minor initiations. In the Orient where the unfolding of the higher powers is taught to advanced and specially selected students only, according to traditional methods, the student is required to withdraw from the world and spend a full year, or longer if necessary, upon the unfoldment of each center, under constant supervision and guidance. Hence, one can readily see how little can be ac-

---

[2] *St. Mark*, IV, 11, 12.

complished with the unprepared by a few commercialized lessons as to methods of unfoldment.

To those who know that initiation and ability to comprehend the mysteries comes only as a result of long and steady spiritual unfoldment, it is obvious that the grandiose promises of commercialised teachers cannot be kept, but are simply bait used by charlatans to exploit for financial returns, the sincere desire of the Soul for spiritual enlightenment. But a little experience will show that no amount of mere repetition of mantrams, of sitting in specified postures or of performing prescribed breathing or other exercises can, of themselves, unfold the spiritual understanding, enable the mind to grasp spiritual truth or bring one into conscious touch with the Divine Indweller that He may become the guide and ruler of the life. At most, such vain repetitions and mechanical exercises can but open one's consciousness to the lower astral — not the spiritual—world with its manifold illusions and terrible temptations.

But even if the inner mysteries are veiled, all who earnestly and sincerely seek for spiritual enlightenment, rather than for wonders, will always be led to where that aspect of truth needed for their next step onward can be found, provided they ask in the inner sanctuary of their hearts for that guidance. For when the outer activities are stilled and the mind quieted there comes a vague memory, almost a realization, of something wonderful that is within, a part of us, yet which just eludes our grasp. But no matter how vague this may be at first, those who persistently enter into the silence of the temple of the Inner Self some day will surely have the great truths which were given to them in the beginning revealed to their outer consciousness, and the truth shall make them free. Then they will no longer waste time, money and effort poring over books filled with biased interpretations and dogmatic statements put forth by those whom Jesus called the blind leaders of the blind.

As we enter this new Aquarian Age we will find it an age

of revelation and understanding. For while the weeds of misconception, falsification and misuse of God's most sacred truths and gifts must first spring up, the forces poured out by the mighty Water Bearer will ultimately sweep away all that is false and will wash clean the minds and hearts of men as the overflowing of the physical waters will cleanse the Earth. And the cataclysmic conditions through which humanity is destined to pass will awaken to spiritual realization all sincere Souls who are eager for spiritual growth and understanding.

Since the creative *laya centers* of this planet were animated and its manifestation materialized in quite a different way from other planets or world-chains,[3] it is here that an entirely new act in the drama of manifestation is to be enacted. Here humanity is entrusted with the use of a new and dangerous power, capable of bringing to them the greatest suffering and misery, but also capable of lifting them into a realm and a state of consciousness higher than any yet reached on other world-chains. Those who have reached the perfection of other worlds have not had the same lessons to learn, for they did not have the same conditions to meet, experience and conquer. They are the advanced Souls who are now learning the lessons of the Earth-chain. For this reason man did not accidentally or through a mistake on the part of the Creator "fall" into generation, but his bodily vehicles were specially designed by the Creative Hierarchies for the purpose of learning the great lesson of this planet, *i.e.*, the use and mastery of the creative powers in duality, that is, manifesting in separated sexes.

"The light of the body is the eye; if therefore thine eye be single, thy whole body shall be full of light."[4] While the obvious outer meaning of this statement is that we must be sincere and whole-hearted in our search for truth, its esoteric meaning is that when the single or Third Eye functions it

---

[3] See Chapter on "World Chains" in *The Voice of Isis*, Curtiss
[4] *St. Matthew*, VI, 22.

permits us to see in the spiritual realm, whose radiant spiritual light will illumine all our bodies and make them full of light This does not mean that we will ever return to the Cyclops stage of evolution and have but one eye functioning outwardly, but that the Third Eye will function inwardly and admit our consciousness to the inner worlds. Nor does it mean that children will ever be created through the functioning of the Third Eye. Children will always be procreated sexually as long as mankind manifests in physical bodies, according to the Law of Duality which rules the physical plane; for by the time man learns to create physically through *Kriya-shakti* or thought-power, he will no longer function through the physical body.

As the Third Eye gradually opens and illumines our consciousness, the power both to create and procreate will be seen in a far different and more sacred light than can be conceived of by the unillumined today. Only when we open the Third Eye and learn to utilize its power for spiritually creative purposes can we create as gods, knowing good and evil.

Chapter XXIX

THE MOUNT OF ATTAINMENT

"Who shall ascend into the hill of the Lord? or who shall stand in his holy place? He that hath clean hands and a pure heart; who hath not lifted up his soul unto vanity; nor sworn deceitfully. He shall receive the blessing from the Lord, and righteousness from the God of his salvation." *Psalms*, XXIV, 3-5.

"Adoration and joy have a most powerful effect as an invocation. Even though the eye of sinful man may not see the descent of the glory invoked, it can be distinctly felt with a thrill of awe and adoration by every sensitive nature. Hence joy which springs from adoration is truly a magical power." *Christian Mystic Hymnal*, Curtiss, 43.

In the mystic legends of many countries we are told of a certain high mountain—which possibly is not physical, yet which all those who sincerely seek shall ultimately find—whose top is enveloped in a fleecy snow-white cloud and around whose base at various places almost impassable bogs and marshes, deep canyons, rocky defiles and precipitous cliffs separate it from the plains beyond.

It is said that upon the mountain-top there is a pool of clear, radiant water from which four streams run to the four quarters of the globe. This pool is said to be the Pool of Divine Life in which the mystic potencies which constitute the life-blood of the Cosmos are focused for this planet, while the streams which come from it are streams of Living Water which flow from the Divine to all mankind, and of which all who will may drink to their Soul's refreshment, and in which all who bathe will be purified and cleansed from all their sins and Soul-stains.

This mountain is the sacred Mount of Spiritual Attainment which is symbolized in various lands by Mt. Meru,

Mt. Olympus, Mt. Sinai, etc.; altho any beautiful cloud-capped mountain would symbolize the same thing, for all such mountains uplift and inspire the Soul with joy and adoration of the Divine. But however symbolized this is a definite Mount of Attainment which all humanity must ultimately find and begin to climb, no matter how many incarnations they may wander in the wilderness at its base ere they definitely begin the ascent.

The great mass of mankind are content to remain and live for many incarnations on the plain at the base of this Mount, amidst the dank miasmas which rise from the reeking swamps, chilled by the cold fogs which settle down and blot out the Sun, and often suffering miserably from the terrible storms and blizzards which howl through the canyons and gorges and out over the plain. Yet all the time there are many open glades and sunny meadows higher up on the mountain-side which continually invite those who are willing to break away from the traditions of their neighbours, seek out the Path, brave the dangers of the unknown and put forth the effort to climb.

The streams of Living Water which flow from the Sacred Pool down over the mountain-side have, in many places, become so broken up and diverted by the obstacles placed in them by man's ignorance, selfishness and materialism that they are scattered and spread out into shallow, sluggish wandering seepages instead of remaining clear sparkling rills of Divine Life-force. And their waters have been so polluted that they are full of fungi and other low forms of life which only add to their impurity and sliminess, so that in addition to the rocks which bruise the feet of the pilgrim who aspires to ascend the Mount, his feet slip and his hands are often defiled and he despairs of reaching the sunny glades he sees above, to say nothing of attaining the top.

Among the masses toiling at the base many look up from time to time and long for the peace and quiet, the sunshine and the green trees they see above. And some adventurous ones have actually climbed part way up out of the lower mists and fogs toward the regions where the Masters dwell, and think that now that they are above the lower mists all their trials are over and the problem of the ascent is solved. Because of this humanity hears many voices calling out: "This is the only way, follow me! This is the only true Path! See how high I have climbed! See how I can demonstrate! Therefore my teachings are the only Truth!"

Yet each points out a different way. So confusing are these different voices that many earnest seekers follow first one, then another, often slipping and falling over some hidden rock and sustaining many a bruise, and often having to retrace their steps to enter another path. But those who cease struggling to obey the loud cries of "Follow me," and who pray to the Christ for guidance, hear a vibrant Voice of poignant sweetness that penetrates through all the confusion and fills their hearts with a divine emotion, saying: "I am the Way, the Truth, and the Life." And as they look up they see small luminous patches glowing here and there among the rocks, each marking out a footstep of Him who has climbed before them and marked out the Path. Therefore they cease to follow blindly the many cries of human leaders, but seek for evidences of His footsteps and follow them wherever found.

Those who will follow this inner Divine Guidance—and through the Christ-challenge they can be sure it is Divine and not mere astral guidance—realize that on the mountaintop stands the Lord Christ holding out His hands and pouring forth His force to help all who turn to Him. They then see that He is not hidden, as so many think, by the clouds which surround the top, for the clouds are but the effulgent radiance of His glory which the eye of sinful man cannot penetrate, for it must be spiritually discerned. He stands in the radiant Light which seems to fill all space, and the Power which streams from His hands thrills each devout seeker, illumines his mind and warms his heart with ecstasy.

It matters not from what country the aspirants come or through what religion. The only questions He asks are: "Lovest thou me? Art thou true and sincere? Art thou trying thy best?" For no matter what our belief, if we follow it sincerely we will either advance toward Him—under whatever name we may know Him—or we will soon come to the end of any mistaken path we have taken and will learn its lesson. When we reach the end of such a path we need not fear either punishment or reproach, for even though we must someday reap the inevitable Karma of our mistakes, especially if willfully persisted in, nevertheless at the end of our blind path or detour we will find the Christ with a tender smile of loving encouragement waiting to point out the luminous footprints of the true Way. Therefore, no matter what path we may have followed, how we may have strayed or how we have delayed our advance, if we have been sincere and true to our best guidance we will ultimately find the Lord of Life and Love and Beauty, even if only to change the direction of our efforts. For often there are lessons on paths leading away from Him which seemed necessary for us ere we could give Him true recognition and allegiance.

Thus many Souls go round and round the Mount, incarnation after incarnation, even after they have climbed to a considerable height. Some of these are wont to discourage other seekers by telling them that there is nothing new to be learned, even as high as they have gone, and that all is contained in the old musty teachings which were suited to past ages and which they had studied in past incarnations, hence had recognized and naturally accepted in this life. This is one of the reasons why the whole world is so filled with unrest and dissatisfaction with former teachings which fail to point out a straight path that can be followed under present day conditions, "Because straight is the gate, and narrow is the way, which leadeth unto Life, and few there be that find it"

Know well that there is not one child of Earth, be he ever so wicked according to the world's idea, who will not ultimately learn—by the inevitable suffering his transgression of the Law creates, even out of the depths of agony and despair, if he will learn in no other way—how to find the Christ; who will not at least glimpse the radiance of His glory and feel the warmth of His redeeming love. The greater the sinner, the greater the miracle of transformation when the thrill of Divine Love awakens him to realization. The more he has striven to serve self or to stand in the market place that the world may exalt him, the more surely will he reach the end of his own greatness, when, overwhelmed by disappointment and humiliation, he will gladly turn at last to the Christ.

The lower slopes of the Mount of Attainment are infested by bandits of many kinds who seek to steal from the pilgrim that which he has gained from the Lord Christ during his climb up the Mount. Even at certain passes far up on the mountain-side occasional bandits are to be met. One earnest Aspirant was once confronted with two bandits, both young, handsomely dressed and very polite. But since the Aspirant had been trained to look deep into every unusual incident or experience of life for its inner significance or lesson, he at once challenged "In the Name of the Christ." The first bandit told him that the ransom he demanded was that the true Aspirant for Mastery must cater more to worldly prosperity and prove the height of his attainment by the degree of his worldly advancement and power. The second bandit demanded that the Aspirant cater more to the intellectual classes and modify his ideals so as to conform to the ideas of the so-called practical scientific world. But upon further challenge and the refusal of the Aspirant to abandon the Heart Doctrine or follow any other guidance than the Christ Light, the bandits disappeared. Thus we see that as we advance up the Mount of Attainment the temptations become more subtle and apparently more reasonable, yet are always amenable to the Christ challenge.

Those sincere and humble ones who are willing to empty themselves of their own conceptions that they may be filled with His consciousness and follow in His footsteps, reach many sunny glades on the mountain-side where for a considerable time they enjoy health, peace, rest and prosperity, and where they expand their consciousness with the realization of His presence or at least the aura of His passing near. But after this period of advance, assimilation and recuperation, as they climb still higher, a new period of trial and testing awaits them. They have been tested as to their ability to hear the Voice and follow the footsteps, as to their sincerity and their ability to climb, but now comes the test of their faith and their endurance. For just as mountain climbers experience various changes in their bodily functions as the higher altitudes are reached and the rarefied air makes breathing more difficult, makes the heart labour and the blood vessels seem ready to burst, and brings on the lassitude of "mountain sickness," so do similar experiences occur as we reach the higher altitudes on the Mount of Attainment. Our whole being must adjust itself to the rarified atmosphere, to the higher vibrations, to the focus of previously unknown currents of force and to the dazzling Light to which we are now subjected.

This type of illness naturally results from an excessive influx of Divine Radiance, for as the higher spiritual forces pour into the body all its nerves and tissues must respond and be transmuted or those which are too dense must break down and be cast out. A similar process takes place with the use of the X-ray. While it is helpful, stimulating and healing in moderate amounts, its excessive use causes terrible burns or even cancers which necessitate the amputation of a limb or part.

Not only must the bodily tissues adjust themselves to the great influx of spiritual forces, but in the mental realm the seed-thoughts of every fear, sin or disease experienced since childhood—together with similar seed-thoughts brought over from past lives—which have been impressed upon the subconscious mind or lodged in the astral body or physical tissues in a latent or spore stage, are fructified and stimulated into active manifestation until conquered or thrown off, because their Karma has been reaped. Hence it is necessary to use every possible means—physical, medical, mental and spiritual—to help Nature make this great readjustment, lest the physical be unable to bear the strain.

Often such latent seeds of fear, sin or disease may have entirely disappeared from the mind and not have been thought of for years, yet they suddenly break out into manifestation without apparent cause. Hence the Aspirant may pass through attack after attack of various severe illnesses, often of an infectious nature with high fever and great prostration, or through attacks of neurasthenia or nervous prostration from apparently trivial causes. But in spite of passing through this "mystical ill health" as it is called, many of whose attacks would kill an ordinary person living on the lower levels of attainment, those who pass through this rapid chemicalization or transmutation seldom die during the attacks and often live to a ripe old age in spite of their invalidism. But when the process is over they return to perfect health, altho still very sensitive to inharmonious conditions of body or mind.

Such persons survive because the main life-centers have been sufficiently transmuted and spiritualised in the past and in this life to be able to withstand the higher forces sufficiently to hold the body together and preserve its life. But this should not be made the excuse for giving way in a negative manner to every little indisposition or inharmony instead of striving to conquer it.

All these experiences are evidence, not of backsliding or failure to "live the life," but of the fact that higher altitudes on the spiritual mountain-side have been reached. But if the various stages of this strenuous climb are understood they need not become "the dark night of the Soul"; for it should be borne in mind that the message of the Christ is essentially one of joy. This is the message that mankind greatly needs. We need to realize the wonderful truth in the words: "Sorrow may endure for a night, but joy cometh in the morning." For the Soul passes through a night-period and suffers only as it loses sight of the Christ-life, and it is morning the instant the joy of His presence illumines our being.

Already we see the Mystic Light far out over the sea of life, the Light which presages the dawn of a New Day for all humanity. We should therefore repeat to ourselves until it becomes a part of our inner consciousness that *we can enter into the joy of the Lord if we will.* We feel the thrill of this joy to the extent that we become one with Him, even if it be but for a moment. No matter if the Earth be shaking, if cities be burning, if governments be overturned and nations in despair, if through climbing up the Mount of Attainment we have learned, by even one experience, something of the underlying, eternal and never-ending stream of joy that is flowing from the heart of the Christ, we can rest in the knowledge that all is well; for all seeming disasters in the outer life are but clearing the way for His coming and for the greater manifestation of His joy.

Chapter XXX

THE ROUND TABLE

"That ye may eat and drink at my table in my kingdom, and sit on twelve thrones judging the twelve tribes of Israel." St. Luke, XII, 30.

"Except ye eat the flesh of the Son of man, and drink his blood, ye have no life in you. . . . He that eateth my flesh, and drinketh my blood, dwelleth in me, and I in him." *St John*, VI, 53-56.

"Man am I grown, a man's work must I do. Follow the deer? Follow the Christ the King. Live pure, speak true, right wrong, follow the king—else wherefore born?" *Idylls of the King*, Tennyson.

Among the many legends handed down through the early literature of the race there is probably none more romantic and interesting than that of the Mystic Quest, the English version being that of King Arthur and his Knights of the Round Table. He is represented as a great monarch, the splendour of whose court, whose riches and generosity, are the admiration of all. His court is made the point of departure and return for the Knights who ride forth on purely chivalric ventures, such as aiding each other, rescuing those in distress, seeking the Holy Grail and the like.

Altho the legends concerning King Arthur were collected and published in Geoffrey of Monmouth's *Historia Regum Britanniae* as early as 1136 A.D., recent historical research tells us that whether there was a historic King Arthur is much debated and often roundly denied.[1] But it makes little difference whether the tale is historical or not, for it contains a marvellous symbology when spiritually interpreted.

Even though Geoffrey of Monmouth makes no mention of a Round Table, such a table is almost universally connected with the story of King Arthur as being one of the three

---

[1] *Encyclopaedia Britannica*, II, 681.

fabulous and mystical tables representing the Trinity. The first table is said to be the Table of the Last Supper, the second the Round Table of the Holy Ghost which was brought to England by Joseph of Arimathea, and the third is the Round Table of King Arthur, at which only the most valiant of the Knights of the Round Table were privileged to sit. This table is said to have been made round so that all the Knights might be seated without quarreling as to precedence.

The legend goes much farther back than the fifth or sixth century, for there is scarcely a time in recorded history when some version of it was not known to the mystics in some form and repeated either as history, legend or myth according to the understanding of the one repeating it. But always there is the central figure of a King, also his Queen, surrounded by a halo of light from a crown of jewels and sitting in the seat of honour, in the center of the Round Table of which there were twelve divisions or seats. The curious part of these legends is that while these seats always hold twelve Knights, often many other Knights are represented as seated back of each chair, so that each division of the Round Table, as it extended outward into space, could contain an infinite multiplication of the original twelve.

Since every legend that is handed down through the ages must have some underlying basis of truth or it could not survive, let us seek for the truth underlying this legend of King Arthur and his Round Table.

Scholars generally agree that King Arthur is a Solar Hero or a representative of the Sun God. This gives the key to the whole legend; for with King Arthur in the center representing the Sun, the Round Table is seen to represent the zodiac, and its twelve seats or divisions are the twelve signs of the zodiac The twelve chief Knights are the Rulers of the twelve signs, while the other Knights who stand back of each seat are all those belonging to each sign who have passed their initiations and have dedicated themselves to serve the Light Bearer in His mission of spreading the Light of Truth to every type of mankind in all the twelve signs.

As we have said elsewhere: "Reference may be made to the twelve zodiacal signs as representative of the Twelve Apostles, of which King Arthur and the Round Table is but another version—as merely a figurative method of typifying the Twelve as a fundamental law of spiritual geometry. Hereby is sought to establish the truth that every Circle of Being includes twelve particular points of spiritual radiation or magnetic departures, whereby a change in the involutionary inbreathing becomes a vibratory foil to its polar opposite or evolutionary outbreathing. . . . Being the representative of the Spiritual Sun, the Light Bearer of every age naturally drew around himself twelve representatives through whom his Light could shine forth and be expressed in twelve phases to the peoples to whom He came, just as the Sun is reflected in its twelve disciples or signs of the zodiac."[2]

"The twelve was a symbol *necessarily* used by every Light Bearer, not to copy some older expression of cosmic truth, but to illustrate the twelve aspects through which both the physical Sun manifests in Nature and the Spiritual Sun manifests in humanity; also to indicate the twelve mighty zodiacal Hierarchies or Rays of Understanding, the twelve mighty expressions of Cosmic Truth; the twelve avenues through which the Sun of Righteousness—the incarnate Word—can shine forth to illuminate the hearts and minds of all classes and conditions of humanity. They also represent the twelve gates to the New Jerusalem, that inner Temple of Truth in which each type of humanity (disciple) can receive the illumination of the inner Mysteries face to face and heart to heart through his own special avenue of thought and teaching; that inner shrine where the one Light reveals those inner truths which cannot be given directly to the uncomprehending multitude, but which are the basis of the

---

[2] *The Key of Destiny*, Curtiss, 51–53.

outer shining forth of every true disciple of the Christ."[2]

"The zodiac also represents the Last Supper or Round Table on which the Bread of Life is placed, the food which sustains the universe; while the life-force (blood) of the Sun, which vitalizes all the signs, is the Wine of Life or the mystical blood of the Cosmic Christ of which all must partake. While all partake of this mystic bread and wine around the Sun's table, only those who are truly disciples and who recognize their Lord of Light, can consciously partake 'in remembrance of Him' with a full understanding of what is taking place."[2]

At the last supper Jesus "took the bread and gave thanks, and brake it, and gave unto them, saying, 'This is my body which is given for you.'" And in *I Corinthians*, X, 16-17 we read: "the bread which we brake, is it not the communion of the body of Christ? For we being many have one bread, and one body: for we are all partakers of that one bread." Both these and many other similar statements clearly indicate that all mankind—regardless of race, color, religion or creed—must collectively be regarded and the body of the Cosmic Christ broken into countless fragments (personalities) that we might share His life, while the Wine is His blood or spiritual life-force which is instilled into all, no matter how differently they may manifest it or by what name they may call it and whether they have been able to recognize and manifest it or not. In other words, just as all animals of a certain species collectively form the body of the overshadowing group-soul of that species, whose life-force and consciousness animates them all, so does all mankind form the manifested body of the Cosmic Christ, who stands as the Group Soul of all humanity. Because of this we rightly speak of the Christ within and say, "Thou are in me and I in Thee." It is the inoculation of man's physical body with this higher spiritual Christ substance which differentiates man's body from that of all other animals. The word "eat" is used to emphasize the fact that whatever is eaten is carried to every tissue and becomes an integral part of our bodies. In this sense, eating of this manifested body of the Christ means that we must cooperate with and assimilate His constructive forces and ideals to the greater nourishment of our individual and collective lives. Hence we should not expect an individualization of the Christ in addition to this collective manifestation until mankind has so far demonstrated its brotherhood as to form an international body of disciples in whose midst the phenomenal manifestation can take place as of old.

When we realize this mighty truth of the oneness of all humanity we will see the essential unity and brotherhood of all mankind, not only spiritually, but also in this physical sense. We will see that all are God's children, all who are born in every sign of the Round Table of the Zodiac. Only as we understand and admit this great truth and recognize the Christ as our King standing in the midst of all mankind, can we consciously partake of that mystic Bread and Wine which shall make us His true Knights of the Holy Grail. Not only does this legend reveal the inner symbology of the twelve signs of the zodiac which surround their central point, represented by the Sun, King Arthur or the Holy Grail, but it also refers to a fact of pre-historical days. For in the very early days of mankind, when the Masters walked and talked with men and taught them face to face, the basis of this tale was an actual fact upon the physical plane. For there was a special court of a King Arthur (which means White Knight) and his Lady. And there were twelve chief Knights, honest, loyal and true, who had their seats at the Round Table, altho there were many other Knights and their ladies in addition. While this White Knight always had his bride, and his bride is always at the Round Table with the King, in the outer symbology she does not appear except as a great mystical overshadowing, representing the Holy Ghost. Hence history has much trouble in locating or placing the Bride.

While history tells us either that King Arthur and his Lady are but mythical characters or that King Arthur was merely a great hunter and chieftain who had to protect his country from marauders, and that his wife was the weaver of the wondrous apparel—spiritual understanding—which each Knight donned ere he took his place around the Table, yet in reality there were two pre-historical characters around whom all the various myths, legends, operas and stories are woven. They were the rulers of the first human dynasty established by the Masters as They gradually withdrew from the outer guidance of mankind. These two were, indeed, King and Queen "by divine right," a doctrine so little understood and so degenerated in modern times. The court thus established was one of peace, harmony and co-operation, and through it the Masters introduced to humanity the perfect and harmonious basic principles of life and government.

Strange as it may seem to some, scarcely believable and almost miraculous, nevertheless it was in those far distant days and at this perfect court of the White Knight and his Lady that many, who today find their true spiritual home in *The Order of Christian Mystics*, made their first touch with the Wisdom Religion now expounded by this Order. There also they first met the Founders of the Order who at that time were first given the accolade of authority and were trained in the ability to transmit the Cosmic Wisdom to humanity. And there are some of you today who sat upon or stood behind the twelve seats; who lifted up the Sacred Cup and sipped its nectar; who swore a mighty oath that while life lasted you would ever be true to the divine principles you then understood and espoused, knowing full well that life is immortal and can never end. And as that mystic vow was taken the Light of the Shekina descended like a dove and rested upon the Cup. And because of the descent of the Shekina, as each partook of the nectar there was instilled into the blood of their mortal bodies the Divine Fire of immortal life. For these Souls, even the mention of that ceremony will bring a thrill of joy and a warm glow to the heart

But as the ages rolled on, life after life and experience after experience gradually overlaid or wiped out the memory of your baptism and your vow. Some of you incarnated in the East, some in the West, some in the South and some in the North. You were born in many different tribes and later on in many different nations. Some of you sat in the seats of the Twelve first in one age and country and then in another, according to the Planetary Ruler to whom you belong or under whose sign you were born, altho often not realizing or understanding the position you occupied or why.

Naturally you forgot the ancient ceremony and the ancient training as you sank more and more deeply into matter, for it was necessary for your consciousness to be occupied with the concerns of the outer world until you learned its major lessons. Yet always there was a vague longing as for something you had known and lost; always an unceasing urge to seek and find your true spiritual home again, even while learning the outer lessons of the physical world. This was because your lips had once touched the Sacred Cup, the Holy Grail, and its Wine of Life flows forever in your veins, even though the memory of that great event is denied you until you have reached a certain stage of spiritual unfoldment. Nor can we reveal more of it to you.

Today most of the devoted students of this Order have gone some distance on their great journey up the Mount of Attainment toward spiritual realization and at-one-ment. At least most of you have consciously turned your faces and your footsteps toward your Father's house, your spiritual home. You have learned that there is no use turning back. There is no use saying: "I am tired of life, tired of sinning and suffering, of dying and being reborn. Let me avoid such further experiences." You have gone far beyond that childish stage and you realize that there is but one way to progress, and that is ever onward and upward and inward. Some of you already say: "Because the Round Table started out from God and goes back to God, I must fight the good fight until I can once more consciously sit in my place with my armor on, with my brain and understanding clear and with my heart aglow. I must do my duty in the place where the Great Law stations me until I can once more see God in the center of the Round Table, radiating everywhere."

In a personal sense the Round Table is the circle of our aura and our environment. In the center stands our personal Light Bearer, the Christ within, with our seven centers and our five senses making up the twelve Knights through which He must manifest in our lives. It is for us so to rule them that they will co-operate with each other without rivalry or striving for precedence, but will help each the other, rescuing those in distress and all ever seeking the Holy Grail. Only as all look within to Him for guidance can we make our lives a peaceful, harmonious and helpful court like that of King Arthur.

In the stories of King Arthur and his Knights it is said that wherever a Knight travelled, even though he went on foot and dressed in rags, people recognized him because of his courtesy, his learning, his kindness and his unselfish desire to help others. So they said: "Surely he cometh from King Arthur's court." As Tennyson expresses it, "When first thou earnest—such courtesy spake thro' the limbs and in the voice—I knew thee for one of those who sat in Arthur's hall." [3] So must those of us today who again aspire to serve King Arthur be recognized by our tolerance, our humility, our loving kindness, our joyousness and our unselfish service to our fellow men.

While those who represented the White Knight and his Lady have manifested through many personalities in many

---

[3] *Idylls of the King.*

long, wearisome incarnations, nevertheless they carry in their
hands the mystic Host. Again today, as of old, the White Knight
is told to take the mystic Bread broken by the Christ and give
it to the hungry world. And she who holds in her right hand the
Mystic Cup which contains the fiery spiritual life-force, the Wine
which once partaken of never leaves the body, cries: "Come and
drink! Drink all who will and live forever!" This is the crystal
Cup from which all must drink ere their ascension can be made.

Today this mystic Round Table at which some few of you
have found your places, is once more revolving out of the dense
darkness of the ignorance and mistakes of the past and is coming
into the light of recognition. Will you, can you, dare you once
more consciously don the armour of the Knight you once vowed
you would be? Will you take up the Sword of the Spirit and cleave
from you every fault, failing and imperfection that holds you back
from returning to your place at the Round Table?

This conscious reseating of the Knights around the Table of
the White Knight must be a deliberate choice, and can be attained
only through willing service from the Christ. This is a mission
which does not concern yourselves alone, but all mankind.
Therefore you must face conditions and realize that as we are
passing through the blackest darkness into the light of a New
Day, all the more reason for you to don the full armour of the
Christ[4] that you may conquer and help humanity to find the Way,
the Truth and the Life.

---

[4] *Ephesians*, VI, 14–17

Chapter XXXI

DIVINE FIRE

"Fire is the most perfect and unadulterated reflection, in Heaven as on Earth, of the One Flame. It is Life and Death, the origin and end of every material thing. It is Divine Substance." *The Secret Doctrine*, Blavatsky, I, 146.

"The Seven Beings in the Sun are the Seven Holy Ones, self-born from the inherent power of the Matrix of Mother-Substance. It is they who send out the seven principle Forces, called Rays. . . . The energy, from which they spring into Conscious existence in every Sun, is what some people call Vishnu, which is the Breath of the Absoluteness." *The Secret Doctrine*, Blavatsky, I, 310.

"He who tells thee he has seen the Sun, laugh at him, as if he had said that the Sun moves really onward in his diurnal path." *The Secret Doctrine*, Blavatsky, I, 310.

The whole universe and all its forms of life are but manifestations of Divine Fire; for this Fire is the cause of motion, and matter is but retarded motion or motion temporarily crystallized objectively into latency. The biblical statement that, "Our God is a consuming fire," refers to that formless Divine Essence, that invisible "cold flame" whose three-fold aspect constitutes the animating power of the invisible Spiritual Sun whose manifestations we call God, and of which our physical Sun is but a focal point or servant of manifestation in the physical universe.

The basic manifestation of this Divine Fire is that akashic energy which composes the internal fires or radiant energy which occupies the central core of the Sun, of the Earth, of the atom, of the proton and of our bodies. It is the basic vibration of our whole solar system and is that which vital-

izes all matter with electronic energy, and all life with *prana*[1]
and bodily heat; for all life requires some degree of heat, absence
of heat being death, according to science "absolute zero" being
annihilation. This akashic Fire is the animating, rotary, centripetal
form of energy which holds the whole material universe in
objective manifestation, from flaming comets and blazing Suns
around which universes circle, down to the red tips of most
sprouts of vegetation as they first emerge from soil or bud, and
also those lowly manifestations of fire or combustion (oxidation)
found in rusting iron and in the decay of old age.

As we recognize the manifestations of radiant energy in suns
and stars, in electrons and protons, in chemical affinity and in
radium and radio-active substances, we should thank God for His
mighty Love thus expressed in these lowly aspects of Divine Fire.

If we are really to understand Divine Fire we can do so only
by studying Fire and its manifestations as we know it on Earth,
realizing the while that this most mysterious and practically
unknown element is but a manifestation of Divinity. Scientific
men have declared that, "The first use of fire, and the discovery
of the methods by which it can be kindled are all discoveries with
which, in ingenuity and importance, no subsequent discoveries
may compare."[2] Yet science also says that, "Fire is that which has
ever eluded definite analysis. . . . The lighting of a fire by a flame
is a scientific difficulty, yet few people think so."[3]

Thus is Fire considered by science as both a philosophical
and a scientific mystery. And well may it be so considered,
for in reality it is not an earthly element at all, but a
vehicle for the manifestation of the Godhead. It is not
surprising then that the very heart of all religions springs

---

[1]   We here use the word *prana* in its generic sense as the master vibration of the life-force,
hence it includes its subdivisions of *apana*, *vyana*, *samana* and *udana*.
[2]   *The Unity of Nature*, Argyle.
[3]   *Logic*, Bain, II, 125.

from the thought of Fire in one form or another, from the worship
of the Sun as its source and the adoration of the perpetual Flame
upon the altars of the Ancients, to the Christian statement that
"Our God is a consuming fire."

That which is known on earth as Fire is but the lowest and
outermost covering of the highest element, that which brought
forth the manifested universe; in fact, air is a fluidic, water a liquid
and earth a solid manifestation of Fire. Fire, being a manifestation
of Divinity, naturally has a three-fold manifestation on Earth;
heat (terrestrial fire), light (solar fire) and electricity (elemental
fire). These three manifestations are sometimes called the Three
Mothers,[4] or the creative forces which fructify all things. They
also stand for body, Soul and Spirit. Thus heat (red) represents
the body, light (yellow), the Soul and electricity, energy or force
(blue), the Spirit. Other synonymous terms are Love, Life and
Will. Fire also represents intelligence—heat, light and electricity
being the vehicles through which Divine Intelligence manifests
or brings forth in the lower worlds and kingdoms.

The Ancients gave to Fire a seven-fold expression, three
of which were Divine and four terrestrial. In the center of the
universe they placed a sphere of "Etheric Fire" which was called
"cold flame" because it radiated Light without heat. It was also
called the "Celestial Sun" in the center of the universe. We would
term it the as yet unmanifested Christ resting on the bosom of
the Father or the Throne of God. Around this Celestial Sun the
Ancients placed a sphere of "Spiritual Energy" or the "Sea of Fire
round about the Throne," which emanated from the seemingly
motionless central Sun. The emanations of this Spiritual Energy
went forth into manifestation as the One Life which is the cause
of the ceaseless and incessant generation of all things.

Next, the Ancients conceived of a sphere of "Invisible Es-

---

[4] See *The Key to the Universe*, Curtiss, 119.

sence" or "mind-stuff" through which consciousness manifests. This was the vehicle of the Divine Consciousness which manifests throughout the universe and through man as the Light of Intellect, Sound and human Speech. This is poetically expressed as, "The Mind is the Bride of Heaven" and becomes the "Virgin of Earth," bringing forth in the fields of earth the seed of the heavenly or Christ-consciousness. The Vedas say that, "The heart, excited by Divine Love, becomes creative and from it the senses emanate." These three are the trinitarian manifestations of God as Life, Truth and Love.

According to one classification, the four terrestrial manifestations or fires are first, Light, the Creator; for only when Spiritual Energy has put the mind-stuff into motion and generated mental energy, and Light was conceived of, could the Word go forth, "Let there be Light, and there was Light." Thus Light becomes the Manifested Creator.

The second terrestrial Fire was Heat, the Preserver, the result of the manifestation of the Light meeting the resistance of Earth, and the vehicle of its life-current; for without heat no terrestrial life can exist. The third was Electricity, which they called Regeneration. It is regeneration because, being the third physical expression of Fire, it stands directly under the third spiritual expression, Invisible Essence or mind-stuff, the vehicle of Spiritual Energy or Divine Consciousness. Hence no regeneration is possible until the mind of man has reached a point directly under and is overshadowed by Spiritual Energy. In other words, until man works consciously with and makes his mind a vehicle for the Divine Consciousness.

Electrical energy is such a vehicle to the lower worlds, that which we ordinarily call electricity being but the outer garment, while its inner essence is derived directly from the Invisible Essence of Divine Fire. The fourth aspect of terrestrial fire they called Subterranean Fire, the Destroyer. The work of the Subterranean Fire is to purify, eliminate and transmute; that of the Heat is to manifest as unselfish love, ardor and service for mankind; that of the light is to produce illumination in the heart and mind and shine forth from all the centers of the body, and that of Electricity is to produce never-ceasing activity and illimitable power, a sense of oneness with all life, and manifest the perfect image of God.

We endorse this seven-fold classification as it correlates with the biblical presentation of the subject which we follow.

The akashic aspect of Divine Fire manifesting through the Sun sends its radio-active essence down into the heart of the Earth, down into the depths of the hard and apparently solid rock where its vibrations are instrumental in the formation of gold and jewels and other precious substances which man can use for the better fulfilling of the Law. It also sends down its actinic and pranic rays which are absorbed and embodied in everything that grows: in the gigantic trees, in the tiny blades of grass, in the flowers of the field, in the modest woodland blooms that hide behind the rocks in shady nooks. Not a thing in the universe is overlooked or forgotten. "It is in the Sun, as it is in the glow worm. Not an atom can escape it. Therefore, the ancient Sages have wisely called it the manifested God in Nature."[5]

And as the rays of the Sun are embodied in all forms of life in Nature they vitalize within all those things—each in its own place in its own kingdom—the inner pattern of its form and the outworking of its destiny. It is as though the finger of God reached down and wrote in one: "Lo, thou shalt be a giant sequoia and shalt lift thy head high into the blue sky and rear thy mighty trunk and spread thy branches to the winds of heaven for many ages. This is the destiny that I have given thee. Fulfill thou it." Then He stooped down and touched with His finger the tiny blades of grass and said: "Grow here. Thy destiny is to spread and be prolific and provide food for the cattle that are upon

---

[5] *The Secret Doctrine*, Blavatsky, I, 311.

a thousand hills. Make a gentle covering for the Earth and a green background, soft and beautiful and restful to the eye of man. May the many little flowers that I have planted find their gem-like homes in the shelter of thy blades." To man He said: "Be fruitful, and multiply, and replenish the earth, and subdue it: and have dominion over . . . every living thing that moveth upon the earth." Thus to each form in Nature is given its destiny and its place in manifesting the great Fire of Divine Love, even though we cannot see the pattern or the mystic rays.

As we view the annual miracle of the changing seasons and recognize the manifestations of the Fire of Life in the swelling buds, in the upshooting sprouts, in the unfolding leaves and in the blossoms bursting into beauty and fragrance; in the warmth of the mother bird that hatches her eggs, and brings forth her fledglings, and in the appearance of bee and butterfly, let us again thank God for His mighty Love manifesting in this higher aspect of Divine Fire.

This Earth might have been created as a world of mere utility and without beauty. It might have been a globe filled merely with the forces and materials necessary for life, with only the substances needed for humanity to manifest here and gain certain necessary experiences in matter. But it is not such a merely utilitarian globe, because Divine Will projected it in harmony and co-ordination and Divine Love brought it forth in beauty.

The Flame of God which emanates from the Spiritual Sun had to create the world in such a way that it would be a focus through which its mighty Rays of Divine Fire might be filtered and their high cosmic vibrations toned down and tempered to manifest in this infant stage of planetary and human unfoldment, much as we dilute food for an infant, knowing that its ultimate destiny is to manifest in the full-grown beauty of perfection. Over these Rays from the Father-Mother-Fire there comes to each of us the power to manifest Their life, love and beauty. And to the degree that we allow these Rays to unfold the pattern of our destiny they will manifest in the beauty of perfection; the beauty and perfection of body, of mind and of Soul.

As we recognize in our fellow men the Fire of Love and brotherhood manifesting in all the races and classes of mankind, even the most unevolved and backward, let us again thank God for His unending Love manifesting in this still higher human aspect of Divine Fire.

The second major aspect of Divine Fire to be considered is that aspect of Solar Fire which constitutes Divine Ideation. This is the animating principle of the mind of the Logos or the Divine Mind, whose individualized sparks were implanted in man by the "Sons of Mind" during the middle of the Third Great Race[6]—the Lemurians—and which were later developed into what we now call mind or intellect during the Fourth Great Race—the Atlanteans. Thus it is that mind, as the vehicle for the manifestation of the consciousness of the Real or Spiritual Self, is the link between Spirit and matter, between life and form. Mind is, therefore, the indispensable channel through which the consciousness of the Spirit finds expression and evolution in the world of matter and form.

As the lower Fire of Life is rotary and centripetal in its form of manifestation that it may consolidate matter into form, so the Fire of Mind is spiral and expansive or centrifugal in its form of manifestation, that it may expand man's consciousness to the Divine. And it is because of our ability gradually to expand our consciousness as we evolve spiritually and unfold our destiny that we are ultimately able to return to that Center of Divine Fire from which we emanated; that Center which is both the origin and the ultimate goal of attainment of the individual. It is because we possess an individualized Spark of Mind that we of the fourth kingdom have independent minds or self-consciousness, in-

---

[6] For details see *The Voice of Isis*, Curtiss, 233.

stead of group-consciousness as found among the three lower kingdoms.

It is because our mind is a spark of the Divine Mind that it must necessarily manifest in a three-fold aspect like the Divine Trinity. These three aspects are called the Spiritual Mind, the human mind and the animal mind, or the Super-Conscious Mind (Higher Manas), the rational mind (lower manas) and the sub-conscious mind (kama manas). But it must be remembered that these are not three different minds, but only three aspects of the one mind of man. It is as though the mind of God reached down into our animal body and implanted in our solar plexus a lowly aspect of His consciousness and said: "Thou shalt be the ruler of the physical body and the consciousness of all its cells, tissues and organs. Thou shalt direct all its myriad complex chemical combinations and all its physiological functions and reflex acts. Thou shalt carry on all the animal aspects of life so harmoniously and wholesomely that the entire body shall be a healthy and happy servant and instrument for the manifestation in matter of My higher forms of consciousness. This is thy destiny. Fulfill thou it." Thus it is that the sub-conscious mind possesses the wonderful intelligence required to carry on all the functions of bodily life, such as circulation, respiration, digestion, assimilation, excretion and repair, as well as those enormously intricate and marvellous reflex acts which adapt the body to the ever-changing conditions of heat and cold, moisture and drought, low barometer and high barometer, variations in altitude, work, play, rest, sleep, emotions, etc.

Then God planted a brighter and higher emanation of His consciousness in our minds and said: "Thou shalt be the vehicle of My consciousness in man and woman, through whom alone I can consciously manifest in humanity. Thou shalt reach outward and respond to the vibrations of the outer world and report them to thy Higher Self in terms of sensation and consciousness. But thou shalt not forget to reach inward and respond to the vibrations of thy Divine Guidance that thou mayest govern the desires of thy animal instrument and the vanities and selfishness of thy personality, and manifest that Guidance in all thy ways. This is thy destiny. Follow thou it."

As we recognize the manifestation of the Fire of Mind in our fellow men, even among the most ignorant and unlettered, let us once more thank God for His all-embracing Love manifesting to us through this mental, aspect of Divine Fire.

While comparatively few minds have embodied sufficient of the Fire of Illumination to be able directly to grasp and express the high ideals and inspirations of the Real or Spiritual Man, nevertheless all are gradually learning to do so more and more in each incarnation, according to the degree of spiritualization their minds have attained. This is not an attainment which comes automatically, but is something that must be striven for more or less consciously in each incarnation. For if we allow our minds to be filled continually only with the vibrations coming into them from the things of the outer life and the appetites and desires of the flesh, we build into our minds corpuscles of mental substance, called "mentoids," of so low a rate of vibration that they respond only to the lower fires of passions and desires and ideas of the outer life. Being thus unable to release our consciousness from such lower vibrations we frequently give way to and experience the negative or destructive aspect of Divine Fire, the heat of anger, passion, animal desire and all the lower and destructive emotions. These lower fires are not creative or constructive but are the destructive fires which upset the normal functions of the body, through their effect upon the subconscious mind, the sympathetic nervous system and the endocrine glands, and thus cause inhibition of the normal nerve currents with the resulting congestion, sickness, disease and suffering. If such lower fires are allowed frequent manifestation they will ultimately burn out and disintegrate our physical instrument and deprive our Real Self of its vehicle of manifestation on Earth and thus prevent the step in its unfoldment which this incarnation should afford.

On the other hand, if we seek continually for our Divine Guidance, through prayer and aspiration, looking inward and upward instead of outward and downward, and responding more to the within than to the without, we will fill our minds with mentoids or corpuscles of a far higher and more spiritual quality which can and will respond to the higher Spiritual Fire and allow our minds to be released from limitations of the lower fires, and thus enable our spiritual consciousness to guide and control all our thoughts and emotions and therefore all the words and acts of the human personality.

Every prayer and aspiration, every effort to live up to our highest ideals, every effort to express peace, love, joy and happiness builds more and more spiritualised mentoids into our minds. And as these grow in number and displace the mentoids which respond only to the lower fires, we experience the warm glow of love, brotherhood, compassion and unselfishness and finally the fire of spiritual exaltation and ecstasy.

Thus, to the degree of our sincere aspirations and efforts to follow our Divine Guidance do we draw down and build into our minds actual atoms of Spiritual Fire whose spiritual radio-activity will so purify and transmute the lower atoms of both our minds and our bodies that they will both rejoice to respond to and express the Divine Fire of our Real or Spiritual Self so that without the usual resistance and opposition of the lower atoms we will do His will on Earth even as it is done in heaven.

"Finally, brethren, whatsoever things are true, whatsoever things are honest, whatsoever things are just, whatsoever things are pure, whatsoever things are lovely, whatsoever things are of good report; if there be any virtue, and if there be any praise, *think on these things* . . . . and the peace of God shall be with you."[7]

(To be concluded)

---

[7] *Philippians*, IV, 8–9.

Chapter XXXII

DIVINE FIRE

"For Simon . . . . Fire contained *all*. And thus all parts of that Fire, being endowed with intelligence and reason, was susceptible of development by extension and emanation. This is our teaching of the Manifested Logos, and these parts in their primordial emanations are our 'Sons of Flame and Fire.'" *The Secret Doctrine*, Blavatsky, III, 466.

"Manas, though one removed on the downward plane from Buddhi, is still so immeasurably higher than the physical man that it cannot enter into direct relation with the personality, except through its reflection, the lower mind. Manas is *Spiritual Self-Consciousness* in itself, and Divine Consciousness when united with Buddhi." The *Secret Doctrine*, Blavatsky, III, 518.

"O almighty Father-Mother! Thou who art all Wisdom and Love Divine! Thou whose messengers like flames are ever hovering near, enter into the midst of us Thy children and manifest Thyself in the greatness of Thy glory! Fill our hearts with a realization of Thy Love, and our minds with an understanding of Thy wisdom and with a burning zeal to accomplish Thy work. Help us to manifest *now*, even as we are destined to do, the glory of Thy indwelling Presence." *Invocation to the Flame*, Curtiss.

The cosmic Divine Fire which composes the Central Flame of the Universe burns in all worlds and in all realms. On Earth it manifests in a four-fold manner through the four primal elements, earth, air, fire and water, and their various subdivisions and kingdoms. In the previous Chapter we have shown how this Divine Fire manifests in the mineral kingdom as the Fire of Electronic and Radio-activity and commonly connected with chemical activity; in the vegetable kingdom as the Fire of Life; in the animal kingdom as the Fire of Mind and in the human kingdom as the Fire of Self-consciousness. We have also shown that in each kingdom the manifestation of Divine Fire is also an expression of Divine Love; for Divine Fire is the outshining radiance of God, and God is Love.

Think you, therefore, that a God of Life and Love and Beauty would thus embody a radiant aspect of Himself in all the multitudinous forms in all the kingdoms of Nature and forget man, the summit of evolution and the crowning point of all creation? Think you that He would embody an aspect of Himself in everything that is and would overlook man who is made in His image and after the likeness of the seven-fold Elohim?

God so loved Nature that He gave her the great focus of physical radiance, the physical Sun, to be her light and life and to manifest her destiny. But to man He gave the great focus of spiritual radiance, His only begotten Son, His first-born, the chief of all His attributes, the Spirit of His Love, the great and mighty Christ-love, to be embodied in each heart in potency, for man to unfold and let it become his light and life, and to manifest his destiny. For what good would the mystic fires of the seven-fold planetary Hierarchies be to man's spiritual unfoldment if there were not this spiritual Sun of Righteousness in his heart occupying the central point or throne of his being and able to respond to the spiritual Hierarchies?

As the physical Sun occupies the throne of Nature whence emanates the forces of its light and life, so the heart is the throne of man whence emanate the forces of his spiritual light and life. Yet that life is but a manifestation of love which is God. The Father-Mother forces of God are the bringers-forth in the beauty of holiness of the Inner Man, the Christ within. And since Love is God, Divine Love is the great and one supreme Fire of the Universe which descends in its seven-fold aspects to each division and kingdom of the universe. And because the universe is thus born of Love, unfolded in Love and fostered in Love, it manifests in each kingdom in harmony and beauty, wherever not perverted by man.

The beauty of the body embraces both beauty of form and beauty of function or perfect health manifesting through well regulated and perfectly co-ordinated organs, muscles and nerves. The beauty of mind embraces not only a harmoniously developed brain, but also intellectual discrimination and the ability to control and co-ordinate our thoughts and their expressions to the greater manifestation of the indwelling Higher Self and the glory of God. The beauty of Soul embraces both a harmonious, happy and loving disposition and the ability to recognize our Divine origin, together with an unquenchable desire to seek union with and to manifest our Divine Self. Only as man has failed to grasp and understand the Divine Plan and the destiny of this marvellous and beautiful world, and also the destiny of humanity and himself, and has therefore brought forth after his own imaginings, lusts and selfish desires instead of according to the Divine Plan, do we find the note of inharmony, impurity and lack of beauty manifested in Nature and in man himself.

But to manifest the beauty of the Spiritual Self man must seek for it, must learn to understand its nature and reach up for it and bring down to Earth and embody it in his consciousness and life through contacting the next higher Fire, the Buddhic Fire. For this Buddhic Fire reaches up to Atma and reflects all that is in the auric envelop, *i.e.*, that which is destined to manifest during this incarnation.[1]

The Buddhic Fire is, therefore, the highest aspect of Divine Fire which can manifest on Earth through a mortal. For to manifest the great Auric Fire we must have entered the fifth or superhuman or Divine Kingdom wherein we are no longer merely separate mortals, but have become one with all, enclosed within the Divine Egg of the great Bird of Life. But since the Auric Fire of the Divine Self and the Atmic Fire of the Universal Spirit are so far above the

---

[1] *The Secret Doctrine*, Blavatsky, III, 375–518.

comprehension of the average student we will confine ourselves to an explanation of the Buddhic Fire.

This Buddhic Fire, while far above the vibrations of the consciousness of ordinary man, nevertheless belongs to humanity, for it is a Ray of the Spiritual Self implanted in the heart of man, just as a ray of the physical Sun is implanted in the seed or nucleus of every living thing in the lower kingdoms. Therefore, if we are consciously to set out upon the Great Quest of how to become Sons of God, or rather how to manifest the Sonship we already inherently possess as "heirs of God, and joint-heirs with Christ" or luminous points of light to reflect His glory, then we must strive until we learn to draw down and manifest this Buddhic Fire in our hearts and lives.

And this Fire is Love. For just as the radio-active essence of the physical Sun penetrates the Earth and there coagulates its essence into gold and jewels and other precious substances, so does the spiritually radio-active essence of the Buddhic Fire of Divine Love penetrate deep into the soil of our hearts and lives and there creates veins of spiritual gold, jewels of great price and spiritual riches beyond compare, which are ours for the digging and bringing to the surface, but which are not thrown into our laps with no effort on our part any more than is the physical gold or jewels.

We need not be discouraged when great occult and philosophical authorities tell us that: "Consciousness *per se*, as understood and explained by Occult philosophy, is the highest sentient spiritual principle in us, the Divine Soul or Buddhi and our own Higher Ego, and does not belong to the plane of materiality," and "is still so immeasurably higher than the physical man, that it cannot enter into direct relation with the personality, except through its reflection, the lower mind."[1] For as we begin to manifest the Fire of Divine Love it will so consume the impurities and dross accumulated in the lower mind through wrong think-

ing, wrong teaching and wrong response to the lower fires—
which impurities make the lower mind more or less opaque to
the Divine Light—that ultimately that Light will shine through
more and more clearly.

It is like a lighted lantern casting shadows on a wall. The
wall is our body and brain and our environment, all our outer
conditions through and in which we manifest. The glass globe
through which the light shines is the lower mind. The light in
the lantern is the Higher Mind, while the fire which produces the
light within is the Buddhic Fire. It is therefore our great duty to
wipe off the dust of material thoughts and the muddy blotches
of impurity which becloud and disfigure the globe or lens of our
lower mind so that the spiritual Light of the Higher Mind can
shine through unimpeded and without casting distorted shadows
on our brain, in our body and in our environment. Thus will the
Divine Light dissipate the shadows and multiply the rays we are
able to manifest as good and constructive thoughts, words and
deeds.

As long as the lens of our mind remains unpurified, the dust
of material thoughts and the blotches of impurity upon it dim
the Light to a murky gleam or perhaps a dull red glare instead of
letting through the clear white Light that is shining within our
hearts. It is this murky gleam of materialism and the dull red
glare of animalism that are called the "lower fires" which burn so
consumingly in the lives of the less developed and sense-ridden
mass of humanity, and which emit their acrid and stifling smoke
and spread their effluvia over all their environment and over all
humanity.

When such undeveloped Souls pass on from the physical
into the astral world they find themselves surrounded by the
corresponding fires of the lower regions of that world. From those
regions many such persons strive to quench the torch of Spiritual
Light which the more advanced Souls are seeking to light and
keep burning in the hearts of mankind.

For that Spiritual Light illumines and reveals in all its hideousness the wickedness and evil with which such undeveloped ones are surrounded. That is one reason why they strive so hard to influence the sensitive followers of the Light, to stimulate their selfishness and their lower fires of passion and desire and subject them to those fires of dissolution which to those in the lower astral realms seem to be life, but which to those who are striving to light the Buddhic Fire would be death or a spiritual darkness worse than death.

Therefore, in this Aquarian Age when the veil between the astral and the physical worlds is becoming thinner and thinner, there is a mighty struggle taking place. The dark, lurid fires of the lower astral, or what is commonly called the fires of hell, are burning fiercely. And *every mortal who opens his aura to them* by giving way to inharmony, anger, lust or selfishness *allows those astral fires to rush in and sweep him away far beyond anything he had intended*, just as the tiny, seemingly insignificant dead leaves in a forest are capable of starting a disastrous forest fire.

But all who are lighting the Buddhic Fire are generating that which will consume the lower fires, both in themselves and in humanity as a whole. They are like forest Rangers who start back-fires, across which the lower fires cannot reach them. Therefore, in using such invocations to the Divine Light as our "Prayer for Light" or the "Protecting Invocation" we invoke the descent of the Buddhic Fire and put around ourselves the Ring-pass-not, the Ring of Flame, *within which no inharmonious or evil thing can penetrate* without being consumed by that Divine Fire. For it will consume all that cannot respond to its spiritual rate of vibration; all the inharmonious conditions it touches in our bodies, in our minds and in our lives, and extract from them their essence of good which has been perverted into evil.

Sudden, unusual and unaccountable bursts of anger, antagonism, lust or destructiveness are in reality astral attacks from those evil ones who have seen the Light of the Torch of Spirituality which we have lighted and who seek to invade our minds, our auras and our lives with the lower fires of their burning hell-like astral conditions so as to make us like unto themselves and, therefore, avenues for their expression on Earth. Everyone who responds to them becomes a fire-brand in every walk of life; in the social, religious, industrial or political life of humanity. On the other hand, all who are striving to light the Buddhic Fire of love and spiritual illumination, also become fire-brands to spread the Fire of Divine Love and Life: become torch-bearers for the Christ whose radio-active Light will consume all evil and stimulate all good.

The Buddhic Fire is the Soul of things, the life of life, whose radiance we call the Christ-light, the Soul's supreme comprehension and manifestation of spiritual light, life and love. And since this Spiritual Fire is above the plane of physical manifestation, *it must be reached up for* by man *and be brought down* and lit in his heart. Even though it be but a tiny glow at first, like all fire it will spread and ultimately consume all evil and bring forth in us the seeds of inspiration, of realization, of power to accomplish and to manifest our godlikeness. For this Buddhic Fire not only illumines our minds and purifies our lives, but it also fills our hearts with Divine Love and a great longing to manifest our Divine Self through our purified personality. This is the great mission for which we came into physical incarnation.[2]

Once our minds have been illumined by this Divine Fire we no longer look upon the world with ordinary mortal vision and see only its imperfections, its sordidness and sin, its ignorance, its selfishness and its spiritual darkness and unbrotherliness. Instead we see the Flame of Divine Life and Love and Beauty everywhere, striving to manifest more

---

[2] See lesson *The Object of Physical Existence or Why We Come to Earth*, Curtiss.

and more nearly perfectly through the limitations placed upon it by the physical vehicles through which it has to manifest on Earth. No longer is our attention focused upon the lack of understanding, hence misconceptions: upon the lack of unfoldment, hence the mistakes, of our less evolved brethren, nor do we carpingly criticize those who are not as evolved as ourselves. Instead, we see the faint glow of the Divine Light in their hearts like a coal of fire, but so covered over with ashes that neither its light nor its warmth can manifest. And our hearts yearn with tenderness to teach all such that the material things to which they cling so desperately that they obscure the Divine Light are but ashes which only clog the manifestation of their Real Selves and prevent them from attaining that peace, rest and utter satisfaction which they are striving to obtain from outer things, but which already exists within if they will but let it manifest.

To light the Buddhic Fire let us turn within and pray: "O Divine Father-Mother fill me so full of the Fire of Divine Life and Love that there shall be no corner of my mind or body or environment that is not touched. Let it illumine every phase of my life and fill it with Thy Love. Let it lie close to my heart and from there overflow and radiate into the most trivial tasks that my hands find to do, that I may demonstrate Thy Presence in all things. Let it go out with my mind to the infinite shores of consciousness and bring me a realization of Thy infinite extension and power. Yet let the realization of Thy imminent Presence within me be like a torch which shall light my Path and be a beacon to lead unto Thee all who can see the manifestation of Thy Light."

Chapter XXXIII

THE GLORY OF THE LORD

"His glory covered the heavens, and the earth was full of his praise. And His brightness was as the light." *Habakkuk*, III, 3-4.

"So the Spirit took me up, and brought me into the inner court, and behold, the glory of the Lord filled the house. And I heard him speaking unto me." *Ezekiel*, XLIII, 5-6.

There is a glory of the Sun and of the Moon and of the stars: a glory of the earth, the sea and the sky, and a glory of every one of the saints and masters, but there is only one God, one divine Eternal Being from everlasting to everlasting, and He is the King of Glory. He it is who sits upon His throne of glory and dispenses the glory of the universe: the mighty, everlasting, universal cosmic forces which are back of all manifestations in the universe. All His manifestations bow before Him and, acting as His handmaidens and servants, do His bidding on Earth and in heaven, even as we His children, the offspring of His loins, should bow before Him and serve Him in our lives. "O Lord, how manifold are thy works! In wisdom hast thou made them all: the earth is full of thy riches." [1]

God is a poor term to use as applied to Him, for it has been made common by being used to designate both the personified forces of Nature and the unseen rulers of the different nations and peoples which are called national or tribal gods. It is even used to designate those artificial elementals[2] which are created by man's imagination and thought-force and which are propitiated and maintained by

---

[1] *Psalms*, CIV, 24-30.
[2] For details see *Realms of the Living Dead*, Curtiss, 78.

savage ceremonies which involve the shedding of blood of fowls, bullocks, sheep and goats, and sometimes of human beings. It is used to designate pictures and images of wood and stone. In fact, it is used for all objects and beings which man in his ignorance worships instead of the Eternal Being. Therefore, we will not call this one, all-inclusive Eternal Being God, but the King of Glory.

At first thought one might naturally suppose that, like the popular conception of heaven, a Being so divine, so glorious, so transcendent, must be afar off. But He is not. While this King of Glory is mighty, like all mighty things He is simple. He is close to the heart of every child of man, wrapped around in Spirit, in great understanding, in unbelievable love and compassion. He is closer than hand or foot, than brain or heart. Therefore, there is no God, no being, no master or teacher so close to us, to our hearts, to our minds, to our understanding, as this Being of all Beings, this one God, eternal in the heavens, the King of Glory. And over our individualized Ray of Himself we can ascend in aspiration to His very presence and absorb the down-pouring of His graciousness until our hearts shall rejoice and be enlarged because of the abundance of His glory and His love. And it shall shine out like a beacon of light upon the troubled waters of our lives and provide a safe haven for us to seek in time of trouble.

But how are we to make the correlation with Him so that our consciousness can recognize His presence and His glory? How can we come closer to Him? How can we bow at His footstool? How stand at His right hand, ready to do His bidding? There is simply one great command: "Love ye one another." For this Eternal Being is not only the King of Glory, He is also the Lord of Love: for Love, Divine Love, is the crowning jewel of His glory. Each one of us has felt His hand of love at some time in our lives and has tried to love in return, but until we came into some realization of His glory and correlated with the outpouring of His

Love we could not know nor comprehend it with our outer, rational minds: for only through the heart can we realize or express love.

Should anyone question that He is the Lord of Love, let some great trial or dread experience or bereavement come into his life or some great disaster to humanity, and when all human comfort or hope fails and he cries out to God for help, He will never fail to come to such a one to comfort and carry him through his trial. It is this glory of His Love that He pours out upon all who call upon and worship Him, upon all who seek Him in humility and receptiveness.

But we must learn how to worship Him truly. When we do this we are told, "That He would grant you, according to the riches of His glory, to be strengthened with might by His Spirit in the inner man; that Christ may dwell in your hearts by faith; that ye, being rooted and grounded in love, may be able to comprehend with all the saints what is the breadth, and length, and height; and to know the love of Christ, which passeth knowledge, that ye might be filled with all the fullness of God."[3]

Every Age, as it begins its manifestation on Earth, has its own definite and particular message from the Eternal One, the King of Glory. If this is so, why does He need so many helpers and ministers to help enlighten mankind and bring them to a realization of His reality and His presence? This question arises out of the ignorance of man: his lack of understanding. For while the glory of God manifests to mankind in all the realms of Nature, on Earth and in the heavens, and while He speaks to each heart in the Still Small Voice, He cannot give His message to mankind except through man; through trained seers and seeresses who can hear and understand His Voice and who endeavour to express His meaning in the best language they can muster, coloured, modified and limited, naturally, by the training and education their minds have received.

---

[3] *Ephesians*, III, 16–19.

The days are coming, aye, are now here, when the world is running too and fro seeking this one and that to teach them. They recognize their ignorance and lack of understanding of spiritual things and are so eager for knowledge that they follow the teachers who make the greatest claims, those who seek out the wonderful, high-sounding philosophies of the past and pour them into the ears of the hungry ones. Yet, in most instances, this is but feeding them upon the dry bones of former expressions of truth not suited to modern times and from which the Spirit has been indrawn to manifest in more modern vehicles. So we hear on all sides, "Lo here! Lo there! I have the truth. All wisdom is mine. Come to me and learn the truth." But while we may be helped by listening to various intellectual interpretations of truth, there is but one Voice which can give us all truth and which we must learn to listen to and obey, the Voice of the King of Glory who speaks in the Silence, yet whose mighty pulsating vibrations fill the universe. Even through the darkness of ignorance and in the depths of misunderstanding and misery we can feel a mysterious something which we are not able to understand. It has penetrated our hearts and awakened our minds, so that there is not a Soul on this planet who has not at some time felt that touch of Eternal Love which comes direct from the King of Glory.

But where two or three are gathered together in His name there His glory shines round about them; there sinks His mighty Love into their hearts and brings forth, if the soil be suitable, some of the seeds of spiritual attainment which are destined to grow into a Tree of Life which will both symbolize and bring forth in the New Age into which we have now entered. What is it that we feel? What do we hear? What thrills all through our body? What vibrates in the air and makes it seem like radiant fire? It is the Presence and the Voice of the Eternal Being speaking to our hearts.

To hear this divine Voice we must be still. We must still not only
our own voice and be quiet physically; not only must we turn our
minds away from the distractions of the world at regular intervals
of meditation, but we must still our minds and our thoughts and
become quietly receptive. We must listen for His Voice in the
rumble of the thunder, in the shriek of the cyclone, in the mighty
crash of earthquakes and disasters, when under-sea quakes are
sending tidal waves to crash in destruction upon the shore. During
all these conditions we must listen to His Voice. And this Voice
is always saying: "Peace. Be still." For there comes a time in the
life of every Soul when this mighty stillness must be attained
and manifested, and the Soul must realize that the Lord God is
speaking in the heart. Then we can send up our aspiration: "O
Lord God! Thou Eternal Being! Thou King of Glory! Thou who
art forever in the heavens and yet who filleth the hearts of all
mankind, manifest Thyself unto me and guide me."

Ere we, as followers of Him and students of His teachings, can
hope to become the centers of radiant life, light, joy and happiness
which we should become; ere we can hope to accomplish the great
work in ourselves and for humanity that we should accomplish,
we must learn, at least to some small degree, this great lesson of
stillness, of listening to the Voice of the King of Glory, not alone
for what we may gain thereby, but for what He may give us to
radiate to others.

Indeed, we must learn to love that Voice, not in a fanatical way,
but reasonably, just as a mother loves her child or a bride loves her
true mate, until that love becomes a natural part of our inner life
which, although too sacred to be spoken of lightly, is nevertheless
the underlying force which never fails us and which makes life a
never-ending joy. When we find our thoughts running hither and
thither, imagining this and that; seeking sympathy and comfort
from others; when we no sooner think we have placed our feet
firmly upon the rock of spiritual understanding than something else

comes up to upset us, then is the time to sit down quietly and say: "Peace. Be still."

Such conditions affect the mind as storms do the ocean. It is just such storms of emotion which make the tears come to our eyes. Sometimes the water does not actually flow from our eyes, but everything seems to go wrong and our whole life seems dissolved. When such negative periods come we should deliberately go apart by ourselves and seek to enter the Silence.[4] There we should look up and listen for His Voice saying: "My peace I give unto you. I am walking on these dark waves. I know all the turbulence of the earthly conditions that seem to overwhelm you and wring your heart. But I say unto you, Peace. Be still."

Realize that the Christ, the Son of God, the outshining of His glory is ever walking on the waters of life which shall, at His command, be stilled for us. Let us make this conception so familiar that we will make it an actual fact in our lives. That was not simply a physical incident that happened only once nearly two thousand years ago, but it happens daily and hourly in the lives of those who seek to follow Him and become His disciples: those who are trying to listen to His Voice and do His will on earth, even as it is done in heaven; those who are tossing in the little boat of their human personality on the mighty and ofttimes terrible ocean of life while trying to draw out of its depths the Great Fish, the Leviathan or the inner understanding of life. When the storms of emotion and discouragement rage and they cannot manage their boat and they lose courage, then the tears flow and they cry out: "The waves of life are too strong for me. I have given up all desire for earth-love and yet Divine Love seems far off."

O, children, Divine Love is all there is. That which we call earth-love is but a reflection, but an image of the real God-love. And if it be a real image and not an illusion, it

---

[4] For practical directions for entering the Silence see, *The Temple of Silence*, Curtiss.

is because we are made in His image and have within us all His powers. It is Divine Love that comes down to man and woman and illumines life and makes our brief life-experience in the flesh tolerable, even happy. Because of that Ray of Love within us we can rise on the wings of light and life and soar into the very Heart of Love and find the King of Glory. Then will our fears and our tears be gone, and we will find our Christ walking upon the waters of our life and saying: "Peace. Be still."

There are many conditions in the lives of each one that seem overwhelming, but, like the storms of Earth, no matter how severe, they are but passing. They are not real in the sense of being permanent and eternal. The only thing in the universe absolutely real is the mighty power and glory and love of the Eternal Being, the Father-Mother of all, and His Son, the Christ. Let us bow, then, before His throne and realize that His Son is the outshining of His glory to mankind. With this understanding and realization, as He descends nearer and nearer to manifestation on Earth we cannot be deceived by the many cries of mortals: "Lo here! Lo there!"

When the time comes for the King of Glory, the Son of the Spiritual world, to rise above the murky darkness of this Earth and manifest Himself to mankind, then all who have learned to be still; all whose hearts have been attuned to Divine Love; all who have tried and proved that Love is divine, that it can dispel all the clouds and darkness from life, all these cannot be deceived any more than a dog can be deceived in his master's voice, even though heard in the dark or from over a stone wall, through a telephone or from a phonographic disk. For they are already overshadowed by the outshining of His glory and will know His voice and recognize His manifestation wherever it takes place.

There are many changes coming to this Earth and its inhabitants.[5] Some may call these mighty changes disasters,

---

[5] For details see *Coming World Changes*, Curtiss.

yet in reality they are only the mighty housecleaning so necessary to prepare for His coming. Already the angelic hosts are at work making straight the paths of understanding which lead to the realization of His glory; changing misunderstanding into light; changing misery into joy, and death into life more abundant. Therefore, when such things come upon the Earth, when the clouds are dark and conditions seem hopeless, look up and see the Light of His glory shining through, and hear His Voice saying again: "Peace. Be still."

Let His Dove of Peace and rest, of strength and power, of sympathy and love, abide with us henceforth forever. Do not weep. Do not grieve. Let His Love dissolve all unhappiness and push it far from us. Have comradeship and friendliness with all, but have *no controversy or intimate association* with those who are not developed enough to understand us or who do not believe in and hence refuse to seek and worship Him.

It is important that as advanced students and followers of Him we should learn to be still and commune with Him daily; for we are entering upon a phase of unfoldment wherein His direct, conscious guidance is necessary to carry us through the turbulent changes that are coming. For although we may seem to be few in numbers, if each student strives to be a radiating center of understanding and light, then we will form a Circle of Light around the entire globe. To accomplish this we do not need to study in the musty tombs of the ancient days; only study *and practice* how to contact Him in our hearts.

Our work, each one of us, is *to do all we can* to bring understanding and comfort in times of distress; to bring peace, light, joy and happiness into our own lives and into the world at large, not as the ignorant and self-indulgent try to bring it today through their jazz music and indecency, turning society up-side-down, but through the spread of the light of spiritual understanding and the radiance of Divine

Love. For there is no true and satisfying happiness except in response to the vibrations of oneness with the divine Eternal Being, the King of Glory, who is the Lord of Love, and whose Ray manifests within each heart.

CHAPTER XXXIV

LESSONS BY THE WAY[1]

PART I. THE ANCIENT CONTINENTS

"Science can, it is true, collect, classify and generalize upon phenomena; but the Occultist, arguing from admitted metaphysical data, declares that the daring explorer who would probe the inmost secrets of Nature must transcend the narrow limitations of sense, and transfer his consciousness into the region of Noumena and the sphere of Primal Causes. To effect this, he must develop faculties which, save in a few rare and exceptional cases, are absolutely dormant" *The Secret Doctrine*, Blavatsky, I, 518.

The oft-repeated slogan "See America First" has a greater significance to the Occultist than others would suppose, for to understand the full significance of the widely divergent scenery he will see it must be seen with the inner sense as well as with the outer.

In the miles of broad luxuriant plains of the Mississippi Valley and its tributaries we find the swamps, sands and gravels which give evidence of the vast inland sea which covered those regions during the Lemurian and Atlantean periods, while the rich deposits of alluvial soil show how the distant mountains have been eroded and washed down and their debris spread over the rocks or mixed with the sands to form the fertile soil of the valleys.

In the wide stretches of the "sage-brush country" which extends through several of the far western states; in the long reaches of desert and "sheep country"; in the arid "bad lands" of the Big Horn region of Wyoming; in the

---

[1] Notes from a trans-continental auto tour made by the authors in September, 1920.

wondrous beauties and geological marvels of the Pike's Peak
region and of Yellowstone Park and in the desolation of the
immense lava beds of Idaho and eastern Oregon; in all these
regions we see the struggle of a new land; of Nature slowly
rebuilding a new earth out of the debris left after the destruction
of the great Lemurian Continent, long before the upheaval of the
Atlantean and American Continents.

The gigantic Third or Lemurian Continent—the home of the
Third Great Race—stretched from the remains of the Hyperborean
Land (Second Continent) in the Arctic Circle—Norway,
Greenland, Eastern and Western Siberia, etc.,—westward to
where the American Continent now stands, and southward across
the Indian Ocean, around Madagascar and South Africa in a great
horseshoe into the Atlantic Ocean, a prolongation of which land
became the geological basis of the far later Fourth Continent of
Atlantis. For the "Atlanteans were developed from a nucleus of
Northern Lemurian Third-Race Men. . . . Their Continent was
formed by the coalescence of many islands and peninsulas which
were upheaved in the ordinary course of time and ultimately
became the true home of the great Race known as Atlantean."[2]

But after the destruction of Lemuria by fire—through terrific
and age-long volcanic eruptions—it sank beneath the waves,
leaving only widely scattered remnants (such as Norway,
Ceylon, Australia and a large strip of California, etc.), while other
portions were again upheaved in much the same conditions as
they went down and were then inhabited by the Atlanteans, thus
overlapping both the Races and the Continents. For instance,
the gigantic statues on Easter Island in the Pacific are not those
of the late Atlanteans who there escaped the destruction of their
own Continent, but represent the much more ancient Lemurians.
Most of the remnants of Lemuria thus remaining today plainly
show the action of the tremendous volcanic eruptions which either

---

[2] *The Secret Doctrine*, Blavatsky, II, 348.

desolated them or upheaved them, after their submergence, during the formation of the Continent of Atlantis. This is particularly true of certain regions in the Rocky Mountains. And just as the Third Continent overlapped the Second and the Fourth, so the Fourth (Atlantis) overlapped the Fifth Continent (America).

Much of the American Continent is really older than Europe, "only a few portions of which were barely rising from the waters in the days of the highest Atlantean civilization"[3] and, before the publication in 1522 of the first map on which America was shown, it was thought to be a part of India. Indeed, the India of pre-historic times was doubly connected with the two Americas. The great cataclysm which sank the larger part of Atlantis occurred soon after the upheaval of America. "The Fourth (Race) born millions of years before the said cataclysm took place, perished during the Miocene period, when the Fifth (our Aryan Race) had had one million years of independent existence."[4]

At the time of its so-called discovery by Columbus, America had for ages been called Atlantis by some of the Indian tribes then inhabiting it. But it must not be supposed that America was unknown to the Ancients, for in those days geography was a part of the Mysteries well known to the sages and teachers but veiled from the ignorant. Not only was it known to the Druids, the Norsemen, the Egyptians and the Japanese, but in the Vedas and other sacred literature of the East there are many allusions to it, it being known as the Antipodes, also Preshkara, etc.

Just as the Continents overlapped and blended into each other, so each Race overlapped and developed from the preceding Race; the Lemurians, gigantic in stature gradually becoming more and more materialized and organized and then differentiated; then the Atlanteans, reaching, during the latter part of the Fourth Race, the extreme of physical ex-

---

[3] *Ibid*, 763.
[4] *Ibid*, 755–447

pression, gigantic, coarse, hairy, yet intellectually and psychically developed but with little spirituality; and then our present Fifth Race overlapping the Fourth and growing less in stature but more and more in higher intellectual and spiritual development. These ancient teachings are confirmed not only by the biblical account of the "giants in those days, and also after that," but by the finding in mounds and caves here in America of groups of skeletons of men varying from nine to twelve feet in height. And we ourselves have seen the so-called petrified body of a large ancient Indian.

And just as the Races and sub-races overlapped in the past, so do they at the present time. Although the majority of the inhabitants of Europe and America are of our Fifth or Aryan Race and are manifesting in the present *Kali Yuga* or Iron Age, there are already beginning to be found Souls incarnating who really belong to the *Satya Yuga* or Golden Age which will follow the present Iron Age some thousands of years hence. Such Souls are the forerunners of the Sixth Great Race who have voluntarily taken up the onerous task of incarnation in this transitional and troublous era that they may help to prepare and set aside as a nucleus for the New Age all who will listen to and obey the Voice crying in the wilderness of modern life, "Prepare ye the way of the Lord, make his paths straight" Only when such Souls, as well as all others who can be spiritually awakened, are gathered from the Four Winds can the coming Avatar manifest in the flesh in this era; for although He will reveal His presence to all who are so spiritually awakened and desirous of becoming His disciples that they affinitize with Him, He will manifest bodily only to those whose development belongs to the Age of His public appearance to the multitude,"[5] *i.e.*, the Golden Age, although living now under the outward reign of the Iron Age.

This is no more of a mystery than the overlapping of the

---

[5] See *The Message of Aquaria*, Curtiss, Chapter XXXVIII

Continents or than it must have been to the boneless and androgynous Lemurians to see the Fourth Race beings develop among them, with bodies quite differently organized, possessing solid bones, erect posture, separated sexes, etc.[6] But in the present overlapping it will be not so much a difference in physical structure—although organs and faculties now latent will develop—as in mental, psychic and spiritual development.

This overlapping of the Sixth Great Race with the present Fifth, which has already begun since we have definitely entered into its sixth sub-race, will continue and be increasingly marked all through the sixth and seventh sub-races of the Fifth Great Race. And even when humanity enters fully into the Sixth Great Race, thousands of years hence, many backward or even degenerate remnants of the present Fifth will still remain, but will then be far in the minority, just as there are today remnants of the Fourth (Atlantean) and even of the Third (Lemurian) in the Tasmanians, Australians, Andaman Islanders, etc.

After this brief geological and ethnological introduction we wish to call the attention of our students to some of the lessons revealed to the inner eye in the vast and wonderful parts of the far western states which we have recently traversed.

After leaving the Mississippi Valley country one of the most interesting lessons came from a visit to the homes of the ancient Cliff Dwellers of Colorado; those mysterious people who lived so many thousands of years ago and who have left such remarkable traces of their lives and habits, preserved in the pure dry air of their now almost inaccessible mountain retreats, yet of whom so little is known to exoteric science as to their origin and fate. By psychometrizing some of their pottery, implements, mummies, etc., we came *en rapport* with their auras and conditions, but we found their emanations and influences so disagreeable that

---

[6] See *The Voice of Isis*, Curtiss, Chapter XVII, "The Origin of Man."

we did not feel like pursuing our investigations further by that method, so we asked the Teacher of the Order for an explanation and were given the following facts:

The Cliff Dwellers were the late and pigmy descendants of certain abnormal off-spring of the degenerate Atlanteans who bred semi-human animals to do their manual and menial work, as we have already explained.[7] Among the services they were required to perform was the embalming and care of the dead. The Atlanteans would not touch a corpse since they considered it both defiling and degrading. We find this same idea among the ancient Egyptians who sprang from a colony of Atlanteans who listened to their spiritual teachers and, warned of the terrible cataclysms which were to put an end to the horrors of black magic practiced by the ruling classes, fled from Atlantis and settled in the valley of the Nile. The tribes of these half-human, half-animal Atlantean servants who had to do with the dead were therefore considered more degraded than those used for house servants, labourers, etc., and hence were outcasts, even to touch whom was pollution. They therefore lived among the sepulchers or in caves and other wild places outside the cities and came in at night to take away the bodies that were to be embalmed.

It was the custom for those who could not afford the complete embalming indulged in by the rich to pay for a partial embalming and for the use of a tomb for a certain period, just as a cell in the tombs built above the marshy ground in New Orleans can be rented for a similar purpose today. After the time paid for had elapsed the embalmers would exhume the bodies, unwrap the mummy cloths and after disposing of the disintegrating remains, hang the cloths around their dwellings until used for the wrapping of the next corpse of the poor. This made their dwellings so polluted that no Atlantean would go near them and the people were considered worse than animals.

---

[7] *Ibid.*

At that time the Lemurian remnants of the Rocky Mountains were still in a condition of constant volcanic upheaval, with such terrible cataclysms that the whole region was considered an inferno and unfit for human habitation. Yet certain tribes of the outcasts, which had been taught the fundamentals of the Wisdom Religion to the extent of their limited capacity by missionaries from the Great White Lodge, refused to continue their degraded life under their Atlantean masters and fled into the so-called infernal regions and there found certain valleys or rather high cliffs, where they could protect themselves from the beasts of the region and from recapture, and where they escaped the cataclysms which destroyed Atlantis. And it was the descendants of these outcasts, interbred among themselves until they became pigmies from three to four feet tall, who composed the Cliff Dwellers whose remains we find today.

Naturally we expect to find some trace of the ancient Sun or Fire Worship among them, and this we do in the circular pit, entered only from the top, which is found in each village. Science thinks this was used to store grain, but it was really a place of worship, traces of the fire altar still being visible. For although degenerate they were by no means lacking in a certain intelligence, as their implements, baskets and the openings of their houses show. The doors used by the burden-bearers were much wider at the top than at the bottom so the bearer could enter without laying down his burden, while the doors used by the higher classes were narrow all the way up.

On this tour we also gained quite a new lesson in regard to the silence, namely, that the Great Silence is something outside of yet including all Nature-sounds, which all Nature feels and vainly strives to understand and express. On the high mountain tops and in the vast stretches of desert and plain we seemed to touch something that was more than silence, for silence or great stillness, dead and ominous, brooded over the "bad lands" of Wyoming and brought no inspiration, for the vibrations of the elemental forces of horror and malignancy still lingered in the ethers around such regions. But in the mountains we seemed to feel the brooding of the creative Breath of Divinity, and in awe we asked: "Is this the Temple of Silence, and can we enter it?"[8]

To find the entrance to this mystic Temple of Silence we do not have to travel to distant places, for it is always near. All we need is to believe, and when we need help knock and it shall be opened to us.

(To be continued)

---

[8] See *The Temple of Silence*, Curtiss.

CHAPTER XXXV

LESSONS BY THE WAY

PART II. THE LESSON OF THE SAGEBSUSH

"Praise ye the Lord. . . . Praise him ye heavens of heavens, and ye waters that be above the heavens (the Divine Mother). . . . Praise the Lord from the earth. . . . Fire, and hail; snow, and vapors; stormy wind fulfilling his word: mountains, and hills; fruitful trees, and all cedars: beasts, and all cattle; creeping things, and flying fowl." *Psalms* CXLVIII.

While passing over the many mountain ranges which we crossed on our tour from ocean to ocean we were struck by the number of large trees which grew from out what seemed to be the solid rock, with scarcely a crevice in which soil could accumulate, and so far above ground that roots could not possibly reach the soil below. This was but another corroboration of our teachings in our *The Voice of Isis*[1] that the life-force of the planet manifests in greatest abundance in the rocks and breathes through the mountains. It reminded us that those who find themselves planted in the hard, rocky conditions of life can nevertheless draw their life-force from the foundation stones of Eternal Truth, even though denied the intellectual and physical conditions which seem to the outer world so necessary as soil for the expression of life in happy and sturdy growth.

In other less rugged regions, where the hills were composed of solidly baked day, scarcely a sign of plant life could be seen, for solid clay soil is so impervious to both air and water and to the currents of the life-force that little or nothing can grow. For growth comes quite as much from

---

[1] *The Voice of Isis, Curtiss*, 311.

the invisible currents of life-force of the planet as from the nourishment received from the physical soil. This reminds us that we must not rely merely upon that which we receive from without, but that we must ever seek to correlate with the inner currents of spiritual life-force from within; that instead of allowing our lives to become hardened with a day-like selfishness we must make ourselves firm as a rock, yet porous to the flow of the finer forces that they may find expression through us.

In the Big Horn Mountains of Wyoming where baked clay seems to the passing tourist to be the universal composition of the region, although the marvellous colourings produced by the precipitation of mineral colouring matters presented grand and inspiring sights, yet there was a notable absence of both plant and animal life, save in the few instances in which the hills have been washed down to form soil along the bottoms of the arroyas. And even there the vegetation was sparse and coarse. Indeed, in those so-called "bad lands" there seemed added to the physical barrenness and desolation a brooding sense of horror and malignant antagonism, as though the emanations and thought-forces of the ancient black magicians who occupied the land in long bygone ages were still hovering about the region whispering of the orgies of black magic and terror which had given them birth and which had not been completely transmuted, purified and redeemed, like the effluvia arising from the decaying debris remaining on the seashore after a great storm.

In the wide lava beds of Idaho and eastern Oregon, the road winds for 20 to 80 miles or more over sharp and jagged volcanic rocks amid the remnants of the titanic eruptions and past mountains whose entire tops have been blown off, leaving barren and desolate craters. Here we recognized the remnants of Lemuria which had been purified by fire and were now just beginning, here and there, again to become habitable, through the combined efforts of the elements and of man. Indeed, in the very heart of this region we passed one beautiful gem of a ranch extending out into the lava beds whose owner, we were told, had in a former life been the chief of one of the later tribes of Lemurians whose evil had helped to bring on its destruction. He had incarnated in this general region many times during the days of Atlantis, and also many times much later as an American Indian, in most cases still following the same impulses which he had so intensified in those ancient days. Only in this incarnation is he working in a definite and constructive way to aid the redemption of the land which his evil forces helped to curse in that far distant past. Thus does the Great Law of cause and effect ever operate. We must each of us become the redeemers of our own creations, sometime, somewhere.

One day, after traveling over a hundred miles through nothing but sparse and scrubby sagebrush with no habitation for thirty or forty miles at a stretch, we became so tired of the vast stretches of drab and dry looking bush and its penetrating odor that we spoke very disparagingly of that humble plant, so much so that the Teacher found it necessary to correct our attitude of mind. It was pointed out that the sagebrush is about the only form of vegetation, save the few cacti and yuccas, which can live and thrive under the hard conditions of the desert. As the sagebrush thus overcomes all obstacles to its growth, as it spreads over the vast regions of arid and desolate country, it proves its power to accomplish that which can scarcely be accomplished by any other plant, namely, even though growing gnarled and scrubby it nevertheless has the power to gather up and retain or draw up from the depths sufficient moisture (water, love) to grow and manifest. It thus helps to redeem the soil and make it fit later for higher types of vegetation; for its fallen leaves help to fertilize the soil, and even its death and decay help to form that "humus" or vegetable matter in the soil without which it will not support higher forms of plant life. The sagebrush also helps man directly with certain medicinal and other properties.

We therefore learned, or rather had a greater realization of that which we had known long before, namely, that no matter how humble the form in which the one Divine Life may be manifesting, each form is accomplishing a definite work in the world, working in its own place and way to prepare for a higher and greater form of manifestation of that same One Life. After this we felt like apologizing to the sagebrush for the attitude of contempt in which our ignorance and lack of realization permitted us to indulge. In fact, we came to look upon it with much the same admiration which we feel for the sturdy pioneers who are willing to live under hard and primitive conditions that they may cultivate and improve the soil and make the region habitable for others, in other walks of life and with other qualities to express, who come later and whose work can be accomplished only after the primitive conditions have been overcome. And who shall say that the life-force now manifesting through and learning the lessons of the sagebrush may not manifest in some later age through noble trees growing in the very soil which the sagebrush has helped to redeem and enrich and prepare?

The sagebrush reminded us of the great mass of unenlightened and undeveloped humanity who seem to be toiling hopelessly and apparently wasting their lives in a dreary and drab existence almost as barren as a desert and with scarcely a bright spot of colour or blossom in their lives. Yet even in their lives there are many tiny blossoms of love—for their children, friends, homes, etc.,—which make an opening through which the Divine Life of the Great Mother-love can flow forth to fill them with the Spiritual Sap and manifest the life expression and experience which their stage of evolution needs to take them their next step onward; to bring forth in their lives the perfume of their highest ideals.

Like a beautiful life amid sordid surroundings we would

now and then come upon an irrigated patch amidst the surrounding sagebrush, fragrant with the delightful perfume and refreshing coolness of alfalfa. For alfalfa has to an extraordinary degree the ability to give off large quantities of moisture and life-force as well as perfume, thus markedly cooling the surrounding air. This is a phenomenon which might not be noticed so distinctly did it not surprise us in the midst of an arid waste. This crop alone is doing much toward the regeneration of such lands.

Through all these regions we were introduced to the beginning of reconstruction. Even the rodents, little ground squirrels, gophers and prairie dogs, by their burrowing through the earth and their life in it are helping it to transmit more freely the life-forces. The elements were also everywhere at work slowly washing the disintegrating rock from the core of the mountains, leaving spires and pinnacles and columns, often weird and fantastic shapes like giant heads with gasping mouths striving to breathe, like stretched out hands seemingly lifted to heaven in protest because the elements were transmuting them into soil.

In other regions we found rugged, beautiful, even awe-inspiring canons where laughing streams had cut their way through solid walls of rock and made it possible for man to construct a highway by which he could climb to the heights above. Here we saw exemplified the lesson that the great stream of Divine Life-force is like a pure river flowing through our lives. Even if their outer conditions be seemingly as hard and dense as granite, nevertheless this stream of Divine Life and Love of the Great Mother will wear a passage through them as the water of a mountain stream cuts through the hills. As the rocks break and crumble or are undermined they fall into the stream, but the water only dashes over them. The greater the obstruction the higher the water lifts itself in spray and the more beautifully it reflects the sunlight. The more obstacles it meets the more determination it shows to conquer.

Just so with the life which consciously permits the great stream of the Divine Life-force to make a pathway through it. It may not find all things smooth and pleasant, but no matter what is encountered it knows that it can gather its forces until the obstacle is overcome, each victory developing great power and endurance, and bringing greater joy and greater ability to sparkle in the light of the Spiritual Sun. Hence the lesson we learned from the canons was to let our lives flow like a river, ever fed from the Eternal Springs on high, our aspirations ever pointing upward like the giant pines; ever gladly meeting obstacles, trusting in the irresistible power of the stream within us to overcome them, not for ourselves alone, but that we may help to make a pathway for other feet that shall lead them from the valleys of life to the heights.

Anrfther lesson was learned from the distant mirages in which we seemed to see cool waters for our parched throats, and shady trees to protect us from the stifling heat and burning glare of the desert sun. Altho they were only mirages, yet in them we recognized alluring illusions similar to those which come to tempt the untrained psychic to leave the well-marked trail of teaching and philosophy left by the Masters of Wisdom and great Teachers which will lead him safely across the illusions of the Astral World to the Hall of Wisdom beyond. Many today are being tempted by such illusions, due to their close touch with the astral. For just as a mother must be open to the astral that incarnation may take place, so as a New Race is being born, humanity is more open to the astral than before, and many new forces are striving for expression.

Many today are finding themselves tempted from the Path by the many self-appointed teachers in the astral who cry: "Lo, here! Lo, there!" so that the student scarce knows which way to turn or whom to believe and follow. Yet if we truly enter the Silence and ask that the Comforter shall bring to our remembrance all that was told us of these times, we will at once remember that it was said: "Many shall come in my name . . . . and shall shew great signs and wonders; insomuch that, if it were possible, they shall deceive the very elect." Yet we need not be deceived. Those who come in the name of the Christ are not always or even often in the flesh, but come in the astral to every awakening psychic,[2] claiming to be Messengers of Light and pouring into the minds of the psychics plausible tales and great promises, telling one that he is to be a great teacher or another that she has been chosen to redeem the world, etc. To all such, and they are many, let the Comforter, the Divine Mother, bring to their remembrance the answer that Jesus gave to those who came asking, "Art thou he that should come? or look we for another?" His only answer was to point to His works, to that which He had accomplished. And His answer is as true today as ever. "By their fruits ye shall know them."

Hence, unless we see such teachers bringing forth the bread and wine of spiritual truth we must recognize that all their fair promises are but the allurements of the mirage which, if followed, means the terrible suffering of losing our Path across the desert. "Do men gather grapes of thorns, or figs of thistles?"[3] Spiritual drink (grapes) cannot be gained from the hard, woody fibre of mere intellectual teachings, be they ever so sharp and penetrating, nor can spiritual food (figs) be found on the stinging growths in the astral which seem so green and tempting.

It is not what some astral teacher tells us we will be or will do, but *what we are doing now*, what foundations we are laying, what principles we are following, that counts. Never does one have to proclaim to the world that he is a chosen one; that he alone can turn discontent and antagonism into brotherhood, abolish war and inaugurate an era of world peace. If he is so appointed and has the power, all he has

---

[2] For details see *Realms of the Living Dead*, Curtiss.
[3] *St. Matthew*, VII, 16.

to do is to go quietly about his work and the world will know it by its results.

But whether chosen for a special public work or not, each one can strive to enter the great Temple of Silence and there receive the accolade of divine power and have the love of the Divine Mother fill him. Then he can go forth and express and manifest as best he may that which he has received, and thus fulfil his part as a humble worker with the Great Ones for the enlightenment and upliftment of his fellow men.

(To be concluded)

Chapter XXXVI

LESSONS BY THE WAY[1]

"Little drops of water, little grains of sand,
Make the mighty oceans and the pleasant land.
Little deeds of kindness, little words of love,
Make the earth an Eden, like the heaven above."

Little Things, Carney.

"I will lift up mine eyes unto the hills from whence cometh my help." *Psalms*, CXXI, 1.

Summer is the season of vacations, of travel and change. Change is essential to growth and progress; change of surroundings, change of ideas, change of outlook and attitude, even frequent changes of costume. All these create new interests and stimulate both mind and body. But the change must be of a constructive nature else its benefit may be lost. Too strenuous a vacation may bring one home tired out and depleted instead of refreshed and invigorated.

Since this planet was created as a great school[2] for the Soul in which man must learn many vital lessons, if we travel over it with only a sightseer's interest in mere surface conditions we may enjoy its scenery and expand our conceptions of how other communities live and thus improve our minds, but if we travel with our mystic eyes open we will see back of surface conditions into the mysteries of life, into the causes of things; will tune ourselves in with Nature's activities and thus have a better understanding of the

---

[1] Notes from a trans-continental auto tour made by the Authors in September, 1930.
[2] See *The Voice of Isis*, Curtiss, 46.

significance of the rapid and remarkable changes that are constantly taking place around us.

We all know that this summer (1930) the whole middle portion of our country has been suffering for months from the most severe drought on record since 1874. One explanation is that the areas of high atmospheric pressure which normally sweep across the northern third of the country every few days from one coast or the other, drawing air currents from both North and South, have failed to appear this year. Hence, the cool air currents from the North could not mingle with the warm, moisture-laden currents from the South or from the coasts, and condense their moisture into rain. But a study of the weather map shows that the storm currents have not disappeared, but have only been diverted far to the North across the wastes of the Hudson Bay region where the rain was not needed for mankind.

One scientific reason given for the diversion of the storm track so far to the North is connected with the swing of the Moon far to the northward in successive decades, the extreme swing this year repeating that of 1874, which was also a year of great drought. But this is only the effect, not the cause. The cause is connected both with the wobbling of the Earth's axis and with the crossing over of certain earth-currents,[3] which crossing coincides with our entering into the new Aquarian Age. During this transitional period there will be many and great changes brought about by cataclysms, great floods, unusual droughts, famines, strikes, wars and disasters of all kinds, as fully explained in our *Coming World Changes*.

That the drought this summer is not a mere local disturbance of the air currents of this country, but has a planetary aspect, is evidenced by the fact that the drought has been far more terrible in other countries. Recent newspaper reports quote Bishop Claes, the chief missionary

---

[3] See *Coming World Changes*, Curtiss, 49.

Bishop of the Belgian Congo, as reporting that the drought in the Ruanda Province had caused a famine so frightful that it had taken the lives of 40,000 natives! in spite of the fact that many thousands had emigrated to the British territory of Uganda. This terrible disaster to humanity is all a part of the travail which this planet and its inhabitants are passing through during the "last days" of the old cycle; those days of "great tribulation, such as was not since the beginning of the world to this time, no, nor ever shall be. And except those days should be shortened, there should no flesh be saved."[4] But we must ever keep in mind that "for the elect's sake those days shall be shortened." And we have explained elsewhere just how[5] this can be accomplished and the responsibility of every thoughtful person in regard to it.

In driving across the parched and sun-baked plains of the middle western states it was brought home to us with great force the vital part which water plays both in the life of all animate beings and inanimate Nature as well. Of the three essential factors for physical life and growth—water, sunshine and food—water is by far the most important, for life can be maintained far longer without sunshine or food than it can without water. For without water—the great solvent and purifier—the food (or soil) cannot be dissolved and assimilated nor the waste products be washed out, so the plant or animal body dries up and shrivels and the life-force can no longer flow through it. Thus do we realize the dictum that, "Life is the basic reality, of which everything else is a form or manifestation."

All this is correspondingly true of the spiritual life. No matter how much spiritual food is provided, unless we imbibe the waters of Divine Love—the great solvent and purifier—the Spiritual Fire will only scorch and wither and the spiritual food which it should vitalize and use for growth

---

[4] *St. Matthew*, XXIV, 21, 22.
[5] *Coming World Changes*, Curtiss, Chapters II–III

cannot be assimilated or our natures be cleansed and purified of the waste products of our minds, our emotions and our desires. "But whosoever drinketh of the waters that I shall give him shall never thirst; but the water that I shall give him shall be in him a well of water springing up into everlasting life."

Seeking to imbibe the Christ-love from the universal ocean of Divine Love, and striving to build it into the structure of our lives, is even more important for our spiritual growth and fruitage than water is for the growth and fruitage of plant life. If there is a dearth or drought of love in our lives our spiritual tassels cannot pollenize our actions, and our ears of manifestation and our kernels of demonstration will therefore be few and puny and not at all nourishing, and our whole lives will be withered and barren of spiritual attainment, no matter how luxuriant the leaves of our outer conditions may seem to grow.

But if we have love, no matter how little learning or how little mental illumination we may have, we can grow to the full stature of the inner unfoldment which we have reached and which our environment (soil) and our Karma enables us to manifest. And so we can help to make the human landscape brighter and more cheerful and happy, and bring forth fruits of character which will encourage, comfort and help others. For just as surely as "little drops of water, little grains of sand, make the mighty oceans and the pleasant land," so is it true that "little deeds of kindness, little words of love, make this earth an Eden, like the heaven above." For it is not by outer achievements that our spiritual growth is promoted and our character formed, but by the assimilative and cohesive power of love which builds in little by little the results of the deeds of kindness and the words of love which the Divine in us prompts us to express.

In our *Coming World Changes*[6] we have described the effect of sincere and earnest community prayer in bringing

---

[6] Page 104.

rain, and how the very lives of both the Hopi and Pueblo Indians depend upon their ability to bring rain annually from what had been for weeks a cloudless sky during the drought season to save the corn crop upon which they depend for food. While driving through the drought-stricken states we felt so sorry for the withered vegetation, the thirsty animals and the suffering humanity that in the middle of the morning, without a cloud in the sky, we prayed that if their Karma permitted they should be given rain. Before noon clouds began to gather and in a few hours the first shower for weeks was falling.

In watching the clouds float over the landscape it occurred to us that the earth, the clouds and the sky might be likened to the physical plane, the astral plane and the spiritual plane. The clouds float over the earth much like clouds of astral conditions and forces float over humanity. The clouds may seem too ethereal and unsubstantial to be seriously considered, but under certain conditions they can concentrate and condense until they darken the whole horizon. Although usually so harmless, upon occasion they become so charged with destructive forces as to wreak havoc upon the earth and humanity.

Similarly, the astral world seems so ethereal and unsubstantial that it is hardly worth while considering, yet it too is capable of concentrating such destructive forces as to wreak havoc upon mankind. Yet in both the physical and astral storms, the effect is but the result of man's own destructive creations, as we have explained elsewhere.[7] But just as there are many beautiful and inspiring effects in the cloud formations—altho they too have a significance but little understood or suspected—as they bring cooling shade and refreshing rain to combine with the soil and sunshine to bring forth the crops of the field and the health and happiness of mankind, so are there many beautiful and inspiring effects to be noted and conditions to be contacted in the

---

[7] See *The voice of Isis*, Curtiss, 116–7, 172

astral world which do much to comfort, inspire and refresh mankind and help them to bring forth their most fruitful experiences. And even though the clouds do often hide the Sun from our sight for a time, the glimpses of the blue sky we see between them is evidence that the Sun still shines whether we see it or not. Likewise, altho unfavorable astral conditions may sometimes overshadow, chill and discourage us, we must never forget that the Sun of Righteousness is forever shining above the clouds, and the deep sky-blue of Divine Love ever arches over us in tender, protecting care, assuring us that *all storms*, no matter how severe, *eventually pass away* and reveal the Sun and the blue sky as friendly and cheering as ever. And if we have faith in the Divine Law and steadfastly hold fast to our spiritual principles and ideals until the storm of discouragement, trial or depression blows over, we will save ourselves much unnecessary suffering.

As we approach the mountains (Rockies) we are at first awed by their vastness and their majesty and we feel our own seeming insignificance. But a little reflection will reveal the fact that we are not insignificant, even in the presence of the mountains, for we are individualized immortal Souls, emanations from the divine Father-Mother, and as such we are Their direct representatives on Earth. The mountains, reaching so far up into the sky, naturally symbolize the heights of spiritual attainment or man's ascent to Godhood. At first sight these attainments seem to loom vast and forbidding before us and we are apt to think that there is so much to learn, so much to attain, and we are so ignorant and undeveloped that the task is hopeless. But if we examine the mountains carefully when we reach them we will find that others have been there before us, intrepid pioneers who have blazed the trails to the heights for us. Indeed, in these days there are splendid highways leading to all the beauty spots and to the richest mines. So today, when many eager, hungry Souls are seeking the Path of Attainment, there are many entrances to the Path pointed out by many reliable guides, and many well-mapped highways of instruction, even broad, well-paved courses of teaching, which will help to quicken our progress and make easy our attaining an understanding of the great truths that seemed so formidable at first sight. Yet ever the top-most heights of spiritual realization must be scaled by the individual initiative, the indomitable courage and the persistent efforts of the aspiring Soul.

But even if we cannot reach the mountains and have to live seemingly upon a dead-level plain, we need not be discouraged. If we cannot go to the mountains they can come to us, not in their vast bulk, but in their essential elements. For as the storms beat upon the heights they are gradually disintegrated and washed down to form the floor of the valleys and the broad alluvial plains. Therefore, if we but seek deeply enough within we will find beneath our very feet and in our own home environment particles of the same granite boulders which form the mountains. Then, too, the air of the higher altitudes is too rare for many of the dwellers of the plains, so they are able to make only brief visits to the heights. Yet no matter in what region we may find ourselves placed by the Great Law, if we will open our spiritual eyes and seek deeply enough, we can find the essence of those eternal truths whose mastering will take us to the heights of attainment.

We often think that as we progress toward the heights that our lives will be increasingly serene and peaceful, but in driving through a mid-summer hail storm four inches deep while crossing a high mountain pass from Cripple Creek, Colorado, it was brought vividly to mind that the heights are by no means always calm and serene. For many are the storms and testings, the black clouds of discouragement and depression, the thunder of our emotions, the jagged flashes of anger, the drenching rains of doubt and the fierce, beating hail of material attractions, which assail the Neophyte until he has passed the four great initiations of the elements—earth, air, fire, water—and has reached the haven of peace above the storm clouds.

These observations may seem to some but trite remarks and obvious platitudes. But what are platitudes? They are not merely dull, stupid remarks, but are simple statements of the eternal verities upon which all civilizations are built and without the observance of which mankind cannot live in peace and happiness. Hence they are absolutely necessary for our communal life. The multiplication table is a platitude to the mathematician and the statement that two plus two make four is a very trite remark, yet we still often need to be reminded of these fundamentals which underlie all mathematics, even though we may have become an advanced authority on higher mathematics.

So do we ever need to let the beauties and wonders of Nature and the events of our daily lives remind us that we are not mere mortals, but are essentially spiritual beings who have temporarily donned the uniform of earth life. But there is no limitation, sickness, lack or inharmony in the Soul. Therefore nothing can prevent the manifestation of the powers of the Soul through the human personality save those things of the earth, earthy—thoughts, desires, deeds, ambitions, emotions, etc.,—which we permit to intrude and divert our minds from a realization of the beauty and glory and the infinite power of the Christ within.

CHAPTER XXXVII

THE KING OF GLORY

"Now unto the King eternal, immortal, invisible, the only wise God, be honor and glory for ever and ever. Amen." *I Timothy*, I, 17.

"Who is this King of Glory? The Lord (Law) strong and mighty, the Lord mighty in battle. Lift up your heads, O ye gates; and the King of Glory shall come in." *Psalms*, XXIV, 8, 9.

"The great Law of the Universe, that which manifests forever in man, atom and world as the law of spiritual evolution, works forever onward and upward." *The Voice of Isis*, Curtiss, 331.

In these days the minds of men are ever turning toward the scientific investigation of the hidden causes of all functions of life. Through the so-called psychoanalysis, vocational-analysis, electronic reactions, photo- and chromo-therapy, iridology or the classification of the markings of the human eye, etc., man is seeking not only the origins of disease, but also of character, disposition, temperament and all those characteristics which make up what is called "personality."

Mankind is, therefore, asking today as never before, What is the Law of Life and how can we know and correlate with it? This is one result of a mighty wave of cosmic force which is now sweeping over humanity, and so many hearts, as well as minds, are responding to it that there is arising an increasing "famine in the land, not a famine of bread, nor a thirst for water, but of hearing the words of the Lord."[1] Many feel that if it could be known just what the Law of Life is and the why and wherefore of our being, an explanation could be found for the diversity of men's minds, their lack of co-operation and the reasons for

---

[1] *Amos*, VIII, 11.

their suffering. Then a solution of the problem could be worked out, just as it has been, through a greater knowledge of Nature's laws, for many physical and scientific problems once thought unsolvable.

In seeking at least to suggest such a solution let us carefully consider such expressions as "the Lord is King," "the King is Wise, eternal, immortal, is a King of Glory," "the Law of Spiritual Evolution," etc., contained in the quotations which head this chapter. This immortal, invisible ruling Power, this "wise King," is not something entirely apart from us, but is a Power which is commonly shut out of our consciousness by certain conditions referred to in the text as "gates" which we, through ignorance of the Law, have ourselves shut. But these gates we can lift up or open and make into "everlasting doors" through which the glory and strength, the love and wisdom of the Lord can enter into our consciousness and become the King or ruler of our lives.

What, then, are these "gates" which shut out the glory from our consciousness and blind us to a realization of the Lord whose Divine Will manifests as the law of our being and the so-called Laws of Nature? In this sense the gates are not merely man's psychic centers which connect him with the invisible realms of the Astral World, and which in other connections are referred to as gates or doors, but in the wider, general sense they are certain conditions pertaining to the personality. First of all, there is the health of the physical body and its functions, which body our Real or Higher Self has built up from the materials ("dust of the ground") and forces of Mother Earth. And the ill-health or inharmonious working of this body, while not entirely preventing the manifestation of its Lord, is nevertheless a detriment and a handicap to the expression of His glory.

A second gate is karmic conditions, which we are apt to think shut down upon us whether we will or not, and seem imperatively to demand that we walk only in their predetermined path. A third gate is the environment in which we have chosen to incarnate. A fourth gate is our general type of mind and trend of thought, together with the character of our ethical and religious training. There are also other conditions which seem like tightly shut gates whose keys are lost; so tightly shut that not only the Lord our King cannot come in, but many men even deny His existence. Others read such quotations as those given above glibly and without serious thought as to their real meaning and significance.

If, however, it is the Law of Life (Will of God) that these gates be lifted up and our condition of life be so purified and spiritualised that the King of Glory may enter this house of flesh which He has builded, and rule our lives—as He ultimately must, as soon as we make it possible through our efforts to correlate with Him and advance, for whatever is foreordained by His Will must and will ultimately manifest according to the Law—then why should we not at once begin to lift up these gates and make possible the manifestation of His glory now? For *all that holds us back* from our realization of God Consciousness comes from *our refusal to respond to* and *obey* our Inner Guidance.

The gate of personality—also health—is so interwoven with the gate of Karma that when we try to lift it we find many traits which at first sight seem really to be ourselves, but which in reality are but the results of the thoughts, habits and conditions which we built up in past lives, but which are just as surely our Karma as are the main events which shape our lives today, the characteristic temptations that assail us and the various persons with whom we are thrown into intimate contact.

For this reason one of the first lessons we must learn, once we have responded to His influence and felt the great urge to let the King of Glory begin to enter into our hearts—our portion of His Kingdom—and rule our lives, is carefully to *examine ourselves each night before going to sleep,* and note each trait of our personality and ask to be shown clearly just which characteristics are manifestations of our Real or Higher Self and which are but the reflected and distorted expressions of Soul-qualities which have either been dwarfed or misdirected as a result of bodily and mental conditions, environment or training and built into our personality through wrong thinking, or which have been brought over from our past lives as inherent tendencies which it is our duty to correct.

In reality that which we call Karma is not so much the actual physical events which come to us because we have set up certain causes in the past whose results must come up to us either to be redeemed or accentuated in the present life. Nor is it particular persons we are destined to meet and with whom we make adjustments. While these are certain aspects of Karma, *yet Karma deals pre-eminently with principles and conditions within ourselves*, often with certain Soul-qualities whose lack of unfoldment results in similar experiences repeating themselves again and again, life after life. For, through lack of this unfoldment, relations with certain persons and our reaction to certain conditions in past lives, we find built into our present personality certain traits, either helpful or detrimental, which have crystallized into ruling principles which bring us either joy or sorrow according as they are manifestations of the Higher Self or the lower self (personality). The results of these traits may or may not be worked out in connection with the same individuals who in the past helped us to build them up.

The point we wish to emphasize is that the expression of our Real or Soul-life is determined by the *principles* which we do or do not manifest, and not by events or personalities. The latter only furnish opportunities for the manifestation of the inherent principles. Hence the axiom, reiterated by all great Teachers: Seek for the cause of conditions and events within yourself, not without. For only within the depths of our own inner consciousness can we discover the principles which shall not only rule our personality, but shall master every event in life.

In the *Bible* we are told, "Dust thou art, and unto dust thou shalt return," yet we surely know that those words were not spoken of the Soul, which is immortal. But they are absolutely true of the body and that which makes up the lower personality, which is but a temporary vehicle of the Soul. In order that it may contact, function in and understand Earth conditions, the Soul, therefore, builds up a body literally out of the dust of the ground, which itself is but the re-fashioned dust of worlds long since passed away.[2] Since we incarnate again and again on this planet, each time we leave it we leave behind our old worn out body, which disintegrates and mingles with the dust from which it came. And since much of this "dust of the ground" is the remains of disintegrated human habitations or creations—bodies, houses, cities, civilizations, also animals and everything with which we have been associated—all things ultimately commingle in this Earth dust.

Often a certain place or region, which we have never seen in this incarnation, attracts us with remarkable intensity, while other places nearby have no special attraction. In certain instances this attraction may be because we lived there in a past life and left our former body there to mingle with the dust. Whatever has been closely associated with us is impregnated with our vibrations and produces either a strong attraction or perhaps repulsion, horror or fear, according to our relation to it and how it affected us in the past. The horror is felt especially by those who were burned at the stake or suffered some form of martyrdom for their religious principles.

Furthermore, since man has within him this Immortal Ego or Higher Self, and since the mind of man can reach up to the highest and down to the lowest, he has impregnated not only the atoms which composed his personality in

---

[2] See *The Voice of Isis*, Curtiss, Chapter XV.

each of his incarnations, but also the very dust of the Earth itself, with not only his emanations, but also the vibrations of his mind and of his Higher Self, to the degree that he has been able to express it in each incarnation. Hence, much of the dust of the Earth is impregnated with more than one form of consciousness, namely, the elemental consciousness of its own kingdom and its builders, together with the consciousness of all the human beings, animals and vegetables of which it was once a part, much as a seed has within it the consciousness of the plant it is destined to become as well as the consciousness of all the kingdoms which go to make up its form, although in its unfoldment it follows the dominant consciousness of its species and grows into the pattern of that species and none other.

A great difference between the plant or animal and man, however, is that the plant or animal, having no permanent individuality, follows the guidance of the Group-soul of its species and will gather up only the materials needed for its form. Man, on the contrary, being individualized and hence having personal responsibility, must ultimately gather up or contact at least the essence, if not the actual particles, of the left-behind dust of all that he has impregnated with the radio-active vibrations of his various principles and life-forces, as well as the thought-forces which he has set up or entertained. Thus do we often build into our bodies particles impregnated with the vibrations of mistaken or entirely wrong principles and habits which have strongly affected us in past lives, and also build into our minds ideas, habits of thought, ancient memories, religious and personal preferences, prejudices, etc., which in truth belonged only to some former personality of ours in a less advanced stage, or to the environment, and not to our Immortal or Higher Self.

No evil force can attach itself to us, be it the aroma of long past ages of wickedness or present day evil, unless there is something akin to it in us, or unless we open the door of our minds to it, even through mere curiosity. For

God has made man in His own image and likeness, hence *he need not respond* to evil forces unless he opens himself and responds to them.

On the other hand, we attract to us and build in all the dust that has been purified and redeemed by our spiritual vibrations, as well as the principles and truths we have learned and proved in the past. And these now manifest in us as inherent convictions, especially those things not directly present in our conscious minds; those things which our Higher Self knows are true and which it is striving to impress upon our minds, but which we so often push aside as mere imagination; for example, a personal realization of the Divine; the reality of a continuous life after death, of reincarnation, of being familiar with the Teachings of this Order, because of having begun their study in past lives, etc. But until we have learned the lessons of the past, whose fruitage we now have built into us and our environment, and can transmute that which is not helpful into constructive expressions of the Divine Self, they will remain with us as personal Karma which will make it difficult for us to lift up the gates through which the King of Glory must come in.

The immortal Higher Self is in truth our Ray of the outshining of the Lord who is the King of Glory, "the King eternal, immortal, invisible, the only wise God." This divine Ray, like radium among metals—radium being but a metalized manifestation of this outshining, through the Soul of the Earth—is made up of emanations of Spiritual Light or is clothed in substance corresponding to its own world. And only as we recognize this Ray in ourselves as the means and source of our illumination and guidance—not merely a friendly guide or astral teacher, still less one who watches to punish and precipitate upon us the Karma of our mistakes—but a spiritual radiation which should permeate every atom of our entire personality, which it can fully do only when we have lifted up our gates, just as we must crush the ore to extract the radium. Only then can the Radiance of the Divine Self shine forth through us.

Remember that we incarnate on Earth not to save our own Souls, as the orthodox teach—for the Soul is immortal and needs no "saving" in that sense, only saving from the suffering which *we impose upon it* by failing to follow its guidance—or from the Karma we have created, as many occultists think, but to work with and for the King of Glory as His ambassadors; to help His divine Radiance to permeate and fill this planet and all its kingdoms with His peace, harmony, love and glory, so that all things shall acknowledge this mighty Lord as their King and express His harmony and glory forevermore. Therefore, no one can live to himself alone, for ultimately the Will of God or the Great Law as "unity in diversity," "co-operation and individuality," must be fulfilled, no matter how far we withdraw from humankind.

The dust of the Earth which we have impregnated with our emanations we must ultimately redeem by impregnating it with the radiant energy of higher ideals of love and brotherhood and also with more purified and spiritual emanations from our whole personality as its advance in spiritual unfoldment raises its vibratory rate. This can be done efficiently only to the extent that we manifest the King of Glory within ourselves; for *whatever we entertain within becomes a part of us and radiates to all we contact.*

Scientists have marveled that no matter how far they wandered from civilization, even where the foot of man had never trod before, they nevertheless found disease germs, hordes of insect pests, savage animals and other antagonistic forces of Nature to combat. But as a majority of mankind open their gates and invite the King of Glory to enter, all the things now antagonistic to man will gradually be transmuted into forms which will co-operate with and help man. Man, therefore, must learn that his destiny is to become the Lord of Creation to the lower kingdoms, but this he can do only to the degree that the King of Glory rules his life.

The Karma he has stamped upon the dust of the Earth is his own Karma and can be redeemed only by him. This is not the Herculean task it seems at first sight, for when man opens his gates "the King mighty in battle" will enter in, and the same cosmic forces which fashioned the world in the beginning will sweep through him and all through Nature, cleansing, purifying and redeeming all, even as the waters of the rivers Alpheias and Peneios, which Hercules turned into, and through them cleansed, the Augean stables.[3]

Many, instead of recognizing as their own the karmic dust which settles upon them, complain that others do not appreciate them; that the world is cruel and unkind; that some friend is hard to get along with; that evil forces persecute them; why should not others take pains to be considerate of them instead of always expecting them to be considerate of others, etc. When such ideas assail us we should seek within ourselves for the cause, instead of praying that God will make others more considerate of us. Neither should we waste time and energy trying to find out what we may have done in former incarnations that we must suffer now, or speculate on what those whom we dislike have done to us in the past. We should simply ask the King of Glory to illumine our understanding that we may realize just what principle or trait our personality is manifesting which calls forth reactions from others which cause us humiliation, suffering and sorrow.

Looking thus deep within ourselves in meditation and courageously facing what we find, is often a hard lesson to learn, for the personality naturally tends to make excuses, to consider only our good intentions, to say, "I intended to be kind, loving, helpful and true, hence should not be blamed if I am not perfect." Instead, why not work definitely to make ourselves more perfect, that we may be one of the first to lift up our gates and let the King of Glory

---
[3] *The Key of Destiny*, Curtiss, 90.

enter in and illumine us and shine forth to others? In other words, instead of expecting others to live up to higher standards, we should strive to let the King of Glory out-picture through us more of the beauty of holiness which He radiates within. Thus, by our example and the force we radiate, will we stimulate and inspire others to live up to their highest ideals and let the King of Glory shine through them.

Once let us understand that Karma is something out of the past which in some respects is like the dust which follows an onward moving vehicle; that we need not be overwhelmed and suffocated by it; that we do not have to breathe it in and re-animate it, then we can recognize it for what it is and brush it off into its proper place. We can also leave behind us new particles full of radiant blessing for all they contact. For, remember, we have as great ability to transmute our Karma as we have ability to brush the dust from our clothing, if we but lift up our gates and let the King of Glory in.

Chapter XXXVIII

THE CHRIST STAR

"Behold, there came wise men from the east to Jerusalem, saying, Where is he that is born the King of the Jews? for we have seen his star in the east, and are come to worship him . . . . and, lo, the star, which they saw in the east, went before them, till it came and stood over where the young child was." *St. Matthew*, II, 2, 9.

"Within each heart a sacred Flame,
The Christ Star's steady blaze,
Help us thy children, gracious Lord,
On it to fix our gaze."
Hymn of Consecration, Harriette Augusta Curtiss.

Looking upon the Gospel story of the birth of Jesus, not from the literal and historical viewpoint, but viewing it solely from the standpoint of its being another expression of the universal allegory[1] of the periodic appearance of all spiritual Light Bearers or Saviors, in all ages and to all races, as well as the birth of the Christ-consciousness in each heart, in a former volume[2] we have answered the great heart-cry which is constantly going up from so many hungry Souls, "Will He come again? If so, how? and where?" But there is still another important phase of His coming which should be better understood, namely, another meaning of the Christ Star.

We are told that His previous coming, at the begin-ning of the Piscean Age, was heralded by the appearance of a Star which is said to have led the Wise Men and to have finally come to rest over His birthplace. We know that

---

[1] See lesson, *The Universal Solar Myth*, Curtiss.
[2] *The Message of Aquaria*, Curtiss, Chapters VI, XXXVII, XXXVIII.

astronomically a star is a great cosmic body or Sun with a relatively fixed position, hence it could not literally appear miraculously and be seen with the naked eye by only three persons, much less travel ahead of them and then stand still over any certain country, far less single out a particular little village in that country.[3] But since every country and nation is ruled over by one of the zodiacal signs, the country which was ruled by the same sign as that of the Great Age in which the Christ was to appear would naturally be the one in which the Great Teacher of that Age would descend into manifestation. For the Light of the Spiritual Sun (Son of God) appears at the beginning of every Great Age—approximately every 2160 years—that all mankind may have renewed spiritual life by absorbing and manifesting the new spiritual ideals thus revealed and which that Age should naturally develop, just as the physical Sun shines forth at the beginning of every lesser cycle— the year—that all Nature might have renewed life by absorbing and manifesting the life-force which it pours forth to be embodied during that season. The light of this understanding should indicate to the spiritually wise men where the manifestation or "birth" is to take place.

We are told that the Star which announces His second coming shall rise in the East and shall shine even unto the West. Because the Sun rises in the East and is the source of physical light and life, the East is used in mystical literature to symbolize the source of all spiritual light and life. And just as the Christ Star which announced His former coming arose in a country in the East ruled by Pisces—the sign that ruled that dispensation—and illuminated first that country and then spread to the West—Europe and America—just so may we expect the Star which announces His second coming, and which is to illumine this new Aquarian

---

[3] The giant star called *Nova Hercules*, which, in December 1934, suddenly flamed out 100,000 times more brilliantly than before, only to wane after a few days, was regarded by many as the Star of Annunciation of the Second Coming of Jesus for the Aquarian Age.

dispensation, to rise in the East of the country ruled by Aquarius, *i.e.*, the United States, which is to become the chief center of the New Age civilization—and shed its light even unto the West. And as we are told that this will take place when we see "the sign of the Son of man in heaven"— the sign Aquarius, the man with the water jar—we know that the time is at hand; for our Sun and its attendant planets has already entered the great Aquarian Cycle.[4]

Since every fixed star, as well as the planets of our solar system, is a radiant center of Divine Light and Life, each with its own particular significance and influence upon all the others and their inhabitants, naturally the divine effulgence and Spiritual Light and Life which radiates from the Coming One as from a star, has its own special significance and great influence, especially upon the inhabitants of the planet to which He descends, *i.e.*, this Earth. This mystical Christ Star has already arisen in the heavens—the higher spiritual consciousness of mankind—and has been seen by many who are able to raise their consciousness to the octave of its spiritual vibration and be "caught up to meet the Lord in the air." This means that their understanding is so spiritualised that they grasp the meaning of events that point to His coming. For the truth of His coming enters into every sincere heart, and to all whose hearts can respond. Hence, to meet Him in the Air means to rise to the mystical heights of spiritual understanding.

This Christ Star has for some time been shedding its glorious Light upon mankind and producing different effects upon the various types of people according to their stage of spiritual unfoldment, occult training and their intellectual understanding of the Laws of Divine Manifestation.

That our students may more clearly understand what to look forward to, in this lesson we will try to place the subject before the consciousness of the sophisticated modern mind in a way that is so comprehensible that it will even awaken

---

[4] See *The Message of Aquaria*, Curtiss, Chapter II.

a thrill of spiritual understanding. For, just as with astrological influences, the influence of this Christ Star can best be understood by studying its effects upon the Earth and its inhabitants.

Since this Christ Star ushers in the Sign of the Son of Man, Aquarius, and the number of man is five[5]—man himself forming a five-pointed star when he stands erect with arms and feet outspread—this Christ Star must ultimately manifest in a five-fold manner and have five Points, each Point being a synthetic center of radiant Light, Life and Love. At the present time, however, it is still more like a great undifferentiated Sun whose Rays are seeking avenues of expression through which they can differentiate and become focused into definite Points or centers of force on Earth. It is this effort of the Rays to find focal points of manifestation which causes such confusion and such conflicting claims of, "Lo, here! Lo, there!" among those who are seeking to follow the Light of the Star. For many advanced Souls are today recognizing the shining of the Star, but since they are of various degrees of development and training in occult philosophy, it is only natural that they should declare to their followers that the individual Ray of the Light they have been able to focus in their particular center was to become the Star itself and the home of the New Dispensation. Knowing the reality of their vision, the truth of their experience and the sincerity of their interpretation of it, it is only natural that many such should look down upon, or perhaps condemn as sadly mistaken, the claims of others who may be just as enlightened and just as sincere as themselves.

As one might expect, the apex of the Christ Star is the first point to manifest, and it would naturally find expression in the East. Later on the focal Points of the two arms may be looked for toward the Middle West, probably one in the North and one in the South, while the two Points rep-

---

[5] *The Key to the Universe*, Curtiss, 181.

resenting the feet of the Star will very likely be located near the Pacific Coast, one to the North and one to the South.

As the various teachers and centers of Light struggle for recognition and supremacy, only in a few instances do they realize that the work being accomplished by other teachers and centers can possibly be a part of the Great Outshining so long looked for and so eagerly desired by all spiritually awakened Souls. Each center, realizing more or less clearly that there must ultimately be established on Earth a spiritual center where the coming Avatar can descend "with power and great glory" to establish His reign among men, feels that to their particular group is this entire mighty mission given. Yet a little thought will show to each sincere thinker that no one spot on Earth could possibly contain the entire manifestation of the living Christ who is the Maker and Ruler of every part of this Earth—which is His footstool—and many await some miracle to establish their claims and prove their credentials to the world. In fact, some leaders, feeling the mighty spiritual force poured out upon mankind by the near approach of the Coming One to Earth, and having so little understanding of the Doctrine of Avatara[6] and the laws governing His advent, they do not know that this time He will not manifest as a mortal born of woman, nor merely overshadow some human teacher, such leaders quite naturally conclude that they themselves are in some mysterious way to be so purified, exalted and transformed that they will embody the Manifestation and become the Christ to the world.

While these ideas of personal aggrandizement are pitiful in their misconception of the Law, and almost hopeless to get the mistaken one to correct, they must necessarily bring disillusionment and disappointment to the followers of such leaders and perhaps cause such centers to disintegrate entirely. For ignorance of the Law cannot prevent the reaping of the results of its misconception, since the truth about the

---

[6] *The Voice of Isis*, Curtiss, Chapter X.

Star has been broadcast spiritually from on high for the guidance
of *all who can lift their consciousness and respond* to its plane of
manifestation, even though personalization and misconception
blind their eyes to the truth. Yet we all know that the light of any
star is not focused in any one spot, much less the Christ Star.

Such failures, even though other groups and centers spring
up immediately to take their places, naturally tend to retard and
delay the establishment of the various points of the Star, for it will
require many teachers and many centers and groups of students
to manifest each point of the Star. Nevertheless they are but sad
mistakes which the resulting disappointment and disillusion
will in tune correct for each center and its sincere followers.
Therefore we should have great patience, broad tolerance and
sincere sympathy for each mistaken group until they recognize
the truth. Yet there are always some followers of such leaders
who are too advanced and too liberal minded to believe that the
glory of the Coming One can be confined to any one sect, center
or society, and many such wise men are asking in bewilderment,
as did the Wise Men of Old, "Where shall we find the young
child—the truth on this subject—for we have seen His Star in
the East, and we are come to worship Him?"

There is only one way to find the truth on this subject amidst
all this confusion of claims and teachings, namely, to make a
careful study of the promise as to how He was to manifest at
His second coming. "In like manner as ye have seen Him go
into heaven."[7] Then we must study, with eager aspiration and
sincere prayer for enlightenment, all that Jesus is represented as
saying, both in regard to leaving the physical plane on the last
occasion and His promised return. One of these promises was:
"It is expedient for you that I go away: for if I go not away, the
Comforter will not come unto you. . . . But the Comforter, which

---

[7] *Acts*, I, 11.

is the Holy Ghost . . . . shall teach you all things."[8] As we have said in former lessons, the Holy Ghost is the Love-aspect of the Trinity, the Divine Mother, and it is only through love that we can receive that "spirit of truth" which shall make us free, or that spiritual illumination which will enable us to understand those mysteries which must be spiritually discerned.

The light of every radiant star can be seen by all, yet only those who watch the stars and commune with their radiance can differentiate one from the other. One interpretation of the above promise is that it is expedient that the blind acceptance of the literal and historical conception of the Christ, which has grown up during the centuries of propounding only the letter of the law, should go away and that we should cease to worship a personality, however great, but should study the law as to the periodic manifestations of the Cosmic Christ, and then utilize the illumination of the Spiritual or Super-conscious Mind to teach us all things.

If we study the events connected with the manifestation of the previous dispensation we will find this question answered just as it was to the Wise Men of old. The glory of the coming first appeared to the humble shepherds while they were quietly going about their daily task of tending the sheep confided to their care. Suddenly the heavens were opened and "the angel of the Lord came upon them, and the glory of the Lord shone round about them," *i.e.*, they recognized a new and most radiant star, "and they were sore afraid." And the angel said unto them, "Fear not: for, behold, I bring you good tidings of great joy, which shall be to *all people.* . . . And suddenly there was with the angel a multitude of the heavenly host praising God, and saying, Glory to God in the highest, and on earth peace, good will toward men."

Since the Divine Light first appeared to, and the Angels' message was given to the shepherds, it is only natural that

---

[8] *St. Luke*, II, 9–14

those who are symbolized by the shepherds should be the ones to form the apex of the first point of the Christ Star to manifest on Earth and be the first to herald His coming. Thus it was that even though the Wise Men could follow the Star to the country where the manifestation was to take place, they could not find the Christ Child, for He was resting in a manger (Capricorn) unknown to any save the shepherds. This humble resting place was necessary at first, "because there was no room for them in the inn." Since an inn is a place to which travelers come, abide a time and then go on their way, in the individual it symbolizes the mind, with its constantly shifting thought-guests, and where there is no room for the Christ-consciousness to be brought forth; for the Christ-consciousness is not born of the intellect, but of the heart. In the world the inn symbolizes the centers of intellectual culture, also the intellectual conceptions of spiritual truth and literal teachings, neither of which have any room for those humble teachings which are striving to bring forth the Christ-consciousness in the hearts of mankind, any more than a study of the heavens in search of a new star can attract the masses. Also when the Wise Men asked of Herod—in the personality, King Desire; in the world, those who rule outer conditions, business, finance, society, etc.,—Herod knows nothing about the birth of any ruler who is to challenge his sway, and the Wise Men have to find out from the shepherds where the Child is to be found. Once more today, amidst the confusion of great claims, those who are wise in spiritual things quietly continue their search until they learn where to find and worship Him; for the world is more apt to listen to claims of greatness and supremacy than to the humble, unobtrusive shepherds who seem to make so little impression upon the world, yet who are the ones who have seen the heavens open, have seen the Light shine forth and have heard the prophecy of the angel and have found the Christ.

(To be concluded)

CHAPTER XXXIX

THE CHRIST STAR

PART II. THE SHEPHERDS AND THE WISE MEN

"And there were in the same country shepherds abiding in the field, keeping watch over their flock by night. And, lo, the angel of the Lord came upon them, and the glory of the Lord shone round about them: and they were sore afraid. And the angel said unto them. Fear not: for, behold, I bring you good tidings of great joy, which shall be *to all people*." *St. Luke*, II, 8-10.

"Grant us Thy grace to carry hence
To all the world this Love:
To help to lead Thy children, Lord
Into Thy courts above."
Hymn of Consecration, Harriette Augusta Curtiss.

Daring the cycle of the previous Great Age, the Piscean, while the Light of the Christ Star was but little recognized, owing to the darkness of man's ignorance, his almost continual wars, his passions and his greed, it was, nevertheless, shining deep down into the sea of humanity, like the two fishes which are the symbol of the sign Pisces. And there were always some Souls whose spiritual perceptions could pierce the depths and recognize the Light, even though to the multitude it seemed but the phosphorescence of the two fishes. But in this New Age, when our solar system is slowly passing out of the influence of the old Piscean cycle and into that of the new Aquarian Age, we are told that every eye shall see the Light of this Christ Star. That is, every school of spiritual thought and teaching, all who are steadfastly "gazing up in to heaven" like the disciples of old, shall see and realize that His coming will be the fulfillment of the old prophecy and the Light of the New Age.

It also means that a new great physical star or planet will be discovered by astronomers.[1]

Today, which should be the great "day of the Lord"—the day or Age for the manifestation of the Law—when the Christ Star is slowly rising above the horizon of man's consciousness, we find that we are still in the shadow of the "evil day" of the old cycle of spiritual ignorance, misunderstanding, inharmony and confusion. As we have pointed out, all the elements of the Christ Star necessary to announce His coming are already manifesting on high and are being poured out upon mankind, but unorganized and without coherence, manifesting as but scattered sparks which few can understand, like a puzzle whose various parts must be searched out and be definitely put together ere its message can be understood, or like a star hidden by fog.

But as the Rays of the Christ Star draw closer to the Earth and spread more widely they tend to focus in five types of seekers who will ultimately individualize the Rays and form the five Points of the Star.

Although the glory which shines forth from the Christ Star and the announcement which follows comes not to any one individual, group, center or sect—for no one of these could confine the message or present it in such a way that all seekers for the Light could find in it the satisfaction of all their ideals and the fulfillment of all that His second coming means to them— but "*shall be to all people*," nevertheless, in this cycle *The Order of Christian Mystics* was the first to focus a Ray of that Light into a center in the East (Philadelphia) which belongs to the first Point of the Star to manifest, *i.e.*, the apex, symbolized by the shepherds. Is it not significant that while the Wise Men have to travel from afar to find the Child, there should be, "*in the same country*" where the manifestation is to take place, shepherds quietly going about their daily affairs and tending the little

---

[1] Written in May, 1925. The new planet *Pluto* has since been discovered.

flock confided to their care? And to them the heavens opened, to them the Angel[2] spoke, to them was given the Annunciation.[3] And as they accepted it and believed, they saw the Babe wrapped in the swaddling clothes which are so necessary to protect it from the world. Then they obediently and trustingly "made known abroad the saying which was told them concerning this child."

In fact, after the Order had established its center in the East (Philadelphia), the first Announcement[4] that was sent out began with the words of the Angel who appeared to the shepherds: "Behold, I bring you good tidings of great joy, which shall be to all people." But the realization of the connection of the Order with the Gospel story, and its function in the world as the shepherds, was not revealed to it for many years, not until it had proved in many, many ways its faith and its willingness to follow the Star and obey the Voice of the Angel. As in the case of the shepherds, the full significance of the Announcement and the mission of the Order could scarcely be grasped, even by the Founders, and "they were sore afraid." But, nevertheless, they obeyed. Only as they grew accustomed to the Light, so that its glory no longer dazzled their eyes as it grew stronger and stronger, and only as the messages of the Angel continued to expound the mystery of the Coming and their consciousness expanded, could they more fully understand. And altho they have had to take many journeys and make many stops and establish many camps by the way in the course of their carrying the "glad tidings" to all people, during all these years—since January 1, 1908—the center in Philadelphia has been continuously maintained and has never ceased to function! Also, they have seen the Light of the Announcement which they presented to the world shine from the East (Philadelphia), even unto the West (Los Angeles and San

---

[2] See lessons on *The Ministry of Angels*, Curtiss.
[3] See lesson on *The Annunciation*, Curtiss.
[4] Now used in the pamphlet describing the Order and its mission.

Francisco), thus fulfilling literally as well as symbolically one phase of the prophecy.

Altho the shepherds—who naturally expound the Heart Doctrine—belong to the apex of the Star, and even though, in obedience to their angelic guidance, they have written many volumes, in which they have endeavoured to expound the Laws of Divine Manifestation and prepare the minds of their followers to understand and their hearts to recognize and welcome the Coming One as He draws ever nearer in manifestation, they cannot manifest the Christ Star alone, for all the five Points are needed for the complete manifestation.

After establishing their center as a part of the apex of eastern point of the Star, the shepherds had to have many testings; for every one who is seeking to manifest a Ray from the Star which shall help to enable It to focus into and manifest one of the Points, must be thoroughly tested ere his Ray of Light can be indrawn into and help form a Point. And one of the first and most fundamental tests is for him to recognize his own place in the work and realize that he must co-operate with all the others who have proven that they too belong to one of the Points, ere the Star can fully manifest and shine forth and be seen and recognized by the world.

The shepherds we speak of had to be tested, firstly, as to their faith—for the first years of their work were performed entirely on faith and without any outer recognition, confirmation, encouragement or help, and with very scanty funds. Secondly, as to their courage—did they dare to "make known abroad the saying which was told them concerning this child?" Thirdly, as to their steadfastness— would they grow weary and disheartened at the world's indifference? at the scoffing and ridicule of the Scribes and Pharisees? at the calumny, slander and deliberate misrepresentation of their Teachings? Fourthly, as to the manner in which they spread the "glad tidings",—were they presented so clearly and logically that even the Scribes had to admit that their philosophy was sound, and yet so simply and lovingly that the simplest mind could grasp at least their essential truth and feed his heart-hunger upon it? Fifthly, would they consider their mission hopeless because they did not possess the gifts of the Wise Men but had only love, devotion, faith and divine revelation upon which to rely and to present to the world?

After the establishment of the Apex Point—the Heart Center—by the shepherds, later we see those who represent the other Points—the Wise Men—begin to appear, all seeking to follow the Light as revealed to them until they too find the Christ Child. These Wise Men are much wiser in many things than the simple shepherds, for they have spent all their lives in study. They have crossed the deserts of outer material conditions, have passed through the swamps and morasses of the astral—through psychic research, etc.,—and have climbed the mountains of intellectual attainment that they might find and lay the gifts they consider most fitting at the feet of the Christ; for they know that the time of His manifestation is at hand.

First comes the Wise Man who brings gold. He represents those whose wisdom has made them financially successful in the world, yet whose success does not satisfy their heart-hunger, and who are seeking how best to utilize their wealth in His service, yet who must seek the world over ere they are willing to ask of the humble shepherds. They also have the physical gold which they must lay at His feet to be used to spread the glad tidings of His coming. The First Wise Man also represents those who have a great store of wisdom, yet who sincerely think that the world should pay them well for imparting it. Intrenched in this belief, many of this class either write books for which they charge exorbitant prices (often from $10 to $100) or they travel from city to city with a great blare of advertising, telling of the great-value of their wisdom. And because they feel that they must have much gold with which to do His work or ultimately to lay at His feet, they charge large sums for their courses of instruction.

The testing of the First Wise Man will be whether, having obtained much gold, will he use it as he at first vowed he intended to? Has he recognized that since he represents but one Point of the Star he should use his gold to help build up and manifest the four other Points as well? all of which the Coming One needs to make the Star the Day Star of the New Age.

The Second Wise Man brought frankincense. This symbolizes that praise and worship whose ingredients must be gathered, laboriously and with great learning, from the study of ancient manuscripts and philosophies—theosophical, hermetic, rosicrucian, mystical, etc.,—and the comparative study of religions. This group includes even some of the liberals in the orthodox churches. And there are many teachers, schools and centers who feel that this resurrection of the best of the ancient teachings is their contribution to His worship. This gift is indeed a valuable one to lay at His feet, for through it the proof of His periodic Manifestation in each Great Age is made known and the reality of His Coming in this Age is assured.

The chief test of the Second Wise Man will be, is he wise enough to give a proper interpretation of the ancient writings? Is he able to separate the dust of the ages and the chaff of decayed ideas and outgrown conceptions—suitable perhaps for bygone ages and conditions, but outgrown today—from the everlasting and living truths which underlie former Manifestations, and without an understanding of which one Point of the Star would be incomplete and lose some of its brightness?

The Third Wise Man represents those who bring myrrh for their offering, the symbol of sorrow, anguish, crucifixion and death. There are many of this class today who are giving forth the doctrine—and trying to exemplify it in their

lives—that if the kingdom of heaven is to manifest on Earth
we must give up all joy of life, must frown upon all innocent
recreations, gaiety and happiness, must sell all that we have and
give to the poor or to their society and live a life of poverty,
austerity and self-abnegation. Their sincerity, their courage and
their devotion to what they believe to be the truth would do much
to help spread the Light of the Star, if they are willing to lay
their limited ideas at His feet. But they must be tested as to the
sincerity and correctness of their conceptions, also as to what
extent their teachings are tempered with loving tolerance for the
views of others, rather than condemnation and self-righteousness.
We are told that there was still another or Fourth Wise Man,
altho he is not mentioned in the Gospel story. Four, being the
number of the earth-plane, the story would not be complete unless
representatives of all four corners of the Earth, and the four great
types of seekers for Light, recognize, worship and lay their gifts
at His feet. The Fourth Wise Man represents a large class of
seekers who start out well and with the full intention of following
the Light of the Star, whose gift is service. Therefore, the Fourth
Wise Man is represented in the legend as being so intent upon
rendering service and giving so much of his time and substance
to those in distress whom he met upon the way that he failed to
keep up with the other three Wise Men and so was not present
when they reached their goal. Indeed, when Herod—the desires
which rule the outer life—sought to destroy the new born babe—
the Christ-consciousness—by killing out all the innocents, all
that tends to awaken the Flame of the Christ-light in the heart—
love, compassion, brotherhood, happiness, unselfish service,
etc.,—this Wise Man is said to have told an apparent untruth
in order to save the Christ-child and His mother, whom he had
hidden in his house. Even though he denied that he had seen
the Child and His mother pass by—for they had not passed by,
but had stopped and stayed with him—nevertheless the Child

and His mother—Divine Love—were safely hidden in his heart.

The class represented by the Fourth Wise Man are very numerous in the world today; for never has the world known such stupendous exhibitions of philanthropy and service for the welfare of humanity; such wealth and huge Foundations established for peace, for the education of the people, for the eradication of disease, for social welfare and for the promotion of the finer arts of life and the moral uplift of humanity. Since their form of worship is service, many of this class of seekers have little time for and see little need of meditation or the special study of spiritual philosophy, hence they are often considered or even condemned as irreligious. Yet they ultimately do recognize the truth and find the Christ hidden away in the love of their hearts. The test of the Fourth Wise Man will be as to how wisely he has rendered service; whether from mere sentimental reasons, or from real compassion and a sincere desire to help suffering humanity; whether personally for the sake of shining in the world as a philanthropist, or impersonally for the sake of the resulting good to his fellow men.

For the Christ Star to send out the full effulgence of its glory among men all these five Points must be established and learn to work in unity and harmony, each giving to and receiving from the other that special form of help which each can give, and working together toward the one great end, *i.e.*, *the awakening of the minds of mankind* to a *realization of the Christ within*, and thus prepare to recognize His personification outwardly in the person of the coming Avatar. For "*This same Jesus* which is taken up from you into heaven, shall so come *in like manner* as ye have seen go into heaven."[5] Only when all five Points of the Christ Star blend their various Rays of Truth can they form one

---

[5] *Acts*, I, 11

Great Light, in the center of which the Eye of Divine Wisdom can open and enlighten the world.

Even though the shepherds work ever so faithfully, they form but one Point of the Star and cannot bring about the complete manifestation. They need the help and co-operation of all the Wise Men gladly laying their gifts at the feet of the Christ that these Wise Men may establish the other Points and permit the glory of the Coming One to shine among men. Remember that these Wise Men are not certain personalities or even groups or centers, but certain classes of seekers. And the gold that one class has gathered is greatly needed in publishing the Announcement of the shepherds and in advertising and spreading broadcast the "glad tidings" unto all people. The ancient wisdom gathered by another class is also needed, but clarified and made so simple that the multitudes may see it rise like frankincense before the throne. Even myrrh—the symbol of misunderstanding, bitter persecution and suffering—has been needed that the shepherds might more fully understand the sufferings of others and comfort and bless with everlasting blessing of the Christ those who come to them in sorrow and tribulation. And above all, there is needed among all advanced seekers and followers of the Star, consecrated service and co-operation which shall be so practical, yet so sincere, unselfish and pure, that the world will gladly accept it and be led to the feet of the Christ.

Only by such co-operation can the five Points of the Christ Star become so unified that the Coming One can manifest in their midst and the world declare: "Behold, the Day Star hath appeared!"

CHAPTER XL

PREPARATION

"Prepare ye the way of the Lord, make His paths straight. " *St. Matthew*, III, 3.

"The first of all commandments is. Hear, O Israel; the Lord our God is one Lord, and thou shall love the Lord thy God with all thy heart, and with all thy soul, and with all thy mind, and with all thy strength." *St. Mark*, XII, 29-30.

"Oh, Christ, the Earth trembles at Thy approach. The water and the air and the Heavenly Lights bow down before Thee. The Earth Thy footstool, on which Thou treadest, gives back its worshipful chants as Thou comest. Oh, Lord Christ, open our hearts that we may recognize Thee. Open our minds that we may know Thee. Open our lives that we may follow in Thy footsteps. We fear nothing that can come to this Earth, Thy footstool—for we are Thy children: born of Thy Love: fed on Thy blessings, adoring Thy Son. Amen." *Harriette Augusta Curtiss*.

As we enter into this wonderful new Aquarian Age we must expect many vital changes,[1] both in humanity and in the Earth itself, for this is the night-period which precedes the dawn of the New day. It is a period of preparation for the rejuvenation of humanity and the Earth. It is a period of intensive housecleaning during which many of the old worn-out things of the household must be cast out and burned as with fire; old ideas, thoughts, habits and conditions which have pinned us down so hopelessly to material things and conceptions, and blinded our eyes to the joys and blessings that are the hidden treasure which the Father hath prepared for His children.

But let us not think of these changes in terms of terrible cataclysms sent by an angry God to uproot evil and destroy the wicked—for the more wicked we are, the oftener we

[1] See *Coming World Changes*, Curtiss.

have to incarnate—but as a necessary preparation of this Earth and its inhabitants for the descent to Earth of the Cosmic Christos.[2] The house itself may have to be torn down in places to replace rotted timbers and that a more beautiful structure may take its place. Since man cuts, blasts and destroys the beauties of Nature and leaves ghastly scars, simply to gratify his thirst for gain and self-indulgence, is it any wonder that God should also permit certain portions of the Earth to be gashed and dismembered and destroyed at certain stated seasons and for vital reasons, that He may bring about better conditions and reveal certain things purposely hidden beneath the waves of earth and water until the appointed time for their use has come?

While all this is difficult to pass through, those of the Household, knowing that it means more comfort and beauty and less accumulated rubbish, gladly wait and watch as the appointed servants fulfil this task; the forces of wind, fire, flood and earthquake which, like servants, flit here and there to adjust conditions at the command of the Father; "Prepare ye the way of the Lord, make His paths straight." But these changes are transitory for: "The servant abideth not in the house forever; but the Son abideth forever. If the Son therefore shall make you free, ye shall be free indeed."[3]

While this necessary but disagreeable cleansing process is taking place, let us, as Children of the Household,[4] prepare ourselves by carefully going over the little things in ourselves that need adjustment, and decide what shall be kept and what discarded; old habits, old ideas and methods of thought: pet foibles secretly hidden away or perhaps flaunted before the world, or which we have insisted be considered sacred and be adored by the world. All such must be considered with discrimination that we may fit ourselves for definite work in preparing for "Him who is to come."

---

[2] See "The Doctrine of Avatara" in *The Voice of Isis*, 137.
[3] *St. John*, VIII, 35–6.
[4] See "The Children of the Household," in *The Message of Aquaria*, Curtiss, 147.

Although all the planets are His temples, yet at this particular time this Earth is chosen as His sanctuary, because He has chosen to come here and manifest to humanity in embodied form, that He may again teach us and perchance again awaken us to a fuller realization of the Christ within ourselves, and bring to our remembrance in a more powerful way the essentials which have made us what we are today and which shall ultimately make us true sons of God. "And if children then heirs; heirs of God, and joint heirs with Christ." For, could we but see into the vast depths of interplanetary space we would realize that every planet, every star, every spot in our universe, knows of this great event and is circling around this little planet in adoration, blessing it and lending their powers to cleanse this Temple and make it fit for the great and wonderful cosmic event so soon to take place. Already in the vestibule of this Temple, where the moneychangers sit and where those who traffic in the doves of innocence and trust await their prey: where ignorance, misunderstanding, selfishness and evil dwell and revel, already the angels are waiting to drive these things out with whips of the Law.

As we enter this New Age and see the sign of the Son of Man in the heavens (Aquarius), we see all things in a new light. We see Nature herself prepare to cleanse herself and greet Him purified and reverent. The sea is ready to flee before Him. The mountains prepare to bow before Him and lay their treasures at His feet. And the inner fires prepare to consume with fire unquenchable the tares of man's sowing. Yet all is brought about in Divine Love and compassion to prepare the ground that we may bring forth the Christ-seed and reap the spiritual harvest.

No longer can the natural questionings of the human mind be answered by decrees of the church which evade the issue and try to smother inquiry. For today many, many hearts are eager to find and worship Him, but are crying out in darkness and disappointment because only the same old outgrown conceptions and explanations are offered them. Only a wholesale housecleaning, both individually and in the church, can clear away the accumulated hampering misconceptions, so long taught as truth, and reveal the Path that leads out of the wilderness of life back to our Father's house. "There is a path which no fowl knoweth," but which each Soul must find for itself. "But where shall Wisdom be found? and where is the place of understanding? Man knoweth not the price thereof: neither is it found in the land of the living. . . . It cannot be gotten for gold, neither shall silver be weighed for the price thereof. It cannot be valued with the gold of Ophir."[5]

But ere we can prepare our hearts and lives for His coming we too, like the planet, must pass through a great purifying housecleaning. For every thought and desire and every atom we throw off is radio-active, and does its part to make humanity either better or worse. And we are responsible for their effects. In this way we are all largely responsible for the conditions in the environment in which we find ourselves. We never can know but that the seed of the thing we see expressed as a wicked or sinful act by another may not have been broadcast from some fiery evil thought of our own which, unless thoroughly neutralized, conquered and redeemed by us, may have found lodgement in some other mind whose soil was prepared for just such a seed. As we prepare the soil of our hearts to bring forth the beautiful blossoms of the Christ-consciousness we must be careful not merely to pull up and cast aside the undesirable weeds, but must thoroughly consume and transmute them with spiritual fire, lest they take root as an ill weed of sin in some less purified garden.

Realize therefore that the whole world needs our help and that we can help all we contact by radiating to the entire world the degree of light, life and love that we have received and realized from the Christ within. For we must

---

[5] *Job*, XXVIII, 7–12–16.

not think of the less evolved as impure, wicked and hopelessly separated from us, but simply as less strong, less advanced and fortunate children, whose minds are beclouded by ignorance and whose hearts are clogged with selfishness and sin, but whom we can help, not only by teaching and preaching, but far more by the radiations of our minds, our hearts, our lives. And as we *consciously* allow the stream of the Christ-force to flow through us, not for our own salvation alone, but that we may become greater channels for it to help others, its radio-active force will purify our own body and make it more and more a Temple of the Living God. And it will also radiate from us to all we contact.

While we are thus preparing and purifying ourselves to become His helpers, the forces of Nature and the Cosmos are preparing the Earth, cleansing, purifying and adjusting it—just as we must our minds and lives—for the coming of a beloved and very welcome cosmic Guest: none other than the descent of the Christos into physical manifestation. But not only must the conditions of the Earth be prepared as a planetary chalice fit to receive Him, but a more definite and human chalice must also be prepared by humanity itself, that He may manifest in human form, and again say to those who doubt: "Behold my hands and my feet, that it is I myself: handle me, and see, for a (mere) spirit hath not flesh and bones, as ye see me have."[6]

The Christ knows that those who love Him will gladly take their part in this great task, the part best suited to them, since it is understood; especially those who are so eager to find and greet Him, yet who are crying out in the darkness of misunderstanding: "They have taken away my Lord, and I know not where they have laid Him."

Many devoted, sincere and well meaning Souls who have realized the necessity of such a preparation of humanity, and who are anxious to be of service, have interpreted their realization as meaning that, since the Earth and all human-

---

[6] *St Luke*, XXIV, 39.

ity is destined to pass through great tribulation, they must gather followers and retire from the world to some remote spot where they can build an ark of safety for themselves: an ark with walls strong and high: with solid doors which they can shut tight against all who do not think as they think, believe as they believe, live as they direct, and accept their dictatorship. But according to the vision vouchsafed to this Order, if there was ever a time when humanity needed advanced and enlightened Souls to forget their own safety and the chances for their own personal advance and to *remain in the world*, ready to give comfort, help and instruction to suffering mankind during the coming days of tribulation, that time is now.

There are many devoted ones who are ready and eager to help in this great work, but they are like children who ask their mother to let them help cook the dinner and make the cake. Yet if they had not been taught how to cook and did not know the difference between salt, sugar and spices, the result would be anything but palatable and satisfying. Therefore, if we are to co-operate wisely it is important that we understand the Law of Manifestation[7] or Materialization, that we may work wisely and without easily avoided mistakes and wasted effort. Yet there is so much work to be accomplished, so many types of mind to be reached, so many hearts to be touched, that we have no time to condemn others who are called to work along other lines — each according to his development and fitness — but must strive only to help them understand the universal law upon which the Great Manifestation depends, yet demonstrating to all that Love which we gain by worshiping at the feet of the Christ and striving to become one with Him, because we have accepted Him as our leader, instead of Super-men or even Masters.

While there are certain Great Souls who, through many ages of seclusion and devotion have so unfolded their higher

---

[7] See "The Law of Manifestation" in *The Truth About Evolution and the Bible*, Curtiss, 33.

faculties that they have become Super-men, who can instruct, help and guide many Souls into the Path, nevertheless for the true spiritual birth we must look only to the Christ, for only Divine Love can transmute the atoms of our flesh into immortal atoms. Only as we, of our own volition, determine that the inner Mystic Christ shall dwell in us, no longer as a sleeping, unawakened babe, but *as a living Christ-consciousness*, the Divine Indweller, only then can we eat of the fruit of the Tree of Life that shall nourish our immortal Spiritual Body and enable us ultimately to take on immortality.

The personalized manifestation of the Christ is coming not to isolated groups or colonies alone; not to certain Movements, Societies or Orders alone, but, *after the cataclysms*, to humanity, whoever and wherever they can prepare an ark or chalice in which He can manifest: not in public to walk the streets, be interviewed, etc., but privately to those properly prepared students and groups who have proved that they are His sincere, understanding and devoted disciples. Therefore, He cries: "Build me a body, not out of colonies and buildings of wood and stone, but out of the atoms of your bodies that you have purified in the fires of aspiration and Christ-love: atoms redeemed from fear, from spiritual ambition, from self-seeking, from impurity and inharmony: atoms transmuted by unselfish service to others." This is not so Herculean a task as it might appear at first thought, for as we allow His force to manifest in us, all our atoms that are prepared to respond to His vibrations will be attracted to Him by the Law of Spiritual Affinity and will be built into a fleshly covering in which He can walk the Earth, as we have explained elsewhere.[8]

It must not be said again: "He came unto His own and His own received Him not." For we will thus be lending back to the Giver of all blessings atoms in which His only begotten Son can be seen of men, so that again as of old it

---

[8] See *The Truth About Evolution and the Bible*, Curtiss.

shall be said: "*As many as received Him*, to them gave he power to become the sons of God (Initiates), even to them that believe on His name: which were born (spiritually) not of blood, nor of the will of the flesh, nor of the will of man, but of God."[9]

In proportion as we strive toward this great end are we able to help bring about the manifestation of the Christ on Earth.

"Blessed is He who cometh in the name of the Lord, Blessed are those who can hear His footsteps afar off, yet so near that He enters into their hearts. Only they can understand. Words cannot express it. Only the experience can bring the realization. Then does the Divine One touch our robe of flesh and whisper in our hearts: 'My children, purify with Love divine thy Temple that I may share it with thee; that within it there shall spring up a fountain of unselfish love that shall help make it possible for this Earth, now so filled with evil and inharmony, to become the abiding place of the Lord Christ, a fount of refreshment for all who hunger and thirst after righteousness. Then shall you fashion a chalice for Me whom the mighty Chariot of Fire is bringing to Earth. Then shall you rest upon the bosom of the Divine Mother, and the Father shall clothe you with the Robe of His Glory instead of the tattered and seamy garment the children of Earth have worn so long. Thus shall you help Me save the world.'"

---

[9] *St. John*, I, 12–13.

PRAYERS

Prayers of *The Order of Christian Mystics*

———

PRAYER FOR LIGHT

O Christ! Light Thou within my heart
The Flame of Divine Love and Wisdom,
That I may dwell forever in the radiance of Thy countenance
And rest in the Light of Thy smile!

MORNING PRAYER

I have within me the power of the Christ!
I can conquer all that comes to me today!
I am strong enough to bear every trial
And accept every joy
And to say
Thy will be done!

HEALING PRAYER

O thou loving and helpful Master Jesus!
Thou who gavest to Thy disciples power to heal the sick!
We, recognizing Thee, and realizing Thy divine Presence with us,
Ask Thee to lay Thy hands (powers) upon us in healing Love.
Cleanse US from all OUR sins, and by the divine power of Omnipotent
   Life,
Drive out the atoms of inharmony and disease, and
Fill our bodies full to overflowing with Life and Love and Purity.

PRAYER OF PROTECTION

O Christ! Surround and fill me and Thy Order with the Flame of Divine
   Love and Wisdom,
That it may purify, illumine and guide us in all things.
May its Spiritual Fire form a rampart of Living Flame around me and
   Thy Order,
To protect us from all harm.
May it radiate to every heart, consuming all evil and intensifying
all good.
In the name of the Living Christ! Amen.

PRAYER OF DEMONSTRATION

I am a child of the Living God!
I have within me the all-creating power of the Christ!
It radiates from me and blesses all I contact.

It is my Health, my Strength, my Courage,
My Patience, my Peace, my Poise,
My Power, my Wisdom, my Understanding,
My Joy, my Inspiration, and my Abundant Supply.
Unto this great Power I entrust all my problems,
Knowing they will be solved in Love and Justice.
(Mention all problems connected with your worldly affairs, visualize
    each and conclude with the following words)
O Lord Christ! I have laid upon Thy altar all my wants and desires.
I know Thy Love, Thy Wisdom, Thy Power and Thy Graciousness.
In Thee I peacefully rest, knowing that all is well.
Not my will but Thine be done. Amen.

PRAYER TO THE DIVINE INDWELLER

Come, O Lord of Life and Love and Beauty!
Thou who art myself and yet art God!
And dwell in this body of flesh,
Radiating all the beauty of holiness and perfection,
That the flesh may out-picture all that Thou art within!
Even so, come, O Lord. Amen.

PRAYER TO THE DIVINE MOTHER

O Divine Mother!
Illumine me with Divine Wisdom,
Vivify me with Divine Life and
Purify me with Divine Love,
That in all I think and say and do
I may be more and more Thy child. Amen.

GRACE BEFORE MEALS

I am a creator.
By the power of my spiritualized Will
I consciously gather all the forces from this food,
And use them to create food, health, strength and harmony
In all my bodies (physical, astral and mental).
And we thank the Father for this manifestation of His bounteous supply.
May we use it to his glory.

PRAYER OF DEVOTION

We, Thy chosen servants, to whom Thou hast given the great privilege
    of becoming co-workers with the Masters of Wisdom, ask that we
    may have Wisdom and Power and Courage and Humility to carry us
    through the work of this day.

We open our hearts that the Divine Love of the Master may fill us; that all irritation, inharmony and slothfulness may be transmuted into Love that shall draw us closer in unity to all our fellow workers both seen and unseen; that we may grow absolutely one with the force of Wisdom and Compassion that is sent forth to accomplish the great work for humanity.

Give us all things necessary, that there may be no hampering conditions.

Lead us through this day, in the name of the Divine, Everliving Christ, that the will of the Father may be done in us and through us forevermore. Amen.

Prayer for World Harmony

Glory and honor and worship be unto Thee, O Lord Christ,
Thou who art the Life and Light of all mankind.

Thou art the King of Glory to whom all the peoples of the Earth should give joyful allegiance and service.

Inspire mankind with a realization of true Brotherhood.

Teach us the wisdom of peace, harmony and co-operation.

Breathe into our hearts the understanding that only as we see ourselves as parts of the one body of humanity can peace, harmony, success and plenty descend upon us.

Help us to conquer all manifestations of inharmony and evil in ourselves and in the world.

May all persons and classes and nations cease their conflicts, and unselfishly strive for peace and goodwill that the days of tribulation may be shortened.

Bless us all with the radiance of Thy Divine Love and Wisdom that we may ever worship Thee in the beauty of holiness.

In the Name of the Living Christ we ask it. Amen.

Prayer for the Christ Power

O Lord Christ! Thou who hast planted within me
The Immortal Power of Spiritual Love and Life,
Help me so to correlate with Thy divine overshadowing Presence,
That all hampering conditions shall be swallowed up
In the Light of the Living Christ Power. Amen.

Evening Prayer

As the physical Sun
Disappears from our sight
May the Spiritual Sun
Arise in our hearts,
Illumine our minds
And shed its radiant blessing
Upon all we contact.

INDEX

A

Adam, 4, 40, 42, 239
Age, Aquarian, 7, 56, 97, 226, 255, 291, 317, 388; of Altruism, 21; Piscean, 227, 345
Agharte, 212
Agriculture, prices, 108
Air, element, 180, 198: meet in, 339; mental, 203; purified, 202-3; vitalised, 6
Alchemists, 158, 189
Alfalfa, 315
Am, the I, 8; visualize, 9, 57, 66, 241
Androgynous, 253
Angels, fiery, 210; Karma, 130; lower, 54; solar, 55
Animal, and man, 252
Antaskarana, 162
Antidote, 239
Ark, 25, 26, 195, 359
Armageddon, Battle of, 31, 102
Arthur, King and Lady, 270; characteristics, 273
Atlantis, 304
Atoms, 81; impressed, 85-8
Attainment, Mount of, 258
Avatar, 56, 153

B

Babel, Tower of, 61-4
Be-ness, Realm of, 216, 219, 220
Bethlehem, Star of, 216
Big Horn, 312
Body, 14
Blood, cosmic, 51; of Christ, 52, 144
Book, of Remembrance, 241-8; of Nature, 246
Brahman-killer, 74
Brain, an instrument, 89
Breath, exercises, 181
Breeding, 91
Brotherhood, black, 183

C

Caduceus, 168
Cancer, 41
Canyons, 315-6
Capricorn, 20, 99
Cards, playing, 169
Cataclysms, 32, 34, 59, 64, 110, 231, 256, 355
Causes, unseen, 96
Cells, select, 82
Chain, earth, 77; moon, 77-9, 84
Challenge, 262
Change, love of, 5, 53, 56, 72
Character, evident, 15
Chariot, of fire, 222
Cheerful, look, 185
Child, Christ, 218, 220
Christ, consciousness, 17, 110, 149, 246; cosmic, 143, 269; force, 91, 116, 144-7, 174, 186, 278; manifest, 360; Saturn, 229; Star, 337-53; within, 7, 8, 24, 147, 155-6
Christmas, story, 217
Clothes, swaddling, 3
Clouds, 323
Comforter, 153
Coming, second, 24; before 1975, 34, 101
Compensation, 83
Consciousness, Christ, 17, 110
Constellation, 45, 46
Continent, American, 306
Co-operation, business, 108; spiritual, 28
Cosmic Causes of World Conditions, 94, 102
Cross, 246
Curse, on Eden, 85
Cycles, of experience, 96; of nations, 19, 56; of the year, 19; rule, 224

www.ingramcontent.com/pod-product-compliance
Lightning Source LLC
Chambersburg PA
CBHW051812090426
42736CB00011B/1450